Feet-on-the-Ground Theology

CLODOVIS BOFF

Feet-on-the-Ground Theology

A Brazilian Journey

Translated from the Portuguese
by Phillip Berryman

ORBIS BOOKS

Maryknoll, New York 10545

The Catholic Foreign Mission Society of America (Maryknoll) recruits and trains people for overseas missionary service. Through Orbis Books Maryknoll aims to foster the international dialogue that is essential to mission. The books published, however, reflect the opinions of their authors and are not meant to represent the official position of the society.

Originally published as *Teologia Pé-No-Chão* © 1984 Editora Vozes, Rua Frei Luís, 100, 25600 Petrópolis, RJ, Brasil

English translation © 1987 by Orbis Books
Published by Orbis Books, Maryknoll, NY 10545
Manufactured in the United States of America

Photo credit: Dr. G. T. Prance

Biblical quotations are from the *New American Bible*

Manuscript editor: William E. Jerman

Library of Congress Cataloging-in-Publication Data

Boff, Clodovis.
  Feet-on-the-ground theology.

  Translation of: Teologia pé-no-chão.
  1. Liberation theology. 2. Christian communities.
3. Catholic Church—Brazil. 4. Brazil—Church
history. 5. Boff, Clodovis. I. Title.
BT83.57.B595313 1987   230'.2   87-7816
ISBN 0-88344-579-4
ISBN 0-88344-554-9 (pbk.)

To the seminarians and priests,
lay persons and religious,
whom I had as students
when I was teaching courses in theology
at the Pontifical Catholic University
of Rio de Janeiro,
for they understood that
the lamp of theology
must be liberated,
cost what it may,
from obscurity and captivity
under the old basket
in which spiritual rigidity and alienation
have tried to keep it again and again;
instead, it must be lifted up,
put on a lampstand,
so as to manifest the greatness of the faith,
illuminate history,
and convey life and joy
to everyone.

Contents

Foreword

This book takes its place among the many efforts today to provide a theology rooted in living practice. It is a book that has emerged out of an experience within a particular local church, one that is very much alive. For some years I have had the pleasure of following closely the church of Acre and Purus, in northwestern Brazil, bordering on Peru and Bolivia, led by its devoted pastor, Bishop Moacyr Grechi. It is a church where you feel the spirit of Christ pulsating; a church where Christian joy is alive; a church where "fellowship" is not a vain or empty notion. For several years it has had a sister relationship with our church in Fortaleza, and our ties as churches have deepened. The church of Fortaleza has been enriched by all the strengths and values it has encountered in the church of Acre and Purus.

Father Clodovis is not just a theologian—he is also a missionary. His apostolic spirit shines through this whole book. Here you can follow the magnificent struggle a church is waging day by day. The most interesting aspect of the book is its author's theological reflections, which are very relevant. It is a theology with its feet on the ground—and bruised feet at that—ever ready to make the kingdom of God real in an inhospitable region, one full of the unexpected. Anyone who carries on apostolic work in the distant and abandoned corners of our country must have a resolute spirit of sacrifice. But that kind of sacrifice has its joyful surprises; they overwhelm the creature with the tenderness of the Creator God.

It seems to me that this book introduces something new in theological literature. It is a new way to do theology and to pose the problems encountered in daily life, problems that do not always have an easy answer. It also reflects a new way of living Christian life, viewing everything in the light of the divine word that illuminates and guides. It is contemplation of the mysteries of faith in day-to-day life.

Congratulations to Father Clodovis, and much joy in the Lord to those who read this work and meditate on it.

Cardinal Aloísio Lorscheider
Archbishop of Fortaleza, Ceará, Brazil

Preface

Dear Reader,

I have written this book primarily for lay pastoral ministers, or activists among the poor. It is for you that I intend the reflections in this book.

But I have also been thinking of members of grassroots Christian communities, BCCs. Nor have I overlooked pastors and theologians.

What you are going to find here is an exercise in how to get above the rush of life, to reflect on it. Especially on the life of faith.

This book is not a travelogue. Nor does it propose theology of a systematic sort.

It is in fact a kind of theological journal, written over a period of some months of living close to the people.

What you're going to find here is theology worked out in clearly defined sets of conditions, in different situations that are quite specific.

This theology is homemade. A reflection that is immediate and direct. It is a thinking-out-of-a-particular-situation.

Don't think, however, that I'm offering you some kind of "off-hand" theology. Not at all. The theology you're going to find here is deeply bound up with the life out of which it has issued.

That's why it is closely interwoven with events. A course of events is described, along with its religious interpretation.

The considerations you're going to find here were written on the run. As things developed, with the people and with me.

I took notes as I went along, often right on my lap. I only added a few things later on, to fill out something missing, complete a thought, clarify an idea, or round out a paragraph.

Hence the title of the book, *Feet-on-the-Ground Theology.*

"Feet-on-the-ground," in the first place, because this is a theology moving along over the fertile earth. An earthy theology, like a stretch of land pregnant with the seeds of future life.

"Feet-on-the-ground," secondly, because this theology is worked out first with the feet. This sort of theological thinking starts with the feet, moves through the whole body, and rises to the head. There are some things you can grasp only by going there and seeing for yourself. This theology says what it has seen and heard as it moved about in the midst of the people.

Finally, "feet-on-the-ground" means that it takes into account the life of those who go around with their feet on the ground. Of those who live on the rock bottom of history, the poor and the oppressed. Those who have been knocked down on the ground, but who keep getting up. A theology of the poor, worked out with them, one that is theirs.

We've all heard calls for a theology "coupled to life." For an education "linked to praxis." For a liberating culture.

In fact, liberation theology aims at being a "critical reflection on the praxis of faith." What you have in your hands is an effort along those lines.

You should note that theology does not necessarily entail an academic background. True, it does entail training and ability. But you yourself could take up a theological way of approaching life, and reflect on it, and communicate the insight that results. This book could awaken that sort of thing and guide readers in that direction.

You should note, moreover, that the theological statements made here should always be seen as open positions. They may have greater or lesser degrees of probability, and so they shouldn't be taken to be more dogmatic than they are intended. Nor, obviously, taken as the last word.

What is said here is like headlights on a car: they light up the road ahead. But they light up only the space just ahead, not the whole road.

Similarly, this theology is based on the journey a people is making, and seeks to serve that people. But it sheds light only on the next steps, not on the whole course of the journey.

You will observe that there is here always an effort to start out from life. Not from life as it is outwardly, objectively, in rough outline, but life as it is lived, filled with all its variety of meanings, especially religious meanings.

It is within the ambit of these meanings, built into life as they are, that this feet-on-the-ground theology is worked out. In this sense, it simply seeks to locate, discern, and interpret those meanings that are inherent in the very life of faith.

The aim here is not a "scientific" theology, a theology whose starting point is its "epistemological breach," a theology that is then built up as a critical, systematic, and dynamic discourse.

No doubt, you will sometimes find here pieces of that sort of thing. Even so, these reflections will stay very close to direct expressions of faith in both content and form. My reflection will be carried out in deep continuity with "religious discourse," even as to the kind of language it uses.

In this sense, theology clings to its originating principle: to start from the faith of the church. From the faith as lived yesterday, of course, but also today.

Thus, theology becomes a hermeneutics that is existential, social, and political, both human and divine. It unveils the presence of Mystery within historical reality.

My aim here will be to try to put living reality into words. You know that reality is one thing when it is simply out there, mute, and that it is something else when it is given a name, and steps forward, and responds to a conscious subject.

But why should we theologize the life of the people? Because it is that life, with its full human intensity, that calls for reflection.

Living faith calls for and demands theology. Theologizing is an imperative of Christian (and, I would say, simply human) existence.

Life doesn't make theological work superfluous, nor does it simply accommodate it. It demands it as something inherently part of its own being. For it is only in theology that faith and the life of faith unfold, and come to self-awareness and perfection.

You should realize that I'm never more stimulated to do theology than when I'm among the people. Much more so than in classrooms or theological congresses.

The theology you're going to find here is one neither of praise nor of condemnation. What you will find is a critical theology. And that means a discourse that discerns, makes distinctions, weighs, evaluates, and judges.

But all this takes place within, and starting from, an initial act of faith. A faith that translates theologic faith *(fé teologal)* and brings it down to the particular: faith in God's people.

Unless there is an act of faith in the people, a people that is both oppressed and religious, you cannot understand anything about that people. Only love can see well.

So don't be surprised if my attitude here is one of basic sympathy with everything that has to do with the common people. That is the starting point for every statement and every judgment here.

You may perhaps think that the life of the people is not as poetic as it is described here. It must be more prosaic than what this book images.

Yes, there is a banal and paltry side to life. That is its most immediate and superficial side.

But alongside that aspect—or rather, beyond it—there is beauty and grace in life. Besides the chaff there's wheat. In the heart of the cold and bare earth there is a hidden treasure.

That's why it's important to always be alert to what is present and pulsating at the heart of life. The theologian is the diviner who examines the entrails of life in order to find there the signs of the Divine.

The theologian is the detective of Mystery. The explorer of the kingdom in the midst of the world.

In this book, I try to set out the fruit of my searching, my research and explorations, in one church, a remnant, yes, but one that is very much alive. To be sure, I'm presenting the wheat without the chaff. That is, I'm pointing out the meaning without mentioning the opaque shadow of the absurd.

For it is obvious that not everything in the life of the people is interesting and meaningful. But it is also obvious that everything can become luminous and full of meaning for a heart that is alert and a spirit that is illuminated. Even suffering and death, poverty and defeat.

The reason is that Mystery dwells in all and saves all.

But when the battery of faith runs low, the lights of theology also go dim.

You may wonder how so many things can happen in so few months, enough to fill hundreds of pages.

It all depends on how sensitive and attentive you are to what is going on within life and is itself greater than life.

In these pages you are going to run into a huge number of things, from religion to popular customs, and even traces of biography and autobiography.

Don't be surprised. Life is an all-encompassing experience. All-encompassing likewise is the faith that illuminates life and leavens it. And so the theology being done here is also all-encompassing. It encompasses the person from head to toe, so to say.

Nevertheless, faith remains the arch of the firmament and everything else comes in under that arch: prayer, family, sexuality, politics, history.

As for theology, it remains the all-embracing fixed horizon that puts everything else into context. It judges things on the basis of the absolute meaning or end, and therefore it is the most comprehensive discourse that can exist. That's why it can speak about everything, although not say everything about it.

I say "theology," but what I have in mind is pastoral work, planning, church life, political struggle. You're going to find all of that here. Because it is in all those things that theology is real-ized—that is, becomes real.

I draw your attention to this point: these pages especially show what BCCs (basic Christian communities) and a grassroots church are, and not on the basis of theories, but through a living exposition of the living process they undergo.

Perhaps that way you may realize that this "new" or "popular" church being talked about is much more traditional than is commonly thought. More traditional in the sense that its roots reach back a long way, all the way to the New Testament. And they nourish themselves from the soil of the Old Testament.

That's why there's no reason to be afraid of a "popular church." The only ones who might be afraid are those who confuse tradition with the way things have been done recently or are still being done now.

Otherwise, reader, use this book the same way we should live our lives and shoulder our faith: in freedom!

Acronyms

BCC, Basic Christian Community (in Portuguese, CEB, *Comunidade Eclesial de Base*)

CIMI, *Conselho Indigenista Missionário,* Missionary Council for Indigenous Peoples

CPT, *Comissão Pastoral da Terra,* Land Pastoral Commission

EMATER, a government land agency

INCRA, Instituto de Colonizacão e Reforma Agraria, Institute for Colonization and Agrarian Reform

LBV, *Legião da Boa Vontade,* Legion of Good Will

PMDB, *Partido do Movimento Democrático Brasileiro,* Party of the Democratic Brazilian Movement

PT, *Partido dos Trabalhadores,* Workers' Party

TFP, *Tradição, Família e Propriedade,* Tradition, Family, and Property

PART ONE

IN THE HEART
OF THE ENDLESS JUNGLE

I

The World of Faith and the World
of the Jungle Dwellers

In the first three chapters of this book I am going to be speaking of a missionary journey I undertook deep into the jungle in western Brazil, visiting rubber-gatherers and newly formed communities. This odyssey was both theological and spiritual, and certainly human.

Monday, August 1, 1983: Manoel Urbano

FROM THE METROPOLIS TO THE BUSH

I've come from the south of Brazil as fast as the wind. As usual, I've spent the first semester teaching theology at the Pontifical Catholic University in Rio, helping out in pastoral work in *favelas,* and traveling to help with consultations here and there. And so, yesterday, Sunday, after the end of the big assembly of religious priests and sisters in Brazil, in which I took part, I took a plane to Rio Branco. And very early today, Monday, I've come along with some sisters and lay women in a pickup to the town of Manoel Urbano, in the state of Acre, on the banks of the Purus River.

I chose to travel the whole way in the back with Sister Otacília in order to get filled in on the general situation of the local church, to immerse myself in the sights of the vast landscape opening up before us, and to get my bearings in this new universe.

To shift from an urban center like Rio to these edges of the world always gives you a jolt—psychologically, spiritually, and culturally. At first it leaves you stunned, but as time passes it seasons you in both spirit and body.

Manoel Urbano is a small town, with little more than a hundred families. Friday I'm going to set out from here on a trip with Sister Nieta to keep some commitments already made. I'll be in the jungle until the end of the month.

I'm quite worn out from the work that kept piling up toward the end of my time in the south, my theological period, so I want to see if I can rest a bit both physically and mentally before facing this new period, my pastoral period.

3

Tuesday, August 2: Still in Manoel Urbano

FAITH AND THE TRANSFIGURATION OF THE WORLD

These days I make it a point to take part in the life and work of the community of the Sisters of St. Joseph who are responsible for this vast region: Sister Otacília, Sister Nieta, and Sister Teresinha.

At morning prayer we were reflecting together on the gospel of the day: Peter walking on the water (Matt. 14:22–36). There's no doubt that of itself faith is not a *force* for *transforming* the *structures* of the world. Faith is rather a *light* that *transfigures* the *meaning* of the world. True, this light is also an energy that is brought to bear on world structures and can change them. Nevertheless, faith doesn't directly change the *form* of things or events. What faith changes is their *figure*. It is not trans-form-ation but trans-figure-ation. It is a *meta-noia,* a subjective revolution, a transformation of the spirit, and it is active in the world.

The world of the believer is not the same as the world of the unbeliever (paraphrasing Wittgenstein: "The world of the happy man . . ."). Thus the world of Francis of Assisi was different, infinitely far removed, from the world of Pietro Bernadone, his father. What's different is the perspective, the vision or the conception, not the external, objective, or physical makeup of things.

Revolution, in the full sense, involves both structure and meaning, world and spirit, existence and consciousness, *physis* and *pistis*.

And so the big question is how to fit together truth and reality, and the ideal and the real, meaning and system, kingdom of God and society. That is what God calls humans to do—and it is also what God promises.

Wednesday, August 3: Still in Manoel Urbano

CHRIST STILL MOVES THROUGHOUT THE WORLD

At Mass tonight, with the whole town present, we reflected on the gospel of the day: the Canaanite woman (Matt. 15:21–28). Today Christ continues to roam to the ends of the earth—participants said—in order to find those who are abandoned or shunted aside. And to find all the persons who are here, and even more those who live in the jungle along the rivers or in the "centers" ("center" here means deep in the jungle, as opposed to "the edge" or "the road"). The Messiah is going to come to visit them, to save them, to liberate them, to bring them the kingdom, which is life, joy, hope, justice, and peace.

I apply all this to myself, for my own consolation, because every time I come from the "marvelous south" up to these remote areas, I'm always overwhelmed by a strange, and no doubt false, feeling that it is all useless, even absurd.

Besides, I recall the gospel passage, "When that day comes, many will plead with me, 'Lord, Lord, have we not prophesied in your name? Have we not exorcised demons by its power? Did we not do many miracles in your name as well?' Then I will declare to them solemnly, I never knew you. Out of my sight, you evildoers!" (Matt. 7:22–23).

That's the most important thing. Not big gestures that attract public notice, but rather humility, fidelity to the Lord of the kingdom in everyday practice. And you should engage in political action or any kind of revolution with the same naturalness and simplicity with which you set the table or weed the garden.

No scene in the film *Gandhi* impressed me more than the one where he's meeting with the great leaders of India, discussing with them the all-important question of the liberation of the people, and he sees a child pulling along a little goat with its left leg injured. Gandhi gets up, breaks off the discussion, and goes over to treat the animal with mud from a nearby pond.

If politics does not take as its supreme value the creation, preservation, and increase of life—and fullness of life—it loses all its meaning.

The Kingdom Is of the Poor and Oppressed—and of Children

Today I spent the afternoon giving children a ride on the back of a bike, riding around on the quiet streets of Manoel Urbano. There were more than twenty of them, waiting for their turn and running alongside the bike through the dusty streets, noisy and happy. These children are dreamlike in their beauty, with their brown hair and Indian features.

Does this have any liberating significance? None at all, it would seem. But it's enough that it's significant in human terms. Isn't that enough for it to deserve our wholehearted attention?

Children are graciousness itself. They are the living expression of receiving, of accepting the kingdom, which is always a gift. In that sense they are the symbol of the highest and noblest activity the spirit is capable of.

The kingdom is to be found here, in children. Indeed, is there more kingdom present when you give a conference to a hundred important adults than when you entertain a half dozen children by riding them around on a bicycle?

True, there's no need to set one thing against another. It would be more beautiful if speakers could give a conference like they give kids a bike ride. With the same freedom and simplicity. Like someone who's a "useless servant." That is perhaps the only way that political practice will not end up being a new kind of "justification by works," something Paul so thoroughly condemned, as had Jesus of Nazareth before him.

Thursday, August 4: Still in Manoel Urbano

JESUS' MESSIANISM—THE MESSIANISM OF THE POOR

Today's gospel, which we meditated on this morning in our own community and discussed with the people in the evening, speaks of how the Messiah must suffer and be rejected and then enter into glory (Matt. 16:13–23). This passage helps us understand how the liberation of this world takes place within the course of history. For if the "messianic people" (Vatican II, Constitution on the Church, #9) liberates, it does so on the basis of its poverty. The Liberator in history is not Napoleon, but the poor person. It is the suffering Servant, as corporate figure of the chosen people, who liberates the world from suffering. That is what Daniel 7 sees in the "son of man" (v. 13), that he represents a people made up of those who have been defeated (v. 21). Second Isaiah sees in the "servant of Yahweh" a symbol of the people, "the one despised, whom the nations abhor, the slave of rulers" (49:7).

The way things go for the eschatological or definitive Messiah is also instructive for understanding the way things go for the messiah in history: the people of the oppressed.

Peter's problem—and he is "Satan," "stumbling block," filled with the "thoughts of men," which run counter to those of God—continues to be the problem of those with common sense, those who are "carnal" and "alienated." But there is more to it.

Observing the population of this little town and evaluating its potential for acting in history, one is overwhelmed by the same doubt Peter had. It makes you want to laugh and ask yourself: What can this lead to? Or: Can anything good come out of this Nazareth (cf. John 1:46)?

Even if the prospects of what can be done in history are obviously quite limited, things are not that way when it comes to "God's thoughts." The standard of real political effectiveness is not the only thing that counts, nor even the main thing. In any case, it isn't absolute at all. It is relative to human beings and their concrete history.

As a final note, didn't today's saint, the Curé of Ars, have a well-known saying, "A single soul is enough of a parish for a priest"? The scope of liberation. . . .

Saturday, August 6: A Settlement Called Roçado

FORCED MARCH

My legs and feet are aching. We went from Manoel Urbano to a little place called Deposito on foot all the way. That was perhaps forty kilometers. That was the day before yesterday, our first day of traveling.

Next, we came here from Deposito, seven more hours. We left at 7 A.M. and got here after 2 P.M. We only stopped for a little more than a half hour to have lunch at Paranã, a settlement on the way.

This is too much for the first couple days, especially for someone like me who has to begin with a trip like this. Yesterday, when we got to where we were going, after greeting the owners of the house—shy, as these folks always are—I couldn't hold out any more: I threw myself on the floor and stayed there like a corpse, with a terrific pain in my legs. I had a horrible swelling on my left leg near my groin and I was limping along the road. I grabbed a stick on the side of the trail and made it my staff. By leaning on it, I could take the weight off my left leg.

Dona Joana, the lay leader, told me, "Father, go take a swim in the river—you'll feel refreshed." I answered jokingly, "You can bury me here; I'm not going to budge." But I ended up going.

That night when I lay down in the hammock, my legs were so tired and sore I couldn't sleep. I would stretch them out or curl up, but I couldn't get relief and go to sleep. I said to Sister Nieta, "Sister, unless I feel better when I get up tomorrow, I don't know how I'll be able to keep going." "But Father," she answered, "the word is out to everyone in the area, and they're expecting us. . . . Don't do this now." I would have to keep going, even if I had to ride on the back of an animal, like an ox or donkey. I massaged my legs to loosen up the stiff muscles, and I finally got to sleep.

Very early in the morning, it got bitterly cold, as it always does at this time of year. I couldn't stay warm even with the two blankets I had brought. Besides that, you could hear a poor child with whooping cough, coughing away as though it were about to stop breathing and die. It was enough to tear your heart . . . and keep you awake. All I could do was wait for daybreak and get up.

Lost in the Jungle by Night

Nieta told me that the sisters who were visiting the communities in this area the year before didn't get to Roçado while there was still daylight. Night overtook them in the jungle, where it gets dark sooner, of course. Because they couldn't see the trail and didn't have a flashlight, they decided to put down their packs, stretch out on the ground, and wait for daybreak. How were they going to get any sleep that night? They could hear a strange beast nearby, snorting vigorously and moving around. They didn't know what it was. Could it be a panther? Horrified, they tried to put this suspicion out of their mind, a suspicion that was all the worse because they'd voiced it. The three women held each other close and stayed there in silence and fear, praying softly. That's how they spent the whole night, in an endless agony, while that impatient pacing and noisy snorting kept up. At daybreak they realized that it really had been a spotted panther that had been wandering around and around the poor women until the night was almost over. The reason was that the sisters had huddled near a pile of leaves that the panther had been using for its bed. They gave great thanks to God that nothing had happened to them.

But why hadn't the panther come up to them and attacked them? Perhaps because it had seen more than one person and was afraid (it's well known that the panther won't attack a group). Or God may even have sent an angel to stand in the way, holding a sword, between the animal and God's servants, and kept them from all danger. That's what a biblical author would have written.

Isn't that what the book of Daniel has Nebuchadnezzar say when he sees the three young men passing through the fire unhurt: "Blessed be God . . . who sent his angel to deliver the servants that trusted in him" (Dan. 3:95)? Similarly Peter, when he sees himself let out of jail in a marvelous way, says, "Now I know for certain that the Lord has sent his angel to rescue me" (Acts 12:11).

In any case, on the stretch of road of such fateful repute, I wanted to move along faster. At noontime, when we stopped to eat in Paranã, the woman of the house, after serving us some excellent game, urged us to stay longer. But the fear of the spotted panther was more impelling than the woman's insistence, and we got going right after eating, so as to get to Roçado while the sun was still high. The forced march made me repeat the same scene that had taken place where we had stopped the previous day: falling on the floor and asking for water. Only this time I added to the already strange scene something that left our host family even more astonished: I stretched my legs straight up against the wall. I had been told that the position makes the blood flow back to the body and especially to the head, and so it relieves tiredness in the legs. It was true. Then, taking a dip in the cold water of the creek did the rest.

Lay Leaders: Of the Same Stock as the People

The lay leader in Roçado is *Seu* Maia. He is illiterate, as is everyone else in the community. There had been a young woman who could read the gospel, but she had moved away. The inhabitants don't come together often, only to pray the rosary during a novena to honor a saint.

Right now *Seu* Maia is away. He caught his foot in an animal trap and he went to the city for treatment. He's not dirt poor: he has a big enough house and a few head of cattle.

Dona Joana, on the other hand, the leader in Deposito, is something else. A lively woman, she can read well and is a driving force in her community. She told me that on Holy Thursday she had organized, in addition to everything else, a community meal, using homemade wine, in memory of the Last Supper of Jesus.

Nieta and I are quite taken with *Dona* Joana and the low-key but serious way she gets things done.

Sister Otacília said *Dona* Joana had lost two teenage children, one right after the other. It was the kind of thing that could drive you crazy. In fact, that's what happened to her husband: he lost his mind from so much suffering. He went to the city and was downing one drink after another. He wandered around the streets, out of contact, unaware of what he was doing. But with the help of friends and the community he eventually overcame the grief brought on by the tragedy.

In the deep gaze and sad smile of this couple you could see traces of all these terrible torments. Only God knows how much they have suffered. They themselves don't say anything. They don't show how much they've suffered. They bleed and weep alone, facing a savage environment, and a society that is even more savage. Who is concerned about what they feel? Perhaps only the "Mystery of our faith" (1 Tim. 2:16), the One who "will wipe every tear from their eyes" (Rev. 7:17).

Sunday, August 7: São Romão Rubber Plantation

OPPRESSION IN THE JUNGLE: A LONELY CRY OF SUFFERING

Seven families live here in São Romão. Their houses are clustered around the shed (a warehouse for merchandise and rubber) and the "big house" for the manager. The owner of this plantation is the mayor of Manoel Urbano, and his brother Raimundinho is the manager.

There are more than twenty rubber-gatherers who work on the mayor's plantation and they have to sell the rubber they get in exchange for other goods. Until recently, he even paid some money for the rubber, but now he pays only in goods, and according to a price that he himself sets. "That's the law laid down by the mayor," a worker tells me.

The worst of it is that the warehouse very, very often doesn't even have basic goods: there's no salt, sugar, milk, kerosene, and so forth. A whole year goes by with no new supplies. So the rubber-gatherer has a hard time. The result: hunger.

Injustice is unleashed here in the bush. Here the law of the jungle holds for animals and also for human beings. The managers or traders set the price for everything: both for products like rubber and the goods they furnish. That way they profit both buying and selling.

But the workers' greatest complaint isn't that they're exploited, but that there isn't enough merchandise, especially basic goods, like milk for children, cooking oil, and so forth. But they think well of *Seu* Raimundinho, the manager, the mayor's brother. They blame his boss, the mayor, saying he has "no concern for the people." When you first hear about this you find it revolting. It's a demonstration of how far cynicism can go.

In other places workers have gotten out from the claws of the company store or of the trader's supply boat by organizing a consumer cooperative. That's what they've done in Icuriã.

Nature and Society against Human Beings

It's impressive to see the hard natural conditions in which the jungle inhabitants live: their houses, their trails and canals, their food, transportation, and so forth. They sit on the ground, together with animals and insects: dogs, cats, parakeets, roaches, spiders, mosquitos, and so forth. Often they don't have a table or even a chair. Is that from their Indian heritage? Their features carry clear Indian traces.

There are very tiny black mosquitos that don't buzz, but they bite you on the arms, feet, neck, and head, leaving a pink swollen spot with a bright red point in the middle. Arms and legs here are full of black dots, left from bites after they dry up.

As if this unpleasant side of nature weren't enough, human beings exploit other human beings. . . .

The Lowly Are Worth Any Effort

"What am I doing here?" That's the feeling I'm obsessed with and it mortifies the *homo carnalis* we all have inside us.

The truth is that it was for the "weak," for those who are last in this world, for all of them, that Christ died (cf. Rom. 14:5). If that's so, then anything done for them is worth the effort. If the least of all were worth the blood of the Messiah, the Son of God, aren't they worth our effort?

I'm beginning to appreciate how much sacrifice there is in the life of pastoral workers here: priests, sisters, and lay persons who labor in areas as harsh as this one. These missionaries are spoken of sometimes with respect, sometimes with scorn, and almost always in ignorance.

Obviously a person doesn't get involved in this kind of life for any sort of pleasure or personal interest. There has to be motivation that is beyond any question or criticism. It is in the realm of Mystery.

Yes, the missionary is impelled by the same Mystery of God that holds the monk fascinated. Only here the orientation to Mystery takes a different tack: urgency rather than fascination, work rather than contemplation, *liberatio* rather than *vacatio*.

Nevertheless, it is ever the same Mystery: always painful, crucifying, but always liberating as well. For God is inscrutable, unfathomable. "God's thoughts are not our thoughts," says Isaiah. Otherwise, how explain the contradictions in life that are here so scandalously obvious? Why does the panther have to chase and rip innocent deer apart in order to eat and live? And why does the manager have to pressure the rubber-gatherers to produce so much, even if it means squeezing them with hunger, and keeping them without supplies? In other words, why this huge contradiction between God, Mystery of everything good and of infinite love, and the reality of both nature and of human history? Job seems to have felt this contradiction with particular force (12:6–12).

It is between these two terms of the contradiction that we must set human freedom and responsibility, including the possibility of sin (as well as the possibility of faith and grace). Without the category of sin, including "original sin" in particular, there is no way of coming to grips with the contradiction between such a God and such a world. The fact of sin provides a theoretical foundation for the mystery of salvation *through the cross*. In fact, without sin, salvation—as the fullness of humankind and of the world—wouldn't be resurrection from the dead, but the self-generated flowering of the movement and history of the world.

Furthermore, the idea of sin is the basis for the imperative of liberation:

"underlying all those situations where humankind is humiliated, enslaved, abandoned, and made an object of contempt"—as a famous Jewish writer of the last century put it. He was only echoing biblical language: "When the Egyptians maltreated and oppressed us, imposing hard labor upon us, we cried to the Lord . . . and he heard our cry and saw our affliction, our toil and our oppression" (Deut. 26:6–7). Or Mary of Nazareth: "He has deposed the mighty from their thrones and raised the lowly to high places" (Luke 1:52).

The Gospel Way of Looking at Things

Looking at the Brazilians of the bush country and their living conditions doesn't lead to enchantment or ecstasy. It doesn't move you to poetry but to indignation and anger. That's why you need conversion and faith in order to look at the people clearsightedly and justly. The gospel way of looking at things passes by way of the death of a "human, all too human" way. It is a paschal way of looking, a view "according to the Spirit," and no longer "according to the flesh" (2 Cor. 5:16).

I'm thinking about the children who come forward to be baptized. Who is even aware of them in this world? How much do they weigh on the scale of history? And yet, in baptism we say they are sons and daughters of God—and given preference precisely insofar as they are ignored. Such enormous greatness!—but *in mysterio*.

To believe in this is already to move into the perspective of the divine vision: seeing the disadvantaged as God does, seeing them in the surest and truest way possible.

The Lord's Supper in the Heart of the Jungle

Today, late in the afternoon, we celebrated Sunday Mass. The sun was setting as we began. It occurred to me that it was just at this hour that Jesus held his last repast with his disciples, and that his command, "Do this. . . ," was echoing two thousand years later here in the middle of the largest forest in the world.

The community had arranged itself in the afternoon shade, stretching along behind some lemon trees. The participants, about thirty of them, sat on benches, on tree stumps, or even on the ground, around the supper table.

While Sister Nieta was teaching the hymns, I prepared myself to hear confessions. Five adults came forward. The confessions were good and valid. Three were confessing for the first time—and they made their first communion during that Mass.

The Mass was unconstrained, focused on essentials. After all, it's not at all appropriate to insist on the letter of the law or the official ritual in a situation where nothing is official.

Everything went quite well. The community discussed who could take the place of the leader, *Dona* Raimundinha, who was going to move to the city.

They singled out Nonato—a young man who can read, sings well, and is very dedicated to the people. We had a ceremony of handing over the New Testament to him, as a sign of investiture and blessing.

By the end of the celebration, you could see the evening star prominent in a soothing pink sky. And the community gave thanks in its spontaneous prayer after communion.

Wednesday, August 10: A Settlement Named Porongaba

HUNTING AND *IMBIARA*

Yesterday we came to the community of Neném Ponte, after going through Centrinho.

A little after our arrival, *Seu* João Paulo, the head of the house, took his gun and went hunting. His nephew, with another youngster, also went hunting in the jungle, but in another direction.

The reason: tomorrow several families will be coming for the get-together, with baptisms and weddings, and the hosts have to "lay out a spread." The jungle is the rubber-gatherer's reservoir: a kind of market, shop, and refrigerator all rolled into one.

I learned from João Paulo's children that the term "hunting" is used with regard to deer, boars, tapirs—that is, large animals; getting monkeys and birds isn't called hunting but *imbiara*.

Night has fallen and I'm in my hammock. In the rose-colored west Venus is smiling, and directly above there is a new moon, shaped like a thin fingernail.

Collaborative Reading

We asked the villagers if they had known we were going to arrive. They said they did. But in order to decipher the letter sent to tell them that we were coming, a group of them got together. It took a collaborative effort. After more than an hour of struggling, all of them huddling around the piece of paper, they managed to understand the main point, more or less. "But there was a lot we didn't get," said a woman, who recounted that strange battle to us. They had agreed to wait for the boatman who was due that evening so he could "read out the rest of the letter."

Poor souls! Someone has to come up with some kind of communication not in writing, something pictorial, for those whose culture does not include writing. To send letters to a group of illiterate persons is, at the very least, a sign of pedagogical carelessness.

Stumbling into a Blessing

My left foot is all swollen up. Yesterday I took a nasty fall, coming from Neném Ponte to São Francisco. I had only sandals on (because they had told us the road was clear) and I banged up my little toe.

Last night, in the Centrinho rubber plantation, they suggested I put on an ointment, but in the morning my foot was more swollen than ever. That was undoubtedly from the long walk during the day.

Dona Maria prayed over my bruised foot, making a blessing over the red area. She rhythmically traced repeated signs of the cross, silently pronouncing a secret prayer. I only saw her lips moving.

Then it was my turn to get into the act. She asked me to bless some saints' pictures she had gotten in the city. Why not? I was happy to bless them. Then she asked me to bless the right foot of her mother, *Dona* Eline, a lay leader. Her foot was really one whole wound. She could only drag herself around the house, but she was going to the hospital soon.

In any case, it was a chance for different religious procedures to mesh together. Our pastoral practice is unaware of, and hence overlooks, the religious resources of the people. But whoever ignores the people is in turn ignored. Bourdieu says the priest tends to consider the natural healer and witch doctor as his rival. But why does it have to be that way? Couldn't this element of the people's religion be taken up into what is a true ministry of the church—ministry to the sick?

Walk and Sing!

Last night in Centrinho we had a baptism ceremony with lots of feeling and participation. Only three families live there, but there were four baptisms.

We had arrived around four in the afternoon, after having gotten caught in some rain along the road. I led the way, singing anything that came into my mind to keep up our spirits as we were walking and to get my mind off the rain and how tired I was. We had been walking since 7:30 A.M. "Walk and sing!" was St. Augustine's recommendation.

After refreshing ourselves at a spring, as is our customary ritual whenever we arrive at a settlement, I put up my hammock and flopped into it. I was numb with exhaustion, and my left foot was all swollen. After just fifteen minutes, they called us to eat.

We were served three kinds of meat from the jungle: spider monkey, squirrel monkey, and deer. We had brought the deer ourselves from São Romão, provided by *Dona* Raimundinha. That was in order to make sure we had something to eat when we reached our destination.

I thought to myself: So much meat! But this is how it is in the bush: they put everything they have on the table. If they have a lot, they put a lot; if they have only a little, they put a little. Why save things? Besides, *how* could you save things? If you have to, later on you can go into the jungle and hunt.

We ate sitting on the floor of the hut.

Night Baptism on the Hill

Around 8 P.M. everyone was gathered in the meeting room, about twelve persons. While Sister was taking down the names for baptism and marriage, I was speaking with Manoel, *Dona* Maria's husband, asking if he would be willing to be a leader and take charge of the community meetings, because *Dona* Eline was going into the hospital. He said he would and that he would go for the training session in Manoel Urbano from the 25th to the 28th of that month. I took his word for it.

At 8:30 we started the marriage ceremony. The two young couples, whose four children were to be baptized, were in a very good mood. They sang and prayed with unusual enthusiasm. They even inspired me in the celebration.

For the baptism we formed a procession toward the creek that was about three hundred meters from the house. That's where they go to get water, wash clothes, and bathe.

At the head of the procession someone carried a huge torch made of *sernambi* sticks. The others came behind with candles and lanterns. As we went we sang "The People of God Wandered in the Desert." It was a miniature reproduction of Israel's march through the desert, with a column of fire leading the way.

When we got to the creek, after a litany composed of a series of "we renounce," "we promise," and "we believe," closely linked to the everyday life of the community, we baptized the children. I cupped the water in my hands and, as I repeated the baptismal formula and poured the water, the adults in the creekbed held out their right hand over the child being baptized and made the sign of the cross, paralleling the words of the minister. Then one of the mothers on the other side of the creek bent down and laid the head of her child in the water, so it could receive the bath of new life. As we went from one baptism to another, everyone kept singing. And the torch of *sernambi* wood stood over the gully, lighting up the waters, the faces of those present, and the trunks of the closest trees, making them stand out against the darkness.

We returned to the house singing, "Our joy is to know that one day this whole people will be freed." In the meeting area we finished the celebration, almost two hours after it had begun. No one was tired or had even noticed the time pass. We were all full of emotion and joy. A holy and unforgettable moment!

"Now whenever anyone goes by the spring and goes there to bathe, they will remember the baptism of our children. Later on we're going to tell them about it, when they can understand," one of the mothers told me. Memory made present, like the Old Testament memorials.

And so, when the children were baptized, their world was also being baptized. The creek became an abiding sacrament.

Daytime Baptism by a Spring

The day before yesterday, in a settlement named Santa Maria, in the jurisdiction of Neném Ponte, we carried out a similar baptism, except that it was during the day. We went to the nearest spring, and in the shade of towering trees we baptized two children out in the open (the gospel we read spoke of how Jesus saw the "heavens opened" at his own baptism . . .). For over two hours we waited for a third child, but the family never came.

Neném Ponte is the name of the hamlet and the name of its lay leader. (Was he its founder?) The community is not well integrated, and Neném knew why: he had married a second time. So when I spoke, I stressed that a person's past is redeemed to the extent that the person is living well in the present and is moving forward. Faith in the forgiveness of sins tells us that the past is always absolvable and that no human life is beyond recovery.

It really seemed stupid to me to expect Neném to send away his present wife, with whom he has lived for five years and by whom he has two children, and to return to his first wife; besides, she's living with another man. The church is church, not synagogue. The gospel is gospel, not Torah; not a *dys-euangelion,* as Barth would say.

We went back home by night with *sernambi* torches. *Seu* Neném Ponte went ahead with one torch and I came at the end with another. The darkness of the bush is absolute night.

That was the first time I'd walked in the jungle at night. It's a unique musical performance. On top of the loud croaking of frogs comes the chirping of hosts of crickets, and the mysterious and varied song of night birds.

Seu Neném's two little children came along with us, one in its mother's arms, the other on its father's back. This one was amazingly bright, and I wondered how the jungle could produce such a child.

The Rubber-Gatherers' Mental Horizons

Life in the jungle might be said to take place outside history. It's like an eternal present, without a differentiated past and auguring the same kind of future. It's something like the experience Carlo Levi describes in his famous memoirs, *Christ Stopped at Eboli.*

The horizons of the jungle denizens are limited to nearby settlements, the rubber plantation, the animals and insects, Manoel Urbano (which here they call by its old name, Castelo), and little else. What goes on around here? Nothing that even deserves mention in our mass media.

Eliene, a very sharp 11-year-old girl, was telling me stories, things that I found quite incredible, but for her were eminently believable. There's one about a soul of a *caboclo,* mulatto, that comes out of its grave to devour humans; there are faces that pass by in the night as though they were going off to fetch water; there are apparitions that shout like nighthawks. . . . In short, a world where the imagination takes over and masters reality. Or better, where the violence of reality takes over and masters human beings and their imagination.

Although this region is one of the most remote outposts for our state and our church, that doesn't mean it stands utterly outside our ongoing process in history and outside the social system we live under—capitalism. Production relationships are still quite obviously precapitalist; in fact they're semifeudal and slavelike. They constitute a precapitalist enclave within the capitalist system and serve that system. Capitalist patterns haven't penetrated this far yet, although that's what's happening more and more all over Amazonia. But they've got to be knocking at the door, for it's clear that the (semifeudal) rubber plantation system is coming apart.

Although all this is real in the life of the rubber-gatherers, it's not yet something they've consciously thought about. Hence their level of politicization, vis-à-vis a system they can perceive only on the outer fringes of their life, is zero.

Extending the Church through the Bush

During our long hikes from one community to another we talk a lot—about everything and everybody.

On our way back to Centrinho yesterday, Nieta, Nonato (our guide and the new lay leader in São Romão), and I were discussing the possibility of lay leaders in the jungle being ministers of baptism. There sprang up a hypothetical notion—actually quite remote—that certain more mature communities might celebrate the Lord's Supper in their own way and with their own means: bread made from *macaxeira* (millet), wine made from the fruit of *açaí* or *patoá* (palmlike trees), and so forth. All this of course in concordance with the church.

The pastoral life of our church has to be decentralized. Religious responsibilities have to be "popularized" in its ministries. In short, the grass roots must become involved in the church's being and doing.

In principle, there don't seem to be any serious reasons for holding up the church's "hinterlandization"—that is, against its really extending itself into the jungle, so that the elements of the local church would be more and more able to stand on their own.

Of course, this would require preparation of individuals and the creation of new structures. The idea alone isn't enough. But the idea has to be raised, the possibility has to be opened, in order to get on to making it a reality.

Thursday, August 11: Still in Porongaba

THE GRIM SIDE OF THE FOREST PEOPLE

I watch the children. They spend their time rolling around the house on the floor, with animals all around, their faces dirty and their bodies grimy and dotted with mosquito bites. They all eat sitting on the ground with plates and food all around. They sit surrounded by dogs and cats, monkeys and other animals. The animals get what's left over, or else it's thrown out into the yard where the rest of the animals—ducks, chickens, pigs, etc.—gather around and fight over the scraps. It's an ecological community.

It's not unusual for two or three persons to eat from the same plate, as was done in the ancient world. As Joseph, Mary, and Jesus must have done. Sometimes the one sharing is a dog, as I saw today: the baby was giving the animal a spoonful of mush and then taking one for himself. And they kept on that way, taking turns.

When you ask a question that would be obvious for us, like, "Why did so-and-so die?," they say, "Of a fever," or "It was a childhood disease," or "It was a woman's disease." And that ends the matter. And you don't know any more than you did before you asked.

Life in the bush is brutalizing. The horizons of awareness remain very limited. Forced to confront a series of problems, these brothers and sisters of ours assume an air of closed impenetrability, and their faces take on a severe and rough look that reminds you of the wild face of the jungle itself. This is just a part of the truth, however.

THE BRIGHT SIDE OF THE FOREST PEOPLE

The other side of the coin is that the rubber-gatherer possesses a deep humanity. There's nothing of the emptiness and flabbiness you can see in the great ones of this world. Here everything is truth, pure and hard—with the hardness found at the center of certain trees and the pit of certain fruits.

There's a strong sense of honesty. There's a similar sense of hospitality, courage, respect for the other person, etc. Sure, that's partly because the conditions of life aren't very developed (because of the prohibitions existing in their society) but it's also because the human quality of life is very high.

There's no comparison between how basic the human life of these rubber-gatherers is and how futile and frivolous bourgeois life is, as it comes out, for example, in novels. Here life is more truly life, the human being more human, and God more God.

Friday, August 12: Still in Porongaba

COMMUNITY MEETING

Throughout the day families kept arriving in groups. They came from far away. Some came more than five hours on foot, the women carrying children in a sling and the men bringing along another child, perhaps asleep, with a piece of burlap that served as both blanket and hammock. They came single file, sweating like animals, giving off a strong, pungent smell. After a few words, they went off to bathe and swim. They stayed there the rest of the day in conversation. When the priest or sister visits, it's a holiday.

Last night, when the meeting began, the place was full. There were fifty persons or more.

I began by proposing to them something I'd discussed with Nieta. Because they live far apart with no church community and no one who can read, they could get together as families and say the rosary. The family would then function as their community, the rosary as their gospel, and the father or mother as the lay leader.

I tried to explain to them how they could pray the rosary. But it was useless. They simply couldn't hold onto five mysteries in a row. So it occurred to me to suggest that they replace the mystery with any intention at all. They seemed to understand and to commit themselves to getting together in families to pray the rosary on Sundays.

But I'm not at all sure they'll do it: when we prayed the Our Father and Hail Mary together, I could see that they were mumbling along rather than really saying the words. They don't even know how to make the sign of the cross correctly.

Perhaps our pastoral work overlooks these simple and basic things in our faith, things the old style of catechism was very careful about, even to the point of formalism, but which retained what is essential in the gospel message. Starting with the sign of the cross, you could get to the central christological mysteries, and starting with the Our Father, all of Christian ethics.

Two important aspects of the rosary, among others, are that it is a prayer of the people, because it is easy and rhythmic, and that it is connected to the gospel, both through the prayers that make it up (Our Father, Hail Mary, and Glory Be) and through its mysteries—a summary of the core events in the New Testament.

True, in order to get beyond formalism, this prayer would have to make room for variation and creativity: with intentions, reading or calling to mind the Bible, etc.

But all that sort of thing is still just a band-aid or a crutch, because nothing can replace living contact with the word of God, and its dynamic confrontation with reality. BCCs are based on that method. But how can you do that in this kind of situation?

Blessing Future Marriages

There were three new couples in the church, and two of them wanted to "get married in the church." But they had lived with other partners before. I reminded them that in these cases the pastoral practice was to wait a period of time (three to five years) for the marriage bond to become firm and the couple to show stability.

In fact, changing partners is very common. This is due to how narrow the choices are and how hard it is to exercise social control in this area. It's relatively easy to get together to make love on the sly. The women are almost always at home, at the creek, or nearby in the field, while the parents or husbands are in the jungle "cutting" (extracting rubber latex).

The third couple was a young man, fifteen years old, and a young girl who didn't know how old she was (like most around here). They didn't want to get married even though they were living together as husband and wife, as everyone knew. How was anyone going to convince them?

I took the three couples aside and I brought over other couples already married in the church (about five of them) and had them stand facing those who wanted to get married and holding out their right hands as a sign of blessing, while I spun out a spontaneous prayer that they would live well so that some day they would deserve to receive the sacramental blessing.

Everything was quite simple. Everyone took part with complete seriousness and conviction. However, only the Spirit can know what was going on in the interior of these men and women.

Another Baptism in the Waters of the Jungle

The baptism took place at the creek. We went there in a procession, with the *sernambi* torch leading the way.

I brought them around to promising that they would keep on meeting in their homes for prayer on Sundays. In subsequent visits, the sisters would be checking. That would be a condition for baptizing their children. After all, living the gospel demands some form of church or community life.

At the end, I sprinkled the leftover baptism water on the surrounding vegetation, in order to bless the rubber trees, the canals, and the cleared cropland. After all, isn't nature also destined to be redeemed (cf. Rom. 8)?

And Then the Fiesta

We had a late supper, after 10 o'clock. There was cassava (manioc), which I had asked them to cook with butter. They themselves prefer cassava in flour form.

Afterward, the younger element brought out a record player and played some popular music and danced in the flour mill until almost midnight. The young girls stayed in the house, looking on but not wanting to go into the dance.

Seu João Paulo, the head of the house, told us that on the day of his patron saint, John the Baptist, he puts on a huge fiesta. More than two hundred persons attend. He assures us that his part is orderly and there's not a lot of liquor ("only about twenty bottles") so there won't be fights and men getting all cut up. But is what he says really credible?

His house is one of the biggest in the area. When you're tired from walking and getting close, and you see the house high on top of the hill, you have the impression it's alive, calling out to you and welcoming you.

Friday, August 12: A Settlement Named São Pedro

POVERTY AND MISERY

On the way here from Porongaba we went through two settlements: Descanso and Boa Fé. They were an hour and a half apart, at a rubber-gatherer's pace—that is, moving along the path with huge strides.

I've just bathed in some stagnant water that smelled bad, down by the riverside here in São Pedro. In the summer, as we are now, many of these channels dry up; there's some water left standing here and there.

I asked *Dona* Maria José, who has a family, for some water. It tasted like dishwater. "Sorry, the water's a bit rancid," the poor woman apologized. Then she offered me some coffee in a fruit can cut in half. It didn't taste like anything—it was just a black liquid.

Three families live in this settlement. All are of Amerindian descent and all are related. One was "his son" and another was "her son." One of them was Daniel, fifteen years old, who had been in Porongaba. Together with his partner, who was still a young girl, he was living nearby—where his mother could keep her eye on him. The other one, Antônio, thirteen years old, had brought us here. He went ahead with a gun. On the way he killed a *macaco zogue* and then a *guariba* (two kinds of monkey) for the evening meal. It's not much meat but it's enough to make a broth to eat with flour. That's what we did. That was it: there wasn't any other food.

Besides, eating is something that doesn't take a lot of time here. You get to a settlement, and unless there's something else, you take some flour, mix it with eggs or fish, or simply with salt or sugar (with sugar it becomes *jacuba)* and there's your lunch. If it's not nourishing, at least it fools your stomach. That's what we ate yesterday, when we went through Boa Fé, and tonight when we got here. No wonder that once on an earlier trip through these parts, Father João Pedro fainted with hunger as he got to a settlement.

There's no question that poverty is the result of exploitation or marginalization. But it goes hand in hand with backwardness or an undeveloped state of things.

I look around the house to see if I can find any fruit, because everything grows around here: pineapple, avocado, banana, papaya, guava, cashews, and so forth. No luck. Folks here plant hardly any fruit, just pineapples and bananas.

Poverty isn't just something economic; it's also cultural. It's a matter of awareness. Overcoming it involves a learning process and techniques. The "developmentalists" have a portion of the truth. It's not enough just to blame the bosses or the government.

Being here, I realize how true it is that there is a distinction between misery and poverty. Charles Péguy proposed that distinction and it's now becoming common (see the interesting book by the African, Tévoédjrè, *Pobreza, riqueza dos povos* ["poverty, the wealth of peoples"]). Leon Bloy defined the difference very precisely when he said, "Misery is the lack of what is necessary; poverty is the lack of what is superfluous." The one is a mutilation; the other a virtue.

The Greatness of the Faith Stands by Itself

I keep coming back to this question: How much political capital do these Brazilians have, in the sense of power for social change? They're spread out over the jungle, isolated by the very way they harvest rubber (spread throughout the forest) and utterly dependent on nature and on the trading post system. Under such conditions the influence they can bring to bear to change their life is minimal. So how can they be expected to change history?

Asking about how much political capital these persons have may not get to the deepest and most decisive aspect of their life, or of the work one might do here—as I see it. After all, why would anyone ruin their feet on these horrible trails (the one from São Francisco to Porongaba was terrible) unless it is simply to meet these rubber-gatherers whom society leaves abandoned, then announce to them the word of hope and liberation, pass on to their children the dignity of being children of God, and encourage them in their struggle for life and fullness of life, and bring them together in communities?

But what can all this lead to? It's really only *sub specie aeternitatis* that all this becomes comprehensible to us, not *sub specie historiae*. In other words, here there's no question of Marxism—here it's Christianity pure and hard.

True, those things aren't necessarily in opposition. But they don't necessarily go together either. There are cases—and this is one of them—where faith and theology say what they have to say without any other mediation. In other words, there is some work worth doing for reasons that have to do just with the gospel, with no other considerations of a political nature coming into play. If you were here for political reasons, you'd be a real loser. I repeat: you have to have naked faith, the faith of the mystics. Going through these forests is like going through the "dark night of politics." Faith has to withstand this test!

As I was coming here today, beating my way through the jungle trail, I felt this in a very lively way: that faith is something irreducible, that the greatness of the gospel stands on its own, that it is incommensurable, and that its weight is something absolute. To reduce everything to politics and to liberation within history means failing to realize the greatness, the dignity, and the excellence of divine realities. Resurrection, eternal life, the forgiveness of sins, the absolute future of life and of history, *agape* between humans—all that is what comes out of this point, manifesting all its meaning and its power.

In our meetings with the communities in this area, this is basically what we talk about, and it's what's most appropriate in the situation. Obviously, the social implications of the faith always come up: community and justice (I've always tried to sum up these implications in these two words). But we have to recognize that we just make a quick run through this area and what we have to say evaporates. That's because the horizon, both mental and real, of those we're talking to soon narrows down again, as does their understanding and interest.

Work Somewhere Else?

I think my practical experience here in Acre is reaching its limits. The local church has formulated its line of work and is moving along. The foundations for a local church with its own characteristics have been laid and are now solidified. There's no longer a need for the kind of theological service I provide. The theology course, now in its third year, is a sign that this church is now capable of using its own brains. My own impression is that we're reaching the limits of comprehension, that there is a kind of saturation point. Maybe I should shift my area of practical work. Some activity in an urban area or, better, on the outskirts of a city, would be fine. In lower-class barrios with a working-class concentration, inspired Christians might feel the faith as a ferment in history, emphasizing its social implications, because that's where the cutting edge of history is. We'll see.

Events are the vehicles God uses to move us along. *Fata volentem ducunt, nolentem trahunt.* You go along, whether willingly or unwillingly.

Saturday, August 13: A Settlement Called Lago

GOOD WATER, AT LAST!

It took almost five hours to get here from São Pedro. We left at 7 A.M. and got here around noon. We didn't see a living soul along the way. We saw only two settlements: Bacaba and Centrinho. Except for a few stretches at the beginning, the trail was marvelous: open, clear, and flat.

There was a fiesta going on in Bacaba. We stopped to drink some water. It was running water, and so clean you could see to the bottom. I rinsed out my insides—I drank loads of water so I could forget the filth I had drunk in São Pedro, which had lodged in my stomach. Sister was drinking like Gideon: lapping up water like dogs do.

We washed our feet, our hands, faces, necks. We almost plunged right in. Refreshed, we sang when we got back on the road. Although I was limping, my sore toe wasn't bothering me too much. I came along with just a slipper on my injured foot, and a sneaker on the other. All the way I was being careful not to trip on the same toe, the way I did the day before yesterday, making things a lot worse. But now the trail was good and the water gave us strength.

Many thanks, Sister Water, that you are "humble, useful, precious, and chaste," as Francis, brother and lover, put it.

The Fleeting Spectacle of the Butterflies

There were millions of butterflies along the way. All shapes, colors, and sizes. I've never seen them so splendid, fancy, and skittish.

It is a pleasure to contemplate how they stand out against the harsh jungle, these marvels of ephemeral beauty, darting among the bits of light that filter down from the crowns of the tall trees that stand over the trail. And there they are, dancing, circling around before our eyes, all around us, moving along with us, going ahead or sweeping behind, now and then landing on the trail, risking being stepped on, sometimes landing on a leaf alongside the road. There they remain with their wings closed, as if to hide their beauty and grace out of modesty. I could see that when they stand still, the tints of their wings blend into the leaves around them.

The wonder and surprise of the butterflies in the jungle lie in how evanescent they are. Their spectacle lasts a few brief moments: the moments when they fly by, darting around and pausing in front of you, and then disappearing. I kept wanting to run after them, shouting like Goethe's Faust: *"Bleib doch: du bist so schön!"*—stay a little longer; you're so beautiful! That is where the really feminine grace of the butterflies can be seen—in how fleeting they are. They show themselves by hiding. They flutter and fly around in a wavy zigzag pattern, but it is only to show themselves. They seem to be offering to surrender themselves, but they don't allow themselves to be taken, by hand or by sight—as mischievous as children or exuberant flirts.

We looked at one of them, magnificent, standing still on a leaf with its wings open, on display. They were a very rich black color. Looking at them made you think of velvet. And against that ebony background there were two spots of a bluish color, a blue so heavenly that it would strike up envy in Fra Angelico. We had a few seconds of real esthetic ecstasy.

Another one, orange peppered with tiny black dots, went on ahead of us, flying at the height of our hands (you could almost grab it) for quite a distance. You could converse with it, and tell it how beautiful it was. It seemed to understand our language and, with even more grace, it showed off its dainty and charming way of flying that would make it the envy of any woman in the carnival in Rio.

It was quite a show! Especially its graceful, fleeting evanescence. It stood in such contrast with the harshness of the untamed jungle with its dangers and animal life: panthers, snakes, parrots, ants, mosquitos—and all the tree trunks, tall and massive, with their spreading tops, some of them rotting, and the *taboca* bamboo with its treacherous thorns spiralling upward, which sometimes take us by surprise, snagging our clothes or even our scalps when we brush against them, making us jump back, shout, and curse. This thorny bamboo! If the Bible had been written here, it would certainly have read, "Cursed be the earth: it will bring forth thistles and *tabocas*." Only original sin could produce things so perverse!

But out of love for the butterflies and their unwitnessed spectacles, I'll forgive even the *tabocas*.

Not Even the Kings of Persia . . .

Another marvel of the jungle at this time of the year are the carpets of leaves stretching along the road and over the floor of the forest. It is one huge carpet extending in all directions, so that you seldom see what is under it.

These natural carpets of leaves vary in color and texture according to the kind of trees you're walking through. Sometimes the carpets are made up of golden leaves that seem to sigh when you step on them. Other times it's the dry leaves of the *taboca* bamboo, long like serpents' tongues, ashen in color. Yet others are green leaves that seem to have been knocked off the treetops by human hands, or by the work of animals or insects.

The most wonderful thing is when these carpets are decorated with flower petals: red, yellow, orange, purple, lilac—all fallen from the trees above. On the mantle of leaves, these splendid petals, strewn by jungle breezes, assume a royal splendor. Without a doubt, not even the kings of Persia had such rainbow-drenched carpets at their feet.

The only drawback is that usually you come through the jungle at a quick pace, like a rubber-gatherer, sweat pouring off, carrying a pack that weighs more the farther you go. (Jesus was certainly being practical when he recommended that we not take any baggage for the journey.) The situation becomes worse when you're not in shape, and when you have a sore groin or an injured toe. . . . Then the spirit suffers, draws in, and doubles up upon itself for self-protection. It doesn't open up and take wing sufficiently to see the marvels of the butterflies and the flowers in the jungle, the way we were able to experience and savor this morning. We had more time, the path was better, the day brighter, the body freer and better disposed. And perhaps because it was Saturday, unquestionably the most beautiful day of the week!

II

Beauty and Humanity in the Wilds

Saturday, August 13: Still in Lago

THE INTENSITY OF THE PEOPLE'S FAITH

On our way here, as we conversed on the road, we got into the topic of the faith of the people, their prayer, the state they get into when they're praying. When men and women of the people are praying, you can see in them a great deal of concentrated spiritual energy. They lift their eyes to the saint's image, bless themselves, hold up their hands, move their lips, kneel down, pause, and close their eyes, contrite or in anguish.

But the most impressive thing is the way they gaze at an image. They seem to be talking with a living person. And in their experience, that's the way it is. And that's the way it is for the eyes of faith and for God.

When I was in Juazeiro, in the state of Ceará, in northeastern Brazil, I saw a woman staring at an image of Padre Cícero, near his grave. It was that popular image of him with his cassock, biretta, breviary, and cane. I asked the woman what she felt when she looked at the statue. She said to me, "He's so beautiful to me, young man." The people's criteria of religious beauty are not the same as ours, or the same as those of Renaissance artists. As a matter of fact, the popular images of Mary venerated around the world aren't especially pretty: Aparecida, Guadalupe, Czestochowa, etc. Is beauty the way to God?

The people's religion is deeply moving—and contagious. One of the steps in Graham Greene's conversion took place in Mexico when he saw the Indians moving along on their knees and praying to the Virgin. This same sight impressed the great Russian film director Sergei Eisenstein when he was in Mexico. Despite his firm atheism, he respected those expressions of great feeling and very deep humanity, and he chose to include such scenes in a film. It was released as a posthumous work, entitled *Mexico*.

Certainly for simple persons religion is not the world of what is mysterious, but of what is evident. That's plain when you see how they are shocked when someone claims to be an atheist. It's easier to deny the world than to deny God

25

and the saints. Faith doesn't belong to the order of what is invisible but, on the contrary, to the order of what is visible. They pray to God, to the Virgin, and to the saints, "as if they were looking on the invisible"—that's what's said of Moses (Heb. 11:7). Of him it was said, "The Lord used to converse with Moses face to face, as a man converses with a friend" (Exod. 33:11), and the same goes for popular religion.

Of course, Jesus found more real faith in the religion of the people than in the official religion. Wouldn't the same be true today? Perhaps Christ would find many more followers in Aparecida, Juazeiro do Norte, Lapa, or Bonfim than in chancery offices, rectories, and monasteries.

Sunday, August 14: Still in Lago

THE EUCHARIST ALFRESCO WITH THE PEOPLE

The only persons living in the house where we're staying are two brothers, Waldemar and Francisco, and a 10-year-old boy, Deda, the son of *Dona* Maria José of São Pedro. They work in rubber, and run a trading post. The house is built on a beautiful spot: overlooking a big lake, more than a kilometer across, with warm water, and full of fish and alligators.

We had Mass at 8 A.M. There were a dozen of us. We all sat on the ground, around a tablecloth spread out before us, on which was placed everything needed for Mass. The Mass was celebrated the way meals are eaten around here: right on the ground, without tables or chairs.

The baptism was done along the lake. It was a beautiful day, as was the landscape all around. Two children were baptized, José Raimundo and José Paulo (I suggested the latter name).

Before the Mass, I heard a few confessions. One young man went to confession for the first time and also made his first communion. That was Antônio, our guide, *Dona* Maria José's stepson.

My conversation with the other young man centered on white rum. He wanted to break its hold on him. I gave him as much encouragement as I could, building on that moment of grace. Rum is a plague all over this area. The trading posts always have it in stock and it is always expensive, more than 1,500 cruzeiros a bottle [approx. $10]. The wretched stuff flows at every fiesta, and with all the predictable consequences: fights, stabbings, killings. You often find empty bottles thrown on the trails or behind houses (and sometimes the rum drinker himself, lying there, on his way back from a fiesta).

Our church has to think about how to end this vice, out of concern for the well-being of the people and for peace in their families.

Alligator Hunting

The folks here are busy skinning the five alligators they took from the lake last night.

After skinning them, they roasted them, served us the meat, and gave it to the dogs, pigs, and chickens to eat. The skin is valuable, but it takes effort to prepare it and it's not worth the 2,500 or 3,000 cruzeiros the traders offer.

They went hunting for them last night. The alligators came up, attracted by a light: when two small dead-blue spots reflected the light of the lantern, that was the alligator. The boat would go up close and the harpooner would throw the spear with all his might. Then they would bring the animal to the beach still alive. There they would kill it with a machete, cutting the head to bits.

When we got up this morning, Waldemar, the lay leader, took us out the door where he showed us an alligator about five feet long with a spear stuck between its shoulders. It was alive and was snorting furiously. Waldemar proceeded to kill it, bashing it on the head over and over with the dull edge of a machete.

It was painful for me to see this slaughter. Everything alive deserves to live. We have to learn from the East and from Africa how to have mercy toward life, compassion toward every living thing. Waldemar tried to explain it to me (or to himself), by saying that the animal is dangerous and harmful: it eats the fish in the lake and the chickens on the shore. "Life for life, brother!" he was telling me. But is it really necessary to kill it that way—after leaving it alive all night with a spear running through its shoulders?

"Respect for life: the basic concept of all ethics"—that's what the great Albert Schweitzer learned in Africa.

The Social Question and Its Future

Everything would seem to indicate that there's no land problem here. Production is still traditional. The rubber plantation owners have the land. I've still not heard anyone speaking with a São Paulo accent and I haven't seen any large land areas being cleared, in contrast to what is going on in other parts of Brazil.

But one thing is sure: the exodus from the jungle to the city. The settlements are being emptied. There's no opportunity there. The trading posts aren't very much concerned about production, and they no longer provide a regular supply of goods in return for rubber. Everyone talks about the same thing: moving to the city. That includes the two brothers, Waldemar and Francisco, who live here surrounded by such abundance.

However, there are no social services here, a school or clinic that might encourage families to put down roots. "I'm moving mainly so my children can go to school," *Seu* Tonico told us. He's the hard-working man with an unusual social awareness who had his two children baptized today.

The government doesn't really seem to have a policy of decentralization. All its concern is focused on the cities, especially the capital. The mayor of Manoel Urbano follows the same policy: he's making the city fancier, hoping to draw the people out of the jungle. A "mayor" [*prefeito*, "prefect"] is responsible for the whole district, not just the town.

How much presence does the Brazilian state have out here? None. You note it only in the ideological programs broadcast by *Rádio Nacional* (which the rubber-gatherers like a lot). The low degree of political awareness around here can be explained by the conditions that have kept inhabitants backward and on the sidelines of history.

As the residents leave, driven not by fire and sword, but by the decay of the trading posts and debt strangulation, it's foreseeable that southerners will come and buy up the rubber plantations for cattle grazing. This much is clear: the equilibrium of poverty can't hold out much longer. The rubber-gatherers can't "hang in there" any more. With their debts they fall prey to the traders or they're pushed out by hunger and the general neglect of the area.

This prospect should have a considerable impact on the pastoral perspectives of our work in this area. If the situation is so precarious, should we try to form communities and prepare permanent lay leaders?

Lay Leaders—Narrators of the Gospel

One of the things that has my curiosity aroused, given the very high level of illiteracy in this area, is the question of why a lay leader has to be able to read. Does it mean that the Brazilian Literacy Movement is a prerequisite for access to the word of salvation? When did Jesus demand that an apostle had to have a certificate in reading and writing? Yet our pastoral practice seems to demand it. Are the supposed cultural demands of our age so fastidious?

Max Weber says that it was their conviction that salvation came through faith in the Bible that led the English colonists to learn to read, which made a great contribution to the advance of the United States. Among us there are individuals who have taught themselves how to read in order to be lay leaders. But are reading and writing really an indispensable precondition for announcing the faith? If so, where does that leave those who can't? And what about communities like the ones in this area that don't have anyone who can read and write, or have a hard time getting such a person? Must they be content with a lower level of community, with praying novenas or the rosary? Can you have access to the word of the gospel without going by way of reading the gospel? Jesus doesn't seem to have thought so: he didn't leave anything written and didn't even give express orders to put things in writing. Nor did the early church, the church of the apostles, which spent decades without writing anything of its own, content to transmit the gospel word orally so it could be heard directly. (It's true that they had the Old Testament, and they were looking at it in a new way.)

Wouldn't it be possible to conceive of a kind of training where, instead of giving a privileged place to the printed word and to reading, you could think of other ways of learning and listening to the word of God—ways that would be closer to the people? For example, why not *narrate* the gospel accounts? Persons could memorize a whole series of biblical accounts and then recount them in their own community.

Lay leaders would then be "narrators of the history of salvation." They would have it all in their heads, in their own style—that is, not mechanically, but in the creative way it was done in Hebrew culture: in the form of the midrashim—those lively extensions of the basic and original word of revelation in the form of stories or commentaries.

Besides, a good deal of the Bible is the result of oral tradition. Why not continue it?

You wouldn't have to be limited to simply *narrating* the biblical stories. They could be *sung*, and in fact, that's already happening. It could also be done in drawings or cartoons. Weren't the cathedral windows in the Middle Ages the *biblia pauperum*—the bible of the poor?

And of course these means (stories, songs, pictures) aren't just for the use of the illiterate. They're useful for everyone, including educated persons and intellectuals. Or are they composed of pure reason alone?

Parabolic Scene I: Option for the Poor

In São Pedro I was watching little Ilíaco ("a name from the Bible," his Protestant mother explained to me) chasing away the chickens, pigs, and dogs that were trying to come up and take the food away from a puppy a few months old.

That reminded me of the role played by the church, which must defend the poor from the assaults of the powerful. One could say that when it does that, it deals with the powerful, and so what you can see there is still a church *for* the poor, a church that protects the humble, but not yet a church *of* the poor—and still less a poor church.

But the fact remains that the church really does have power in history and society, and that force can be brought to bear on one side or on the other. It should be exercised on behalf of the poor. Anything else is unrealistic or hopelessly idealistic. The church's function as a tribunal is very important today.

Now the whole point is to see if this "for-the-poor" is heading toward becoming a "with-the-poor" so that it will eventually become an "of-the-poor." This is a historical process that advances by a twofold movement: the church coming closer to the poor and becoming identified with them, and the poor emerging within the church as ecclesial agents. This is the option for the poor and for the poor as leaders—at first potentially and then in reality. "Church of the poor" is both an ideal and an emerging process.

Parabolic Scene II: Those Who Devour the People

Yesterday I observed a huge, fierce dog energetically devouring what was left over from a hunt and angrily snapping its teeth at any animal—dog, pig, or chicken—that dared to come near.

An expressive image for so many great lords in power, who show all their teeth (laws, police patrols, army units) to intimidate anyone in society who dares to make the slightest hint that others might share in the banquet where they're having such a good time. In fact, they're dining on the blood of the poor. It reminds me of the great harlot of Revelation 17, an image of the Roman empire and any similar system; John saw it as getting drunk on the blood of the martyrs. Such a macabre vision filled him with horror (v. 6).

"Will all these evildoers never learn, they who eat up my people just as they eat bread?" (Ps. 53:5).

Parabolic Scene III: The More Powerful Oppress More

I notice the way some animals go after the leftover cassava that Waldemar is throwing to them. The big hog is eating almost all of it. With some effort the smaller animals manage to get hold of a piece or two. That's when the big hog is distracted and doesn't pay enough attention.

Whoever is big and powerful in society wants more and can get it. The lowly are always lowly—if they haven't been simply left out or wiped out.

Is the logic of the market economy or free enterprise any different? Don't you have to be very stupid not to see that, or very unethical not to admit it? In our capitalist society, the poor are Lazaruses who scarcely manage to pick up the scraps that fall from the table of the wealthy (after they've had the Lazaruses produce, cook, and serve the food they're eating).

Jesus saw this very clearly: those who have more power, dominate more. And he reverses the logic, by saying: let those who are more powerful serve more; let those who know more teach more; let those who have more give more; let those who are stronger struggle more (cf. Mark 10: 41–45).

Jesus accepts the logic of capitalism (maximal profit) only as a metaphor for things related to the word of God and to faith: "Whoever has will be given more, but the one who has not will lose the little he has" (Luke 19:26).

Parabolic Scene IV: Unity without Self-Defense

I went down to the lake for a swim at noontime and I saw large swarms of tadpoles swimming together and trying to defend themselves against the fish that were trying to eat them. Sometimes you could hear the splash of a fish coming out of the water and eating one of those poor creatures. I felt sorry for them, swimming together to flee from voracious fish.

They really were defenseless. Even together they remained vulnerable. They were united, but not organized. There certainly was a bonding among them, but they had no means of self-defense. That's how it is with the oppressed: unless they have their own independent organizations, how are they going to defend themselves? Solidarity is not just a feeling or a summons. It is a soul seeking a body.

Bees are different. When they're attacked, they fight back together, with a common strategy, just like an army that's well organized and well trained.

Getting Back to the Language of Jesus

Perhaps the prophets, and Jesus even more, grasped the Mystery of God on the basis of what they saw in nature and in human life. For them the world and history were both a font of revelation and a pedagogical resource.

I'm also learning that parabolic language (Hebrew, *mashal*) is the essence of the people's language. I notice that when I use comparisons taken from life in order to explain God's word and the things of faith, the people react with the kind of spontaneity that shows that the point has gotten through, that something new has been seen. They say "That's just the way it is," "That's it," and "That's true"—just as they do when you're talking with them. And you can see on their faces the kind of expression you see when someone has made a discovery or has been touched in the heart.

In Santa Maria I said to the community that to baptize children and then leave them alone at that point, growing up like pagans, was the same as making a clearing in the forest and then letting the vegetation grow back. I saw them nodding their heads in agreement. On another occasion, in Porongaba, I grabbed a lantern that was on the ground and held it up in front of the community and said, "This flame is the light of faith. But the light of faith needs kerosene: that's the word of God. And the kerosene needs a container: that's the community." I went on from there. They stayed with me, paying attention, showing approval in their eyes and faces, and nodding their heads.

Unfortunately, from Aristotle onward, rationalism has looked down on parabolic speech, in the broad sense of *mashal* (proverb, comparison, maxim, riddle, colorful sayings, allegory, parable, and so forth—in fact, any kind of figurative language), considering it to be a detour around the truth.

For Plato, and even more for the Bible, parable is the way to truth, especially that deeper and more transcendent truth that can be glimpsed only through the roundabout way of parable. But rationalism has restricted parable to the narrow confines of examples and illustrations that serve rules and abstract principles. It becomes a mere teaching device. That may be true for understanding the world (the sciences), but not for the transcendent and essential truths of human destiny. For these truths parabolic language is the royal way. Such is the case of myths.

Scholastic theology was aware of that in its theory of analogy. But contrary to the practice of the Bible, scholasticism favored the conceptual analogy over the metaphorical. It's one thing to say that God is good and merciful, and another to say that God is the father of the prodigal son. One way explains, the other paints a picture. The concept wants to conquer; the image invites.

Theology and pastoral work have still not taken seriously enough the fact that the rabbi Jeshua of Nazareth transmitted his message—the good news of the kingdom—in parables, something that astonished those who first heard him. "To them he spoke only by way of parable" (Mark 4:34). We have to go back to the gospel, even for language and methodology.

One way to neutralize the power of parabolic language is to reduce the parable to its "rational core," to an abstract interpretation, a doctrinal truth. Carlos Mesters, a master of parabolic language, says that holding onto the meaning of a parable while disregarding its specific form is like taking the juice from an orange and throwing the rest away. The whole orange is one thing (with its color, fragrance, peel, shape, beauty, and so forth) and its juice alone is something else. Again, the entire fruit is one thing and its "essence" (today industrially processed) is something else.

We have to get deeper into this issue, but always with a view toward pastoral work. Otherwise, it doesn't get beyond academia, whose tradition is abstract and rationalistic—and opposed to popular culture.

Nobility in the Jungle

The two young brothers with whom we're staying are very good-hearted, incomparably friendly and kind. Despite how hard life in the jungle is, they retain that nobility of spirit, that sensitivity, that comes from charity. They show the greatest respect toward Sister Nieta and myself, calling us *Irmã*, "Sister," and "Father," *Senhor Padre*. And they provide us with the best of whatever they have.

They're always rushing here and there, working around the house, down at the lake, out in the field, in the jungle. This morning I watched them get up early and in a flash they were ready and off to work. Little Deda (who's in front of me now "admiring how fast Father writes") hopped out of the hammock, grabbed the dishes and pots that needed washing, and dashed down to the lake. There was still a hazy white mantle of mist on its surface.

Waldemar and his brother have an impressive work spirit. I've tried to keep up with them in work in and around the house, but I couldn't. I ended up back in the hammock. I'm not used to it, especially with the suffocating heat and the hard living conditions.

Waldemar asked if we wanted some *patoá* wine. I went along with him some five hundred meters into the jungle. He climbed up a very tall tree, perched near a cluster of coconuts, and cut it off. Then he came down. We picked up the hard, black *patoá* coconuts and carried them to the house. We organized a wine-making bee, with everyone having something to do. We got two pots of it. With sugar or manioc flour added, you get something very tasty. I said, "Not even the pope has a drink as distinctive and tasty as this," and they laughed.

Later on, in the jungle, Waldemar said to me, "If you're not familiar with it, getting to know the jungle is like learning to read. It's all very hard, those tiny letters and all. But then, with time and effort, you finally learn."

He's a lay leader and his brother Francisco is his helper. But they don't call meetings very often. He's willing enough, but not well prepared and not used to it. I stressed that he should come to the training session at the end of the month. He pointed out how far it is to Castelo, four days each way. He has to take care of his crops, the rubber, and so forth. I let him know I understood that, but I still emphasized that it was important that he come to the training session. Nieta backed me up.

All that aside, the persons I met there are very wholesome. Although they don't talk about religion a great deal, they have a really Christian spirit. From the confessions I heard before Mass, I could see that their life is almost like that before Adam's fall. They don't commit outrageous sins. They're upright and rough like the tall trees in the jungle. And their sins are as natural as the falling of a tree trunk in the forest. The sanctity of the jungle is a primeval, wild sanctity. But it also has the delicacy of the flowers and butterflies we've seen.

Denture Stories

During a meal I look at the two brothers. They have good-looking faces, and to me look almost Greek. With his curly beard, Waldemar reminds me of the famous bronze Zeus (or Poseidon) I saw in the museum in Athens in 1976. It's too bad that at his age he has false teeth.

Last night in our conversation Waldemar showed me his dentures. With all the ease in the world he told me how he had bought them from someone else. The original owner "had a very big mouth," as he explained to me laughing, so he had had to file the dentures down in order to fit them in his mouth.

At this point Francisco came in and recounted how once he almost lost his own precious dentures. He was in a boat with a girlfriend, coming back from a Protestant worship service (his girlfriend was Protestant). The boat tipped over. The young woman got ashore easily, but Francisco was swept downstream by a current. He had to work mightily against it, but he didn't want to open his mouth to breathe for fear of losing his dentures, and thereby his girlfriend. Fortunately, he got to shore safe and sound: he, his dentures, and . . . their relationship.

Monday, August 15: Still in Lago

LAST THOUGHTS

I thought today was the feast of the Assumption. But Sister told me that here it's celebrated on Sunday. Early in the day I was meditating on the meaning of this mystery for us today, especially for the forest dwellers. It occurred to me that this mystery should be complemented by another, that of the "descension" of Jerusalem from on high to bring human beings together, as described in chapter 21 of Revelation. Human destiny is summed up under two aspects: the assumption of humankind into God and the "desumption" of God into human history. Moreover, that's how Mary's mission in salvation history comes out: she rises to heaven as Our Lady of Glory but she also comes upon the earth as Our Lady of Apparitions: Lourdes, Fatima, Guadalupe, Aparecida, and so forth.

For our part, we're about to leave and go to the next community, Ilha. From here, inside the house, looking across the long porch—all the rubber-gatherers' houses have them—I can see fish swimming in the transparent waters of the lake. A little while ago, Waldemar went running to get his gun, and then, standing just outside the door, shot a huge fish, an *aruanã*. Then he ran down, carrying a net, and with Deda got into a boat and went chasing after the wounded fish. It's not that this fish is especially good, but they wanted to give us a treat before we left. How kind they are! I recall that Francis of Assisi recommended that his followers be courteous, saying that in so doing they would be imitating God, because "God is courteous." That's an attribute theologians have neglected—but it's very Christian. I had to come to the jungle to be able to pick this beautiful flower of gospel *agape*.

In the Green Hell, a Man Solemn and Noble

We're staying in the house of *Seu* Vócio, a lay worker who helps *Seu* Esmeraldo, who lives in Ilha, some 40 minutes away "at a woman's pace," as they say here.

The name of this settlement is Guariúba. *Seu* Vócio, who has been here a long time, originally came from Rio Grande do Norte. He is a "man of great respect and always speaks well," a local rubber-gatherer told me.

Seu Vócio really does have a patriarchal look. He belongs to the stock of those grave and noble men Aristotle praised, and whom Dante saw in limbo and described with these remarkable words:

> There with a solemn and majestic poise
> stood many people gathered in the light,
> speaking infrequently and with muted voice.
> [IV, 112–14, Ciardi translation.]

In one part of his moral theology St. Thomas Aquinas has some interesting remarks on magnanimity as a human and Christian virtue (*Summa Theologiae*, II–II, q. 129).

Royal Road

The trip here from Lago was pleasant. It took us an hour to get from Lago to *Seu* Enoque's house in the settlement of Limoeiro. The path was but somewhat grown over. Our guide was little Deda, whom I nicknamed Juca Mulato, because his liveliness, quickness, and hard-working manner reminded me of the character with that name invented by Menotti del Picchia. On a shoulder strap across his back he carried his small gun. When he turned around to go back home by himself, we heard a shot. He did it to say good-bye—or to show his valor. Just like Juca Mulato.

The second part of the trail, from Limoeiro to Ilha, took us two and a half hours. But that road was far better than any of the others. We came across only a few sections that were partly grown over, especially one where we had to go down on our hands and knees and crawl through a tunnel of vegetation.

Otherwise the road was cleared and lined with leaves. It was an uninterrupted carpet, a genuine royal road, made up of a series of rugs that would make the sheiks of the East envious. From a now uninhabited settlement called Lago Nova Olinda, where we gazed at a marvelous lake, in sleepy silence, as it were, in the midst of the vast forest, the road went almost the whole way along the bank of the Moaco River. The terrain there is clear and open and it's great just to walk along and look around. As you walk through the vegetation you feel like you're in the middle of a well-tended park. The tree trunks are smooth, the ground is covered with vegetation, and the branches overhead provide a humid and tranquil shade. It would be a fantastic place for a picnic. Not even the forests of Versailles, which I got to see again this year, are so superb, so magnificent. Magnificent—that's the adjective that fits everything here, persons and things, nature and weather. Out here you don't even feel the weight of the backpack any more, and you don't feel tired or hungry.

I said to Nieta, "What if we held the training session we've been dreaming about, the one for 'lay narrator/singers of the gospel,' out here on this open riverbank? We could tie the hammocks up to the trees. For food, the lakes and the Moaco River are nearby and they're full of fish." "But, Father, what about the mosquitos at night? Who could stand it?" she answered. "They would be kept away by fires among the hammocks. Isn't that how our Indian brothers and sisters do it?" I pressed the point: "And what if they recounted, and sang, and drew, and dramatized the sacred stories of Israel, of Jesus and the apostles. They would stick in the minds of the new lay leaders and they would take them back to their communities. And there everybody would discuss them and 'apply' them to their lives and struggles, like the Jews with their midrashim."

Nieta smiled. I thought I saw a trace of Sarah's skeptical smile (Gen. 18:12–15). But on that occasion the Lord of the impossible got even (Gen. 21:6).

Tuesday, August 16: Guariúba

THE SEEDLING OF GOD'S WORD HAS TO BE TENDED

The communities in this area are really weak. It's partly because the conditions they live in are very difficult. And the lay leaders haven't been able to take part in a training course. The work of forming BCCs started only a little more than a year ago around here.

The lay leaders find it hard to accept the proposal that they should take part in the training session planned for the end of this month. They bring up the distance, work to be done with rubber, and so forth. And that's all true.

Yet the cause of the gospel is worth any sacrifice. "Whoever wishes to be my follower must deny his very self, take up his cross each day, and follow in my steps" (Luke 9:23). "I have bought five yoke of oxen and I am going out to test them" (Luke 14:19). "Those sown among thorns are another class. They have listened to the word, but anxieties over life's demands, and the desire for wealth, and cravings of other sorts come to choke it off; it bears no yield" (Mark 4:18–19). I've reminded the groups of these passages several times.

This morning when I reminded *Seu* Esmeraldo, who was still holding out, of some of these thoughts, he was struck, and made up his mind: "That's true. I'm going." Up to that point he was intending to get out of it, saying that he had some unbreakable obligations, especially hauling rubber with his ox. The words about the five yoke of oxen reduced him to silence, because they applied to him so tellingly.

Nieta was insisting with *Seu* Vócio that he come also. But from the beginning he simply kept saying, "I can't go." And he didn't explain it any further. He didn't feel he had to say anything more—our solemn one!

In addition to the motivation of the faith itself, training is justified by the way it makes persons conscious of their own specific rights and so can help them overcome the longstanding and harsh oppression they live in and the way they're kept marginalized. Besides the gospel as such, the cause of the people makes the effort worthwhile. Once awakened themselves, lay leaders would help their people awaken.

In any case, faith and community don't grow by themselves like mushrooms. They have to be sown and then cared for. The notion that it happens by itself is a product of ignorance.

But it's true that the jungle dwellers here have grown used to their oppression. They are enslaved and they enslave themselves. It's like a bird that grows up in a cage: you open the door but it doesn't want to get out. . . .

Fiesta Creates Community

Talking with the young ones who came here for the meeting, I learned that they had spent the whole night dancing in Esmeraldo's house in Ilha. "From six to six," they told me. There were about ten couples. They assured me that there was no liquor being passed around, because they didn't have any. There wasn't even any coffee, because it was out of stock in Esmeraldo's trading post. Is what they said all true?

Vócio had already given us a hint. I'm sure they brought us to sleep here instead of in Ilha so as to leave the house available for the party and the dance. It's obvious that here in the jungle they don't get together very often. One of those occasions is when a priest or sister comes through. So they take advantage of the occasion to have a party and have some fun. The party and dance clearly help social integration. It brings people together, creates relationships, entertains, breaks the monotony of the harsh life of the jungle, overcomes the isolation of scattered settlements, and creates bonds of friendship and love among the young, possibly leading to marriage. After all, how else can the young come together and be seen by others, given the way they're lost in the depths of an unending jungle? At a party the young men and women come out of their green hell, come out publicly, take chances, and make choices.

Perhaps we shouldn't moralize too much, and disproportionately, about dancing. No doubt we should be concerned when there are abuses with drinking and fighting. But "abuse doesn't invalidate use."

A Full Agenda

This morning we had a meeting of the community of Ilha and Guariúba. It lasted an hour and a half, and included four parts:

1) *Singing practice.* Nieta took care of this part. I can see that a songsheet isn't much help for illiterate persons, especially when the music is complicated. What's needed is a kind of song that's simple, evangelical, concrete, and repeats the refrain a lot. That way it's easily learned and everyone sings. The best kind are those that have a nice melody and lots of repetition.

2) *A review of community experience thus far.* Sister also took charge of this part. She stressed that they would have to go back to meeting again, that that was an essential condition for community life and growing in faith. Without faith and community, there would be no point in having baptisms. "Unless the community meets, Father and Sister aren't going to perform any baptism or marriage"—she ended on that note.

Nevertheless, with their promise and with the hope that meetings would begin again, we baptized and married all those who came forward. Although the celebration was lively and everyone was active (though not exactly "participating"), there are no grounds for trusting in their easy enthusiasm, which had other motivations behind it. What they really want isn't the gospel and it isn't community: it is to bring their children to be baptized so they won't be, as they say, "animals" or "pagans" any more. Anything else comes after that, and it's at that point that they go their own way.

Certainly their appreciation of baptism has a value. It's an affirmation of their own dignity: rubber-gatherers are human beings, Christians, children of God! But this affirmation is abstract: it remains on the level of public, formal recognition. You can't see consequences in the realm of church (gospel, community, sacraments, etc.) or in the socio-political realm (union, justice, solidarity, etc.).

3) *Celebration of baptism.* We baptized two adults. They wanted to be baptized, although they had little knowledge of matters of faith. Still, they promised to go to the meetings and I especially entrusted the lay leaders with the responsibility for instructing them. They accepted the responsibility very willingly. But here again there's no guarantee. That's why you're left with a skeptical feeling. I was reminded of that strange statement in John: "Many believed. . . . For his part, Jesus would not trust himself to them because . . . he was well aware of what was in man's heart" (John 2:23–25).

Because the nearest spring was far away, we did the baptism outside, in the shade of the house.

As a sign of the commitment to go back to meeting together, we went around the house twice, our hands lifted up, and singing "The people of God were wandering in the desert."

Next, all together, we blessed the water, everyone with their hands stretched out over the basin, and repeating after me the words of the blessing. Then we baptized the two adults and one child.

4) *Marriage ceremony.* Here also I invited the whole community to extend hands over the couple asking for the sacrament. As is usually the case, they were already living together and the bride was pregnant, though she was only fourteen! In response to my invitation, all present lifted their hands in a sign of invocation and—something I hadn't foreseen—they came forward very close to the couple, almost touching their heads, huddling together. I was surprised, but delighted.

Then for the vows, I invited the two witnesses, *padrinhos*—significantly, they were the two lay leaders—to take hold of the linked hands of the couple with their own right hand so as to bless them along with me. It was very expressive. They repeated with me the formula in the ritual, "May God confirm this commitment . . . in the name of the Father and of the Son and of the Holy Spirit." They then traced over their linked hands a large sign of the cross. The venerable and solemn *Seu* Vócio, with great conviction and solemnity, made not one but two large signs of the cross over his new "godchildren." How could that blessing fail to take?

Lessons Learned from the Meeting

I've learned that there has to be a certain amount of order imposed when worship is celebrated. The jungle dwellers don't normally get together very often, so when they come for a church service, they take any position whatsoever. The children come up and sit on the chairs or benches, leaving the mothers standing behind with babies in their arms. They don't see anything wrong with that. So somebody should tactfully step in to make sure that at least the couples getting married and the mothers having children baptized are assigned a special place.

Still, I could see today that this order shouldn't be rigid. There should be freedom to move about during the celebration. But not too much, the way it is here—they have no qualms about coming or going or moving around when they feel like it. Community teaches its members how to live together and act with one another.

There should be a certain amount of choreography, or planned group movement, for going from one place to another, or clapping, individuals coming out into the middle, the leader making some expressive gesture calling on the group to do something, etc. That, incidentally, is something the Evangelicals do, and it is obviously very attractive.

When worship involves movement, a celebration can go on over an hour and yet worshipers do not feel tired, even if they're standing, as is the case here. After all, that was the custom in St. Augustine's time in Hippo where there were no pews in the churches and yet celebrations went on for hours.

On the other hand, I realized that the movement of the celebration came almost exclusively from one focal point: the celebrant. I was the one leading the liturgical action and all the initiatives came from me. The people might consider it "nice" but it was "Father's business." I've always been disappointed when someone comes up to me after Mass and says, "That was a very nice celebration you gave us." A celebration becomes a show or performance.

In this case, even Nieta, who could have had a more active and creative role, especially in the celebration of the word and in the examination of community life, was definitely overshadowed. The same is true of the lay leaders, who should have occupied the same place in the celebration that they do in the life of the community.

In short, there was community participation but it reflected dependence rather than autonomy, and was reactive rather than self-starting.

Even though this community is germinal, barely a promise of community, there certainly could have been more group participation. After all, the task of anyone working with the people, whether the end be religious or political, is the same: to expedite participation. I regard all this as self-criticism.

Fragmented Population, Shaky Church

We got to the settlement of Santa Clara, but nobody was there. *Seu* Francisco Cobal, the lay leader, was gone and his whole family as well. So we turned into a side trail and went to the house of *Seu* Francisco Poeira. Living with him are his wife and two sons, twins, who help him work his plot of land.

We had been on the road for four hours. After a marvelous dip in the Macapá Creek I felt like new—the way I always do after a swim.

The whole path, or almost all of it, had been excellent: clear and flat, with a thick carpet of dry leaves that rustled and popped under our feet. Our guide, young Antônio, the son of Esmeraldo, the lay leader, explained that this noise from the leaves makes hunting difficult at this time of year. Animals are easily frightened off, especially deer, which are more skittish than the other animals.

Seu Chico Poeira talks like everyone else: he wants to get out, to go to Feijó, where he has relatives. The hinterlands are being depopulated. And that raises serious questions about training lay leaders and forming communities. Does it make sense to train lay leaders when you're not sure they'll remain where they are much longer? Of course, if they've been trained, they'll be active wherever they go. When persons have advanced in consciousness, they don't go back. Training is never wasted; it's not dropped into a bottomless pit.

But the issue is more serious when the roots of a whole population are quite weak. How can you form church communities when social communities are crumbling? If the population of the jungle is declining, how can you form local churches?

A church community can confront social disintegration if the church is well established, and if it has concrete (especially economic) prospects for surviving. If these conditions are missing, no BCC can possibly be set up.

On this point the relationship is like that between nature and grace. Grace can elevate, perfect, and even heal nature, of course, but only on the condition that nature already exists as its basis ("grace presupposes nature"), and that that basis is dynamically open.

Similarly, the church creates society, BCCs form labor unions and other kinds of associations, faith encourages the growth of political awareness, etc. But this is possible only where the church, BCCs, and faith are already in place and where there is a potential for society, unions, and political awareness—or better, where they are beginning to emerge. That's the way the dialectic goes: church community—political community.

"Life—Downhill after Thirty"

When we arrived, *Seu* Poeira's wife started fixing something to eat. We gave her the two eggs and a bit of flour we'd brought, things the community in Ilha had given us to help with our meal when we arrived. I must say that they did help the woman avoid the embarrassment of not being able to provide enough.

How would the FAO (Food and Agriculture Organization) classify the local population? Starving? Certainly undernourished. I look at *Seu* Chico Poeira: he is skinny, withered, covered with scars, and his teeth are missing. It certainly makes you feel sorry to see persons, even the young, here in the bush with no teeth. What happens is that the traders push antibiotics onto the people and the rubber-gatherers use them as a panacea for everything. And the rare dentists who come into the jungle are simply students doing their practicum—or worse, just teeth-pullers.

Despite all this, the rubber-gatherers exhibit an incredible stamina in their work. Here the demands of life overcome what's missing in their bodily constitution.

For that reason, at age thirty a person in the jungle is already old. *Seu* Poeira tells me, "Life is on the rise until you're thirty—after that, it's downhill."

When will the prophecy of Isaiah, part of the dream of the kingdom of God, come true?

> No longer shall there be in it [the city of jubilation] an infant who lives but a few days, or an old man who does not round out his full lifetime; he dies a mere youth who reaches but a hundred years, and he who fails of a hundred shall be thought accursed [Isa. 65:20].

The Jungle: A Hieroglyph

Fortunately, as we've gone from one stopping point to another, we've always had a guide. Otherwise, we would have ended up lost in the forest. That's especially true in this area where leaves cover the ground and you can't see clearly where the trail goes. Besides that, the trails crisscross one another: rubber trails, trails for avoiding rapids, and side trails. It's easy to wander from one to another.

This morning, when I was half impatiently looking for someone to go along with us as a guide, a 10-year-old girl told me, "It's all straight, *Seu* Padre. Just go straight ahead and you'll get there. You can't miss it." I smiled to myself and thought: "My God, how easy it is for her! But for those of us who aren't from here, the forest is as indecipherable as an Egyptian hieroglyph. We're illiterate, or just beginning with our first primer, when it comes to moving and living in the jungle."

Finally, Antônio came along. But as we were getting to Santa Clara we got a scare. He stopped in the middle of the road and said, "I'm going to take you around to the other side of this lake and then I'm going home. You just keep going straight ahead all the way. In two hours you'll be in Bacia. You can't miss it." I held my breath and Sister Nieta almost fainted. She pleaded, "Don't do it, Antônio. We'll get lost." And I added, "We'll walk right into a panther's lair. We don't know how to go straight and we can scarcely see through all this vegetation." And he said very simply, "Just go where you see the leaves most crushed."

But which of us has eyes for that, to see which leaves are more trampled on than others? Finally, I said, somewhere between anxiety and firmness, "Okay, if you're going back, so are we. If we go on alone, we won't make it." At that, he gave in. He took the lead, in silence, and we followed behind, relieved.

Pan, a Forest God

All the while we're traveling through the virgin jungle, an inexpressible feeling of fear comes along with us: the fear of a "pest"—the understatement the jungle dwellers use for snakes or the wild boars that move around in herds leaving a wide sweep of jungle smashed as though run over by a steamroller. Or the "pest" could be a great anteater, or a tapir, or a panther, the uncontested queen of the virgin forest.

The jungle dwellers have a thousand panther stories. Once they start, they never stop. They praise the animal's cunning and its strength. They say it only attacks when attacked, or when it's very hungry, or when it's guarding its young. That it goes along with you, following your footsteps. That it cuts in front of travelers to attack them, out of hunger. That it sees you without letting you see it, etc.

They say you can defend yourself by climbing up a tall tree, But it shouldn't be very thick, or the panther will climb it too. In any case, you're always apprehensive in the jungle: anything can happen. Even at night when you're lying in a hammock stretched out inside a house (with doors and windows open) that fear stays with you: maybe a panther will come by. . . .

Personally, I'm not afraid of snakes. I know there are terrible ones around here, like the *pico-de-jaca* or the *cobra-papagaio*, a pit viper. About that one the rubber-gatherers have a saying, "If it doesn't kill you, it will leave you crippled." The animal that does worry me somewhat is the jaguar. So both in the jungle and in houses I joke a lot about the jaguar: that if I meet one, I'm going to tie its whiskers together; that I'm going to send it off running with a shout, and so forth. The jungle dwellers have a big laugh when I brag about my valor, which is more to keep my spirits up than to amuse others.

Pan, the Greek god who frightened humans (origin of the word "panic"), dwelt in forests. If this fear makes us dream of all kinds of wild beasts when we're in the hammock, how much more will it make the children of the jungle dream—but with their eyes open—and create a forest mythology: of *mapinguaris* (giants with tortoise-shell armor), striped cuckoos, and other fantastic creatures.

The Jungle, Creator of Wonders

It's not just fear. Often the jungle puts on shows that are surprising and marvelous, displays that sometimes are also lessons.

That's the case of the *apuí-cipó,* an epiphytic woody vine. It climbs up a tree, wraps around it, and strangles it, drawing off all the sap. The tree dies and the *apuí-cipó* grows in its place.

The interesting thing is that the vine keeps growing, loops down from the treetop, sinks into the ground, and produces another trunk. And so its branches keep going up and down and end up crisscrossing a number of tree trunks diagonally.

Yesterday *Seu* Vócio took me to see an *apuí* wrapped around a rubber tree in a deadly embrace. And he remarked, "That's a good-for-nothing tree." He said the people compare a parasitical kind of person to the *apuí*: "That person is like the *apuí*," they say. I think to myself: Is there any more expressive figure for capitalists?

Another surprise! Near Neném Ponte's house we saw a marvelous bridge leading across a deep and long natural canal. It was a palm tree rooted on one side that had fallen across and reached the other side. But from that point it had shot up again some five meters and from that height spread out its beautiful branches. Something worthy of inclusion in an earthly paradise!

And to complete the picture, alongside this palm tree bridge, you could see an old tree holding out a branch that was curved but long and firm, as though it were providing a guardrail for someone who might go across on the rounded surface of that strange bridge. "Now we've seen it all!" I thought with amazement.

But there's more! Yesterday when we were heading toward Ilha, we went over another natural bridge, once more a large tree stretching across a river. But there wasn't any handrail to grab onto. There were, however, some vines hanging down from the trees, thin, straight, and strong, curving over the river. By taking hold of them one by one you could keep your balance and cross safely. There are wonders beyond imagination out there!

III

Apostolic Communities

Wednesday, August 17: A Settlement Called Castelinho

"THEY WANT TO STARVE THE PEOPLE TO DEATH!"

We're on the last leg of our missionary journey. Before getting to the last community that we're scheduled to visit, we stopped at the house of *Seu* Sandro and *Dona* Francisca.

We found only the woman and three children at home. They told us *Seu* Sandro had gone to get some plantains for food. The situation was so bad that there wasn't even flour and sugar for making *jacuba*—a basic dish when nothing else is available.

I got surprised when I took out the bag of flour we had brought just in case there wasn't anything at our next stop. The littlest child came running up aching with hunger and grabbed the sack. Her eyes brightened as she grabbed some flour and ate it.

I noticed a man in the house, the woman's brother-in-law, *Seu* Francisco. Stretched out in the hammock like a Turkish pasha, he went on and on criticizing the traders for not keeping things in stock and for their high prices. "They want to starve the people to death!" he asserted angrily.

He bragged that he brings in more than a thousand kilograms of rubber a year, but even so, he said he can't manage to make ends meet. "It's no good for a living and it never has been," he complained. He explained to me that a rubber-gatherer on the average gathers about seven hundred kilos of rubber a year. Rubber fetches 600 cruzeiros a kilo, so he is taking in something like 420,000 cruzeiros a year (approx. $280). A rubber-gatherer's family never spends all that on goods (I'm still following his reasoning). They get much from the jungle: flour, meat, fish, poultry. But they have to buy oil, milk, salt, sugar, soap, etc. And so all their income is used up in the trading post. "It's a den of slavery," he told me.

It seems to me that rubber-gatherers are more like slaves than workers. They're bound not by iron chains but by the invisible chains of need and debt.

We had to get back on the trail, so to close the conversation I told *Seu* Francisco that the rubber-gatherers are like dogs that don't know how to hunt down panthers. Instead of all attacking together, they each go their own way. The panther tears them apart one by one. Only if they unite will they be able to chase the panther away. He laughed and stopped talking. He prefers the tactic of flight. He's going to start life over somewhere else.

Traders as Lay Leaders?

We've come to the last settlement on our trip: Bacia. We're staying in the house of the lay leader, *Seu* Bena. He's a rubber-gatherer, but he's also—and primarily—a trader: he buys things in the city and sells them in his trading post, to about ten rubber-gatherers, who, for their part, have to sell him their rubber. But he isn't the owner of this rubber plantation. That's someone from São Paulo, *Seu* Carlos, whom he serves as a kind of manager. *Seu* Carlos is also the owner of a large farm called Sudam, on the road between Rio Branco and Feijo, not far from here, where he has 3,000 head of cattle. Obviously, social position makes things ticklish and problematic from a pastoral viewpoint.

As a matter of fact, I've only now realized that several of the lay leaders in this area are really traders, or closely affiliated with them. That includes *Seu* Raimundinho in São Romão, *Seu* João Paulo in Porongaba, Waldemar and Francisco in Lago, *Seu* Vócio in Guariúba, and *Seu* Bena here in Bacia.

This is symptomatic. Perhaps we're repeating, in a diminished form, the same error that was made in the past. We used to go to the house of the one who held economic power—the boss—and now we choose to go to the house of the one with cultural power—the one who can read—and that person is well established socially and economically. The traders are really the "middle class of the jungle." Being able to read raises them up to the position of being managers of rubber plantations.

It is important to be careful here, because if we want liberation and justice, the traders aren't the most important agents. Like any "middle class," they'll go only as far as their interests carry them, and there they stop. True, they're oppressed (by their boss) but there's no question that they're also oppressors.

Such is the class dynamic in the jungle. It's obvious that with this structure it will be hard for a community to get very far in the conscientization and social struggle.

On the basis of information I got from persons in situ, I put together Table 1 showing how prices compared in the different settlements we went through.

As you look over these prices you realize that *Seu* Vócio of Guariúba is the one who gives the best deal: he pays more for the rubber and sells goods at a lower price. He says he doesn't want to exploit, because he doesn't have to. "I live from my own work, not the work of others." One rubber-worker told me he doesn't exploit "because he's a Protestant"! Perhaps because you don't see Catholics acting like that. . . . In any case, the example of *Seu* Vócio shows it's possible to be a trader and yet be on the side of the people.

Table 1

Price Comparisons
in Cruzeiros
August 1983

	São Romão	Porongaba	Lago	Guariúba	Bacia
1 can of powdered milk	1,500	2,000	3,000	1,000	2,500
1 can of cooking oil	800	1,000	1,500	1,000	1,800
1 shotgun shell	700	800	900	800	1,000
1 kilo of rubber (selling price)	550	550	50	865	950

They say the difference in prices is explained by how far away the particular settlement is. But that's no explanation for the very high prices. Those prices are a scourge and they have an impact on absolutely everyone. So it's no wonder that a rubber-gatherer gets over his head in debts, and becomes "subject" to the trader, as they say around here, and that the tendency is to get out by running away.

Thursday, August 18: Bacia

CELEBRATING COMMITMENT

At 9 o'clock this morning we brought the people together for a celebration. There were a few adults and a lot of children. The reason is that word didn't get out that the sister and priest were coming.

First, we had a penitential rite. The community carried out a self-examination on five points that were quite concrete, a sort of "pentalogue": alcohol, gossip and backbiting, fights and violence, infidelity, and community participation.

Then each one freely came out into the middle, put their hands into a basin of water, and said which sin they wished to be rid of. Each time the community would sing "Forgive your people, O Lord."

It worked out well. Nevertheless, I can now see that those five points could have been summed up in a single sin: breaking the "basic option"—following

Jesus Christ and his gospel. Otherwise there's a serious risk of falling into a kind of casuistry.

We then went over the life of the community. Sister Nieta led this part. She began with a reflection on Matthew 18:18–20: "Whatever you bind. . . . When two or three are gathered. . . ." Those words are decisive for characterizing a church community: the forum where decisions are accepted by God, and the ambience wherein Christ is present.

Some important conclusions were reached and some decisions were made:

1) Sandro and Francisca, a married couple, are going to be auxiliary leaders in the sense of helping the community come together. They'll do this with *Seu* Bena, especially when he's away on business. In that case, they'll lead the rosary; they don't know how to read. And they'll do it in their own home in order to vary the meeting place and decentralize the life of the community, because there's always a danger of its being monopolized by just one person.

Still, we had to teach this couple how to lead the rosary. It was a real struggle to get them to where they could remember the order of the five joyful mysteries, which summarize the infancy gospel. We chose these mysteries because some of them already knew them. At each decade they could recall the whole story of that mystery, and make some kind of commentary or personal application. We then put it into practice, reciting the rosary while walking in a procession.

2) Punctuality. The adults insisted that the time and place of meetings should be fixed with exactitude so everyone would get used to coming at that time. They found it very annoying to come to a meeting and then be stuck there waiting hours for everyone to arrive so they could begin the meeting.

3) The last decision was that of insisting with *Seu* Bena that he come to the next raining session in Castelo. *Dona* Maria de Lourdes, his wife, added that this training session would be very good for him, in the sense of helping him control his drinking and other inappropriate behavior. What we had in mind was more the growth of social awareness he might get there, with faith as the starting point.

As has happened before, I came on strong during this part, which Sister was actually in charge of. She got left in the shade a little. This is certainly not good, because the sisters are the ones who will remain around here, and they will be carrying on the work. Besides, even limited participation is always better than trying to do things to perfection.

At the end we had a procession of commitment. We all went out singing, walking on the grass around the house. We stopped in the shade of a tree and there everyone who wanted to—and they all came forward—could put their hand on the book of the gospels, giving evidence of their commitment to keep coming to the meetings and taking part in the life of the community. It was a gesture that everyone felt deeply. But I don't know how far it will take them.

We turned back and finished with prayer in our own words and a blessing.

Waiting

When we were just about to start the last stage of our journey, going back home, we learned that some families were coming for baptism.

What should we do? We talked it over with the others and asked their opinion. Contrary to what we expected and hoped, they concluded that we should wait all day, if necessary, and leave tomorrow.

We gave in. Even knowing that these others don't take part in the community, we decided to provide them with the sacraments, as long as they promised to come to community meetings in the future. Most of them live an hour or so away, so they *can* come (that's a short distance in terms of life in the jungle).

That procedure seemed correct to us, because the communities in this area don't make it easy for members to participate. The communities aren't well organized, and their leaders have little preparation or experience.

So until the others came I got into my hammock. The hammock here is the equivalent of an armchair. I'm spending the day as though it were a holiday, a mini-retreat, and a time for reviewing the work we've done.

The weather is pleasant; it's a marvelous day. The temperature is neither too hot nor too cold. "It's a kind of *friagem*," *Seu* Sandro tells me. *Friagem* means a sudden drop in temperature when cold masses from the Andes pass over.

I gaze at the edge of the forest in front of the house. I see several yellow and red trumpetbush flowers. A wonder, sheer ascension! Why are there flowers?, I ask myself. How can you explain the human pleasure of contemplating these trumpetbush flowers arising out of the green sea of the jungle? Might this not be a sign of what surpasses the jungle, flowers and all? Isn't it a sacrament of supreme and irresistible Beauty?

A Mini-Retreat

I decide to pray and meditate the gospel—in fact, make a mini-retreat. I realize that of its very nature missionary work can't succeed without prayer. Prayer leads all life, all history, including the contradictions, back to God and God's plan. So I take the gospel of Mark and sink into the passion account.

But why a retreat? Certainly faith means commitment. But what motivates this commitment and moves one to it? There has to be something that pushes, stirs things up, lifts things up. A practice is made great only by the soul that informs it. Lying in the hammock I have a strong intuition: behind all action toward liberation there's a dream, a love, an ideal, a madness, a spirit, a mystique—whatever word you want to use. It's what makes you "hang in there" in the middle of the storm.

But the Bible has a word for this: it's faith. It's a kind of attraction, seduction, or passion that holds sway over you and leads you beyond your limits. Faith is not action; it leads to action.

Now that's what a retreat is about: cultivating this secret and decisive force.

It's of the same order as listening to a symphony, making friends, lying out in the sun, admiring flowers.

Hence, that's where the reason for a retreat is to be found: deepening within us faith in the Father and in the reign of God, increasing enthusiasm for the liberating gospel, "stirring the flame" of mission in the midst of the people (cf. 2 Tim. 1:6).

Otherwise, why would anyone wander around these vast jungles? Faith is a gust of wind, a call, a concern, a spirit—the Spirit, who comes before, in the midst of, and underneath everything else: walking, stopping for the night, holding a meeting, dealing with animals, stumbling, hurting your toes, sweating, being bitten by ants, eating unfamiliar food, being unable to sleep at night because of the cold, sloshing through stagnant water, etc. And not getting discouraged or sad in all this but feeling courage, conviction, and joy. And why? Because you see in all this a wonderful meaning, value, greatness, and a definitive purpose.

A retreat means reinforcing the inner drive to bring encouragement and salvation everywhere. It means watering the hidden roots of our being so it will grow, and provide shade, flowers, and fruits. Like this huge chestnut tree I see in the clearing in front of me!

The People of God

I think about these persons who are coming out of the depths of the jungle. This group of poor jungle dwellers coming to have their children baptized, with that faith of theirs, vigorous and wild like the rivers around here—they are the people of God. This is the people chosen by God.

In these poor forest dwellers the kingdom of God is manifest with more power and truth than in the most majestic pontifical liturgies.

Even with their faces the way they are, hardened and bruised from all the beatings life has dealt them, faces that sometimes remind you of the inexpressiveness of a chestnut tree, they are God's beloved children, those whom the Messiah honored, the protegés of the Spirit. The Lord becomes their "avenger," *Go'el,* as the Scripture says, and *Redemptor,* as the Latin writers translated it.

The great and unfathomable mysteries of the kingdom are revealed to them. As for us, we're simply "administrators of the mysteries of God" (1 Cor. 4:1) for them. The pope, bishops, priests, and the whole ecclesiastical system exists for them, to serve them.

In their poverty and abandonment, they reflect the riches and closeness of God. In them we can see that God is the Father of those who are abandoned, the Son is the Messiah of the oppressed, and the Spirit is the Paraclete, the one who encourages and consoles those who have become embittered.

This is all true, despite—or perhaps because of—the "religious ignorance" of these poor persons, their lack of community, formal religion, piety, prayer, sacraments, church, and all the rest. Because they will be liberated from all this; they are being liberated. From whatever they don't have!

They're like the *'am ha'aretz* in the time of Jesus—the poor of the earth—among whom he sent his apostles and who were his starting point for building his church.

"It was not because you are the largest of all nations that the Lord set his heart on you and chose you, for you are really the smallest of all nations. It was because the Lord loved you . . . that he brought you out with his strong hand from the place of slavery" (Deut. 7:7-8). The Marxist loves the oppressed because they're strong, not because they're weak. The Christian, however, loves the oppressed as God and Christ love them: not because they're actually strong, but so they can become strong.

Friday, August 19: Still in Bacia

THE RUBBER-GATHERER: ANYTHING BUT LAZY

We've been in Bacia for three days. That's enabled us to see how life in one of these settlements is very much in motion, contrary to what one might be tempted to think.

All day long everyone is running here and there. And that's everyone—children and adults, men and women.

Nothing at all like Jeca Tatu (Brazilian stereotype for the "typical" *caipira,* backwoods man, assumed to be slow and lazy). Quite the contrary. Despite the scanty food and harsh living conditions, they're always working.

I also note the very special way they have of relating to one another, one of bantering and making comparisons. "You look like an old blind man." "You've gotten to look like a jungle animal." I've heard *Dona* Maria de Lourdes scold her children like that.

Their language is usually indirect, especially when they're criticizing or correcting. When they do that, it fills up with metaphors and roundabout expressions. The susceptibility that outsiders observe in them is a particular expression of this delicate nonconfrontational strategy.

Children show radical obedience to their parents. It's obvious in everyday life and even more so in confessions: it's rare that the question of obedience to parents or even to uncles and aunts, grandparents, or older brothers and sisters goes unmentioned. A readiness to obey immediately is part of the ethos of the rubber-gatherer's life. For example, it's enough for a father to call on his son to go along with the sister and priest to another settlement (and that can even take days); the son will obey without hesitation and without any objections.

I also note the high proportion of rubber-gatherers who are injured or crippled, showing the effects of broken bones in an arm, a leg, or elsewhere. They don't have any way to get treatment so they just keep going the way they are. It's obvious: life in the jungle is itself wild. It leaves marks on their bodies: scars and broken bones. Whatever passing injuries you might suffer on these missionary trips pale into insignificance in comparison with the blows this suffering people endures.

Yet Another Day of Waiting

Again this morning we were all set to go. But once more the people insisted that it would be good to wait for *Seu* Bena, who was going to be arriving during the day. Once more we gave up our plan and stayed.

During these days the family has been laying out a very good spread of food in comparison with what we had been eating. We've been eating beans and rice, which we hadn't seen for two weeks. There was more cassava flour with soup broth. And I was stuffed. I kept on dreaming, whether awake or asleep, of the tables of my communities in Rio de Janeiro and Rio Branco. . . . I had a curious dream: I was in the company of Roman cardinals facing a table full of bread, meat, vegetables, and fruits, at a Christmas supper. . . . My suffering stomach was using these daydreams to get even, things really proper to the "fleshly man," as Paul would say. A good occasion to fortify instead the "spiritual man" who is not nourished by "eating or drinking" but from the "justice, peace, and the joy that is given by the Holy Spirit" (Rom. 14:17).

In any case, I'm inclined to think that the *patoá* wine we drank today for the second time on our trip wouldn't be so out of place on a fancy supper table!

The Bible and Its Persuasive Power

I continue reading and meditating on the passion of Jesus according to Mark. This reading material is more appropriate for the present than anything else: the passion of Christ continues in the body of those who are scorned in this world. It puzzles me why the passion isn't read more often in the official liturgy or in the readings in the BCCs. Why limit the passion to Holy Week?

I note how the children of the jungle find it convincing when you argue from the scriptures. To say "That's the word of God" is to present a proof that is plainly apodictic, irrefutable. The Evangelicals know that, and they quote scripture all the time, to the point of misusing it. On the other hand, theology has always recognized the argument from scripture as the most basic one and the one on which theology, all theology, is based. This vigor of the word of God is being rediscovered in pastoral work with the people today.

Reading Mark, starting with chapter 11, Jesus' ministry in Jerusalem, it's striking to see how, when faced with the authorities of his time who use and abuse sacred scripture, Jesus also quotes it often. Thus, for example: Mark 11:17, 12:10, 12:26, 12:29, 12:36, and all chapter 13 (eschatological discourse), which is interlaced with biblical formulations. In chapter 12 alone there are four Old Testament quotes. In dealing with the masters of his age, Jesus goes into combat with the very same kind of weapons.

On the other hand, Jesus didn't write anything and didn't order anything to be written. It was his preaching and practice that give rise to all the Christian scriptures. Sacred scripture is always the crystalization of the holy word. Writing always takes second place to speaking.

Historians and anthropologists tell us that writing arose not so much as an instrument of communication but rather as an instrument of domination. "The letter kills," says Paul. Plato had already put forth the observation that the written word is like a "deaf interlocutor who doesn't answer when questioned." He considered the book a degradation of living dialogue. For all these reasons, scripture can be understood only within the tradition that gave rise to it, and gives it meaning and life.

And so the scripture that produces a living and creative word is good. And the scripture that only produces rabbinical commentaries is disastrous. The point is to reencounter the spirit in and under the letter, to re-create the oral meaning from the scripture as recorded and written down.

In pastoral work it is certainly important to return to the scripture, but we must go further. Pastoral work has to go from the scripture to the originating word. That will make a "spiritual" reading really possible—that is, a reading of the spirit or of the meaning that is prior to the letter and is in it like the heart in the body. Scripture is an unavoidable step on the way to the word of God, but in itself it's not enough. We have to go through it in order to get to its root, which is the Spirit.

Isn't that what our pastoral work with the people is trying to do in terms of a creative reappropriation of the Bible?

Popular Religion

Dona Francisca, an auxiliary lay leader, has just explained to us how to cure a toothache with prayer. We had spent a good deal of time talking about prayers for curing and when she saw that we were interested she decided to reveal to us the prayer for getting rid of a toothache. "But it has to be hurting a lot, because, if you pray it when there's only a little pain, then it starts to hurt more," she explains with conviction. "Here's how you say the prayer. Put your finger above the tooth, and then pray":

> Saint Pelônia
> Was sitting on top of a rock.
> She had a toothache.
> And Our Lady came by and said:
> "What's the matter, Pelônia?"
> So she answered:
> "I have a toothache."
> Our Lady answered,
> "Because you have faith
> In the rising sun
> And the waning moon
> There's no reason for you to feel any more pain
> In your jaws
> Or in your teeth.
> By the powers of God
> and the Virgin Mary.

Francisca then explains, as a kind of rubric, that you must immediately pray the Our Father, the Hail Mary, the Holy Mary [sic], and the Glory Be three times each. "That's the power of prayer," she concludes.

Then she teaches us how to pray in order to cure *vermelha* (swelling in the foot):

> Jesus came from the mountains
> And he found Pedro and Paula [sic].
> —Where are you coming from, Pedro and Paula?
> —I'm coming from Rome.
> —What's going on there?
> —There's a lot of sickness.
> —Go back, Pedro and Paula,
> You're going to cure *vermelha*
> with three lumps of pure salt,
> A branch from the bush,
> And water from the spring.

Here again you have to pray the Our Father, the Hail Mary, the Holy Mary, and the Glory Be three times each. The ritual consists of putting some water in a glass, taking a small branch, and using it to bless the person with crosses while saying the prayer.

We can ask if this "works." Well, if it didn't work the people would have given up these things. Perhaps you could say it "works" through the power of suggestion or of some similar force. Okay, so what? Does it mean that the divine power can't also go along the same route? The medieval theologians used to say, "God isn't tied to the sacraments." It's all the more moving to observe with how much good faith and conviction the poor carry out these gestures—gestures that are simple and unpretentious, like themselves, gestures that aim at the same thing as many of Jesus' miracles: healing, restoring wholeness of life.

The pastoral question that always remains is whether the church couldn't take up these practices, evangelizing them—that is, purifying and enriching them, and recognizing their value.

The Kingdom of God: Not Just a Metaphor

Reading the passion according to Mark—my meditation matter during these days—makes this much clear: it isn't just Jesus' life that's deeply connected to the message and practice of the kingdom, but also his death. As a matter of fact, Jesus is condemned as the "king of the Jews," and therefore as king of the kingdom he was announcing. It's curious: the primitive community didn't retain the title "Christ the King," perhaps because it could be misleading, and because of the contemptuous way it had been used by

Jesus' enemies. But the corresponding term "Lord" was retained.

"King" and "Lord" aren't just metaphors. True, Jesus wasn't a politician in the sense that Herod, Pilate, Theudas, or Judas the Galilean were politicians. He was fundamentally a prophet and, even more radically, the one announced by the prophets. But from that angle he called everything into question, including the structures of society. Therefore, with the kingdom of God as his starting point, which for him meant "absolute revolution," he included society as well, with its revolutions.

So the Sanhedrin and Pilate weren't completely wrong in trying to get him out of the way. It wasn't simply a mistake, a misunderstanding. Power doesn't often deceive itself. The tremors were reaching their thrones, and so they were obliged to wipe out the prophet of total liberation.

The same is true of the church: its evangelizing mission isn't formally and directly political, but getting into the area of politics is implied and involved in that mission.

And just as it happened then, today also power can only condemn the church by calling it "subversive" and "communistic." The Sanhedrin condemned Jesus as a "blasphemer" and Pilate condemned him as an "agitator" and someone striving to take power. The fact is that those in power can only use categories that come from their own realm. They have to pigeonhole those who question power; they have to put them in their slot. It just shows how legalistic and obtuse powerholders are.

Life in the Christosphere

In the passion according to Mark there is a clear idea of Christ's body as temple: "another temple not made by human hands" (14:58); "the curtain in the sanctuary was torn in two from top to bottom" (15:38). Jesus' death is the death of a temple, any temple—which stands for any cult or religion. From now on, religion is Christ rather than Christianity.

The mysticism of John—the mysticism of the risen Christ as temple—and that of Paul—the mysticism of the Christosphere, within which "we live, move, and have our being" (Acts 17:28)—is not very common among Christians today. We tend to feel God's presence more in a general way, an abstract presence, one that is disincarnate and spiritual (in the Greek sense), a presence without any "material," concrete aspect.

I find a great richness in the spirituality of the body of Christ, extended everywhere, spread throughout the universe, filling the world with his energy and constituting its absolute content, its pleroma, what holds it together. Teilhard de Chardin could speak about this in terms of the "cosmic body" of Christ, which he saw expressed in Paul's captivity letters and in the church fathers.

There is a splendid *agraphon* (unwritten saying) attributed to Jesus that goes, "Raise the stone—this is me. Split the firewood—I am here!" This "I" isn't God or a vague and general spirit, but Jesus Christ. And not Christ the word, but the risen Christ, the paschal and eschatological body—"spiritual body" and "body of glory," in Paul's terminology.

This mysticism of cosmic communion seems quite appropriate for the experience of our jungle dwellers. They don't have any church buildings or worship services; their temple can be the body of the risen one, and their life can be experienced as one great liturgy. And the jungle, with its trees, flowers, rivers, lakes, and animals, large and small, would all be within the Christosphere. That confers an absolute dignity on the humble life of the rubber-gatherers and shows how their lives entail greatness.

Looking Back on Our Mission

Nieta and I took this afternoon to do a review or evaluation of our activity these days.

Among the positive things, besides those already mentioned, I would single out the fact that there were no major accidents: we didn't get lost, we didn't run into any wild animals, we didn't have to spend the night in the jungle, we didn't get any serious illness, we didn't undergo real hunger, etc. We've also felt good and been in a good mood the whole time.

Among the "less positive" aspects, there are some things I've already mentioned: the weakness of the communities and their lay leaders, the lack of a critical consciousness, the exodus from the jungle. But I will now emphasize some that deserve particular attention.

First, neither of us had had previous experience working in this area. It would have been better if at least one of us had had some previous knowledge of the communities.

A second point was insufficient involvement in the life of the people we were visiting. It would have been very useful if we had been able to go along with the jungle dwellers in their daily work and routine: cooking, fishing, hunting, working in their fields, etc. We have to admit our physical and psychological limits, but these limits can be stretched with effort and good will.

A third point relates to our failure to coordinate our work and make it mesh. We didn't plan and carry out our meetings and contacts *together:* neither Sister and myself, nor us with the lay leaders, nor us with the leaders and the people. This flaw is quite serious because it leads to one side running things and the other side being dependent. "It's better to take one step with a thousand, than go a thousand steps with one." It was pressure and concern with efficiency that led to this mistake. The fault is mainly mine, of course.

Saturday, August 20: Bacia

LAST NOTES BEFORE LEAVING

It's morning. We're about to leave. Last night the lay leader finally arrived. He came with his four pack animals loaded down with goods. It dawned on me:

he's more concerned with business than with the community.

In the afternoon we had two baptisms and at night we baptized the son of *Seu* Francisco Cobal, who came with *Seu* Bena. I then found out that he wasn't a lay leader at all, and that the leader in Santa Clara was a *Seu* João or José, but that he had moved.

In the baptism I strongly encouraged participation in the meetings and life of the community. It was celebrated at home, as befits a baptism where everything has to be done by rule of thumb.

Sunday, August 21, Feast of the Assumption: Back in Manoel Urbano

DONKEY PATHS

We got back today at noon. We had left Bacia yesterday at around 7 A.M. We came on a new trail to a settlement called Pau Ferrado. There's a newly married couple living there. We stopped a bit to drink some water. The young man was radiant, simply because we had stopped there. "It was a blessing that Father and Sister have come into my hut," he said, quite moved and obviously happy. He said that the Evangelicals are active around here, especially a minister from Castelo, named Salomão, but he doesn't let them in. As usual, Nieta went to speak with the lady of the house in the kitchen, while the young man and I stayed in the main room, sitting on boxes.

At noon, we stopped in a place called Buretama, an hour away from the national highway. We ate two papayas, green and sweet; we were quite hungry. As we were about to go, the woman of the house came with a dish featuring palm squirrel; we hadn't realized she'd been fixing it. It was excellent, even with the inevitable cassava flour.

At 1:30 P.M. we got to the national highway connecting Rio Branco and Feijó. We stepped onto the road. The sun was fierce and we were sweating like animals.

At this time of year the highway is a series of winding donkey paths and some straight stretches. It's always overgrown with brush, leaving only a narrow path down the middle. That's where humans and animals go winding around looking for straighter stretches.

Every year around this time, the government sends machines out to clear the road. Then cars can use it for three or four months. Then once more it's surrendered back to the invading vegetation, erosion from the rains, and the impact of donkey teams. In the worst stretches you have to walk on the tops of the chips, hard as rocks, deposited by pack animals as they move along.

The Poor: New Actors in the Church and in Society

Our first stop along the road was at the house of *Dona* Joana, an auxiliary lay leader. The only ones at home were her three little daughters. We were dying of thirst and they offered us some water. Then they went to call their mother who was out in the field. She arrived a few minutes later, partly happy and partly shy, and surprisingly well dressed. What had happened was that one of her children had taken her a clean dress from the house. She apologized for not offering coffee; there wasn't any. She offered water, and we drank again. We talked a bit and then left, because we wanted to get back to Manoel Urbano that same day, even if it was at midnight.

Along the way we were talking, Nieta and I (we didn't need a guide any more), about the persons God chooses as ministers. That poor woman was an apostle, a servant of the word, an executive of the church. The way she received us, with only water, but full of kindness and human feeling, certainly had more nobility about it than the demeanor of so many "grand ladies," with their whisky and caviar. The whole immense mystery of the kingdom of God is germinating in the hidden heart of this humble and fruitful land. The poor are the ones who are making things happen in the kingdom.

The new people of God, the church of Jesus Christ, is there, in these illiterate and unknown persons who give of themselves for the cause of the gospel and for their brothers and sisters, poor like themselves.

There's little point in trying to find the church anywhere else. It is there that we must grasp the mystery of the church: in the fact that such persons begin to get together, and together they hear the word of God, pray, sing, speak about their life, and set out on a journey together. The poor are the new subjects, not objects, in the church.

There's no way of knowing what can come out of a community like this in the course of history, how they might react to exploitation and what sort of struggle they might undertake for their liberation. Experience shows that whenever like-minded persons get together to think, to speak, and to act, a force is set loose there, a dynamic is unleashed, and in time it yields its fruits. A potential gets set in motion, a source of energy that can issue in kinds of practice that are effective for changing things. This shows clearly that the masses aren't ignorant and inactive; they are simply blocked, forbidden to speak and act.

The method used by the BCCs to systematically bring the gospel and life together is extremely important for what will happen in history. The large landholders around here, who won't allow grassroots Christian communities on their land, have certainly understood that. When the oppressed can meet and speak freely about their problems, they're always creative. When there's a specific issue, no outside agent has to think of solutions, but simply get the people together and let discussion flow by itself. Things always happen, and they're quite surprising. The poor are the true subjects of history.

When we got to Macapá, at kilometer 27, we ran into a lay leader, Raimundinha. She and her husband are a congenial couple. They wanted us to spend the night there, but we wanted to put more distance behind us.

Afterward we found out that Sisters Otacília and Mariazinha came to the same house somewhat later, also on their way back from a mission. Although they were trying to follow our tracks, they didn't manage to catch us. No wonder, at the pace Nieta and I were going, even though the road was terrible.

On the Go from Seven to Seven

We stopped to spend the night with *Seu* Marcos Ribeiro, a trader, the husband of *Dona* Joana, a lay leader. We had run across another trader!

We got there at 7 P.M. It had been dark since 5:30. We were walking along in the radiance of a beautiful new moon which was lighting up the road ahead, halfway up the sky between the horizon and overhead. We intended to get home, even if we had to walk by moonlight. By that time we had walked some twelve hours, from seven to seven. We'd been stepping from clod to clod and our feet couldn't take any more. Our legs were about to give out. And I still had a shoe on my right foot and just a slipper on my left foot, which was wrapped in a cloth, because the toe I'd stumbled on hadn't decided to get well yet.

So we stopped at *Dona* Joana's house. We got cleaned up on the other side of the road. We had piranha to eat, which, incidentally, was quite delicious. Then, the hammock. At such moments, the hammock proves so sensational (that's the word) to an exhausted body, that it makes you feel some time you'd like to put up a statue honoring the inventor of the hammock. . . .

The early morning, cold as it always is, kept everyone awake after 2:30 A.M. Someone was coughing, someone else was getting up, two persons were talking, a few dozed off, and everyone was waiting for dawn to arrive. We got up at five, and by six we were on the road again, on the last stretch.

After going two kilometers we saw at the end of the road the rising of the magnificent and beautiful Sunday sun. It was "brother sun," as Saint Francis would have said.

An Archaic and Biblical Ritual

At 9 A.M. we stopped in the house of *Dona* Neném, the fourth woman lay leader we met along the road.

She served us warm milk. The cow had just been milked. It reminded me of my childhood when I used to milk the cow and take advantage of the moment to sip a cup full and foaming over with the white liquid.

Then *Dona* Neném offered us curds. She brought out a big bowlful and gave me a ladle. When I dipped into the heavy white mass, I felt a sensation of life, purity, and power that was inexpressible. I remembered Abraham offering his three divine guests curds and milk (Gen. 18:8). It was an ancient rite that was being repeated at that moment. The curds were so marvelous and delicious that I had two helpings. In fact, this was our breakfast.

There's practically nothing left of archaic experiences in our industrial and urban culture, where food comes fast and packaged, laced with chemical additives, artificial coloring, and other artificial ingredients.

Our Lady in Glory, a Pathbreaker

Dona Neném invited us to the meeting of the community as it was about to begin.

The readings for the day, the Assumption of Mary into heaven, were read. There were about ten adults, and countless children.

The reading of the visit between Mary and Elizabeth served to show Mary as a simple woman of the people. The Magnificat, which appears at that point, served as the occasion to reflect on the figure of Mary at Nazareth as a woman who was prophetic, fully aware, and liberating.

Revelation 12 gives a good sense of how ordinary persons like to represent Our Lady of Glory, full of beauty, radiant, splendid. The link between both figures of Mary, in Nazareth and in glory, is clear: through the path of humble service one comes to victory. A lesson for us also.

In that discussion the image of the *mateiro* (from *mata,* jungle, bush) came up. The *mateiro* is one who goes ahead in the jungle blazing a trail for others to follow. That's how it is with Our Lady assumed into heaven: she went ahead to open the way for her children. She was a pathbreaker. After Jesus Christ, that is; she was the first person after him, for he was "the firstborn from among the dead" (Col. 1:15).

Sister Nieta and I were doing most of the talking; there wasn't much dialogue with or among community members. When a sister or priest is present, community members are content to listen. Only after some time, when they have gained confidence, do they put aside their fear and speak freely.

Today I'm wondering whether in these fleeting contacts one ought to go along with what community members expect, or whether one shouldn't be more pedagogical and use some device to frustrate their expectations, so they can be brought to speak for themselves. This second possibility seems possible for someone who works with them in an ongoing way. But it's questionable for someone who just visits and whose encounters with the community are infrequent and random. Perhaps in that case a more forceful and compressed presentation is advisable. *Salvo meliori judicio.*

Apostolic Communities

Dona Neném can't read. But she brings the community together. I asked her what they did. She said they sing, pray the Our Father and Hail Mary, say prayers of intercession, and so forth.

I could see she is a lively and intelligent woman. I could see that by the things she said about the readings.

An active woman, she and her husband own a small farm. They take very good care of it and it produces lots of milk. She has only one son, gotten, she tells me, "through a promise to St. Francis of the Holy Wounds." She's from Ceará.

I liked *Dona* Neném. She made it clear how happy she was to have us at her meeting. It delayed our return to Manoel Urbano, but that wasn't so important.

Farther along the way, we ran into two men who gave us the address of the fifth lay leader along the national highway. "It's at the start of the spur running toward Manoel Urbano. That's where the community meets. We're going to get some cattle, and on our way back we'll stop at the meeting."

There's a new kind of Christian and a new language here—about community, and meetings. And there's another church springing up, one that's closer to the people, simpler, more biblical, more apostolic.

But isn't the church apostolic of its very nature? And doesn't each ecclesial community, as a cell of the church, or as the church at the grassroots, "the cell church," reproduce itself? BCCs enrich the note of apostolicity, living today a Christianity that's quite close to that of the church of the apostles, the community in Jerusalem. That takes place through meetings, reading the word of God, prayer in common, sharing goods, and making efforts to transform the world (cf. Acts 2 and 4).

Hence, the church's apostolic character is to be found not only in the uninterrupted succession of mission and authority, but also, and particularly, in a way of life, in a way of being church, which is just what the first chapters of Acts teach us.

And to think that Mary, the mother of Jesus, today Our Lady of Glory, was part of the primitive community, a model for all communities! She took part in the community of Christians. She is an image of the whole church!

Monday, August 22: Manoel Urbano

WORK IN THE FIELD

This afternoon the sisters and I went out to the field to pick beans along with *Dona* Olímpia.

There was scorching sun and the mosquitos, called *meruins,* were attacking freely. Different from others, called *piuns,* these mosquitos don't leave any mark on your arm but just an itchiness.

The clearing was about a kilometer from here. Working all together, we picked a big sack of beans. Then we went to get some ripe papayas and a bit of cassava.

We all carried loads on the way back. Just like when I was a youngster. My mother always carried us, along with firewood and vegetables. "They shall come back rejoicing, carrying their sheaves" (Ps. 126:6).

Back at *Dona* Olímpia's house we split things up: our share was some beans, a half dozen papayas, and all the cassava.

On the way we ran into two peasants, clearing brush with machetes. They were surprised to see a priest and a sister in the fields. They shouted to us from a distance, "This is really quite a surprise, *Seu* Padre!" I answered something or other in a kidding tone, and we kept going. I don't know how it struck them, in their own way of thinking, while they continued to sweat, hacking away right and left at the brush.

There are bits and pieces of the old mental images in the peasants' heads. Now these peasants know that the priest and sister can actually go out to the field. That gives the field some dignity. The sisters here make it a practice to go out with the people for planting and harvesting rice, beans, cassava, etc.

While we were on our way back, with me toting the sack of beans on my shoulder, Sister Ota kidded me, "It's different from teaching in the university, isn't it?" But that impression of contrast isn't something natural. It's the product of culture, it's arbitrary. It's our culture that favors the intellectuals and shows contempt for those who work with their hands. This situation can't last, because it's abnormal, pathological. A human being should be able to exercise the same degree of skill in picking beans and doing research, hauling papayas and consulting books.

Work: Something More Than Production

I recall researching the difference between production and work, even checking Marx. I can now see that there's a vast distance between the two.

Work is a lot more than just producing. Work assumes a whole way of relating with other human beings, with the earth, and with things; it goes far beyond mere economic interest. That's always there, of course, heavy and silent. But it's not the whole story.

Today, for example, there were a number of things that were going into our human experience of work: the afternoon sun going down, the shade of the jungle cooling the air and the ground, the tiny birds singing at the end of the day. But note that they aren't counted among the factors of production. Work is an overall human experience: bodily and spiritual. Certainly goods are produced, but the human being as a particular human being is also being produced. Work is self-production. Hegel defined it that way, Marx repeated it, and it has continued up to John Paul II in *Laborem Exercens*.

In this connection, as we were picking, I was listening carefully to the conversation between Sister Otacília and *Dona* Olímpia. You realize that in work there is so much spontaneity and freedom that things seem to come to the surface effortlessly. When persons are working, the reality of the world and of human nature comes bubbling up to the light of consciousness.

That's what explains how workers understand the contradictions in society easier than do nonworkers. That's also why, if an outsider wants to understand a people and its life, they have to go to the people at work. That's the privileged place, the vantage point for understanding the life of the people. And that's true not only for the experience of a people, but also for its language.

Tuesday, August 23: Manoel Urbano

LAY LEADERS, SUCCESSORS OF THE APOSTLES?

At Mass tonight there were some lay leaders who had come for the training session that begins tomorrow.

Together we meditated on the theme of today's feast: St. Bartholomew, apostle and martyr. I told the community that according to tradition this apostle evangelized India and died a martyr's death. He was literally skinned alive. Rubber-gatherers know about this, for they often skin the animals they bring home. Images of this martyr in the famous mural of the Last Judgment in the Sistine Chapel, and also in a big statue of him along with two other apostles in the Lateran Basilica, show him holding his skin in his own hands. It's a powerful image of what it means to "risk your skin" for the gospel and the people.

Together we reflected on who might be the successors of the apostles. They are the foundation—around here people would say the stilts—for the church today. Besides that, in the first reading, Revelation 21, we had heard it said that the names of the twelve apostles of the Lamb were written on the twelve gates of the Holy City.

Certainly bishops and priests are successors of the apostles. But so are the sisters. And also the lay leaders. Why? Because the lay leaders also continue the mission of the apostles, which is preaching the word of God and founding the church, creating and giving life to communities.

It was wonderful to see how the eyes of the lay leaders lit up when they realized that they had attained such a great dignity and had such a great mission!

Materia Mater—*Mother Matter*

Today we took a marvelous swim in the Purus River. Clear water over a golden, sandy bottom.

Sinking into nature: water, hot sand, the air, even when it's full of mosquitos—it all refreshes body and soul. The spirit is freed and takes wing. Matter is our mother—"holy matter" (Teilhard de Chardin).

It's true: "Human beings are human only when they're at play" (Schiller).

History Read from the Periphery of the Periphery of History

I've read the papers Father Heitor has sent over from Sena Madureira. I'd spent three weeks without any contact with the "world of history."

News? The same old stuff, such as the IMF (International Monetary Fund) and all that. I'm almost ready to admit Léon Bloy was right in saying "When I want to know the latest news, I read St. Paul."

I conjure up what all this about the IMF and the government's policies must mean for the jungle dwellers and their mode of production. They have a different economy: one of subsistence, an "invisible," "informal," or "submerged" economy, according to the experts. They're relatively autonomous. At least it seems that way.

Nevertheless, the IMF does touch their lives, whether they know about it or not. Decisions made in New York reverberate in Brasilia, pass through Rio Branco, and even hit here in Manoel Urbano. The fact is that whether we realize it or not, we live in one world, especially in terms of the economic system—a spider web in which we're all caught.

But isn't that just what immorality is: treating others as *objects?* And that's what you experience here on the periphery of the periphery: these persons are never recognized as *subjects.* They are only acted upon; they never act. They are victims of decisions made by someone else, never themselves actors. Some few of them are accomplices.

But to treat others as objects, even for their own good, means demeaning them, the opposite of loving them. Love, after all, means treating the other as subject, loving the other as a being who is free, conscious, responsible, able to assume his or her own life, to decide, create, grow.

What we're seeing is the *reification* of persons. In Brazil we have more than 100 million things, not persons. That's how those who are supposed to be "responsible" for the nation, the capitalists and their acolytes in the government, treat the people. There's no place where it's more evident than here, although the small scale of things here means that human relations still retain a remarkable degree of humanity.

This also often happens in the church: treating the people as the object of love, of liberation, and of evangelization. But Jesus never treated anyone that way. He always demanded faith, and faith was a personal decision, as Bultmann emphasized. "Jesus was the guide for those who are awake," Plínio Marcos, the theater critic, told me this past June, when we met for the first time. And Dostoevski's portrayal of the Grand Inquisitor shows that magnificently: to love is to promote the freedom, not the happiness, of the other.

Hearing about Alceu's Death

Only now, reading old newspapers, have I learned that Alceu Amoroso Lima died. He passed away on the 14th. I read that his death brought expressions of condolence from the whole intelligentsia of the country, from right and left, believers and unbelievers. He was regarded as the best expression of the whole cultural history of Brazil.

I only got to know him personally in the St. Teresa Hospital, in Petrópolis, along with my brother Leonardo, one Friday, a month before his death.

He was obviously quite encouraged to hear the news we brought of the meeting of BCCs in Canindé. He looked young. He urged us to write an article for the *Jornal do Brasil,* but he immediately added, "I realize that paper is obviously opposed to the work you two are doing."

Alceu was an extremely decent and courageous man. A humanist and a Christian. Perhaps his thought wasn't especially original, rich, or provocative. But he had what counts more than anything else: he was critically and prophetically militant and always open to what was new and to the future. That's what he takes with him and also what he leaves behind!

Wednesday, August 24: Manoel Urbano

POST MORTEM IMPRESSIONS: CULTURAL DIFFERENCES

All the time I was wandering through the jungle, taking notes, I always felt a bit of embarrassment. What does it mean to take up pen and paper in the midst of persons who can't write?

It's understandable that they would stand there observing "the priest" writing away, admiring the technical skill of someone who can write rather than the actual written content. "He fills up a page in a flash!" they would say, grinning at one another.

The observer observed! At such a moment it was I who was the strange, curious, and exotic figure, even though from a position of dominance.

Being able to write puts you beyond their world. It underlines your position as external, from the outside—the position of an intellectual. You're not like them. That's just a fact.

This sense of embarrassment merges into something else: the personal and impressionistic tone of this account. There is a particular personality behind every observation or idea here. This also produces some unpleasant feeling. And also a certain amount of shame. All the more insofar as this personality is that of an intellectual with a degree, a professor who writes.

Is this something to be ashamed of? Certainly not. But why keep on exalting the intellectual?

Actually, if what's said here arouses any interest, will it only be because it's the work of an intellectual who spends some time with ordinary persons? Certainly a rubber-gatherer wouldn't write down the things noted here, and wouldn't have any interest in doing so! For this is his own life—a prosaic life, without any theological poetry of any sort.

I have the impression I'm some kind of astronaut transported to another planet. I'd like to have a space suit duplicating the living conditions on my home planet.

Consolation comes from transforming unpleasant cultural distance into a means of service, something that enhances the life of the other.

Tuesday, September 6: Rio Branco

AFTERMATH

It seems that I'm not quite finished. On Wednesday the 31st, I came back home to the city, totally exhausted: headache, with shooting pains on the right side of the brain, fever, chills, and a general sick feeling all over.

I went to bed, without eating. At night my fever went up to 102°. I suspected malaria and went into the hospital. A blood test showed that my suspicion was right. It's vivax malaria, the most common and least harmful type.

I stayed in the hospital for a week. Yesterday I got back home completely recovered. They say there are aftereffects, because you remain a bearer of the virus. But with the vivax type that's not always the case.

While still in the hospital, I heard two bits of news that weren't very encouraging. The first was that Sister Nieta, who went on the mission with me, also got malaria. But she was braver: she took care of it out there.

The other was that for the training session for lay leaders held in Manoel Urbano, the only ones who came from our area were Joana (from Depósito) and Antônio (from Timorantes, near Bacia).

That was disappointing; I had been counting on at least five of them to attend: Joana, Raimundo Nonato, Neném Ponte, Esmeraldo, and Bena. You never fully understand the people. . . . So now, without more preparation, how are they going to be able to conduct the meetings, and through those meetings, lead the whole community along?

Plantatio ecclesiae, how hard it is!

Nevertheless, we have to hope that the mysterious logic of the cross and resurrection will transform all pain and death into divine joy and life!

The famous Manaus Opera House, which was built with money from the Amazon rubber boom. It is filled with European marble, and lavish furnishings; the ceiling was painted by Italian artists. Such groups as the Milan opera company sang here, but contrary to many popular accounts Caruso never did make it to Manaus.

A typical rubber-gatherer's dwelling near Tarauaca in the state of Acre, Brazil.

A Brazilian caboclo *felling a large buttressed tree to clear a plot of land for his cassava field.*

A Brazilian rubber-gather–Brazil nut collector opening the hard outer case to extract the nuts, which are actually the individual seeds of the fruit arranged inside similar to segments of an orange.

Rubber-gatherers starting a ball of crude rubber by wrapping a sheet of rubber around a pole. This will be used as the nucleus for coagulating more latex with smoke to build a large ball of rubber for trading.

The process of coagulating rubber is done by pouring the latex onto a spinning ball of rubber in the presence of an acrid, acid smoke. The rubber then sets and the ball is gradually built up until it is a marketable size.

Rubber-gatherers know the forest well and use many plants. During the dry season, the water vine is a life-saver for the workers. The stem is cut and held up and a copious supply of potable water runs out.

A group of rubber-cutters and their families on a Sunday morning. There are two balls of crude rubber behind them to the left.

PART TWO

COMMUNITIES AND LEADERS

IV

BCCs: The People of Revelation

Friday, October 28

REVELATION—A BOOK OF THE PEOPLE

I've come to Xapuri to help out with a five-day training session for lay leaders, catechists, and other lay ministers.

I'm responsible for the first three days. I have to present the book of Revelation and help the trainees get deeper into the main chapters. The fact is that a lot of ordinary persons are reading this book. Actually, it's a strange book only for those who haven't been given the keys for interpreting it. In itself, as I explained to the lay leaders today, this book has three features that make it popular in the communities.

1) Revelation is the book of a *persecuted* people. It speaks of the Wild Beast and its followers oppressing God's children, ripping them up, leaving them all bloody. But they don't give in. They keep the faith and the hope for victory. And that victory eventually comes. Hence the immense joy, the alleluias you can feel in Revelation, alongside the blood that gets spilt.

2) Revelation is a book of the *people*. Its language, full of metaphors, is one of the things that makes it popular. Many beautiful figures make their appearance in human form, such as the Son of Man, the pregnant Woman, the angels; others appear in the form of animals: the Dragon, the Wild Beast, the Four Horsemen. Local communities are enchanted, contemplating this whole fantastic bestiary roaming through the world and through the skies, and these figures in glory appearing in heaven and continuing on earth.

3) Finally, Revelation is a *political* book. The forces that come into play are collective. It is the whole people of God that is set in motion, as well as the whole of society. Moreover, it is the only book of the New Testament that undertakes a systematic political reading of history. So it's a marvelous book for opening communities to the political dimensions of the faith and of the church in the world. There's no better and more penetrating Christian introduction to politics than Revelation. I realized this before, when I was asked to

67

give training sessions on this book in local communities. Its heuristic power (for uncovering and making clear the contradictions in society) and ethical/ critical power (for morally de-legitimizing the structures of injustice, which it represents with animal-like figures) are unparalleled. Obviously this doesn't excuse anyone from a rational analysis and a concrete strategy, but it is a powerful way to open Christians up to do just that.

"Who Are These Leaders . . . and Where Have They Come from?"

On the first night, Thursday, the participants introduced themselves. I made notes on whatever struck me.

Clóvis says it took him three days "on feet" (that's the way they talk in this area) to get here. "Thank God, I got here okay and I'm happy," he concluded.

The community of Santa Luzia, where Pedro is involved, has no less than four leaders. Together they coordinate the life of the group. Besides them, there are catechists.

A young lay leader, just seventeen years old, speaks up: "The priest and sister chose me as a leader, but I don't even know what that means." But he says he's come to learn. "Thank goodness for that," I think to myself.

Elzira, who's over forty and a mother of twelve children, says she's a lay leader, a catechist, and a minister to the sick. Concentrating tasks in one person that way doesn't seem like a good idea to me, but it's no doubt inspired by the same kind of generosity that led her to have so many children.

Socorro, from the barrio of Sibéria, says she's twenty-one and has been working in the community for seven years. She's a Christian whose life has been marked by a different kind of church.

Raimundo says his group is "quite encouraged because they have so many persons to baptize." That made everyone laugh as though to say, "we understand." It's the same eternal problem: so many come for baptism but most of them go away later.

Of some fifty-five present, twenty or so belonged to unions. That's a significant proportion.

The vast majority were from the jungle; fewer than ten were from the city. Not many have been involved in community work for more than four years.

Behold the Army of the Lamb! Actually his apostles were of just as humble a background. And it was on them that the church was founded (cf. Eph. 2:20).

Monday, October 31

SELF-ANALYSIS OF THE LIFE OF THE PEOPLE

The lay leaders broke into groups to discuss what they felt were the main problems in their areas and what the causes of those problems were. When they came back together they pictured things as follows:

1) *Lack of unity and organization among the rubber-gatherers.* The city

dwellers hit on the same point, adding immediately that it was due to fear: fear of losing your job or fear of the mayor and the police. Note how these persons, when they point out problems, blame themselves. It's not very helpful to be moralistic and blame others when oppression only takes place because it's tolerated and accepted by the oppressed themselves.

2) *Land threatened by large landowners* (buying it, moving onto it, taking it away).

3) *Exploitation when they sell what they produce and buy goods from a trader or a company store.* Those from the city spoke about shortages of goods, hunger, and low pay. Those are their main problems, not the same as those in the jungle.

4) *Lack of schools and health care* (medicines, clinics).

It becomes clear that they can themselves provide a full vision of their situation. But only when they reflect on it together, not individually. Their knowledge is essentially collective and can be apprehended only collectively.

What's Behind All This?

This is the question that always comes up in a discussion at the local level. It leads questioners to look for the roots or the causes of specific problems. Such an effort of looking for the causes of the issues mentioned above led to this:

1) Government and capitalists (landowners, business persons, etc.).

2) The fact that persons aren't organized in what should be their instruments for struggle: communities, unions, cooperatives.

That shows that they've gotten beyond the kinds of explanations that are fatalistic (that being poor is one's destiny) or developmentalistic (that it's due to backwardness, etc.). If any lay leaders have such ideas, they would drop those illusions under the effect of a collective socialization of consciousness: those who are further along lead the whole group forward.

Note that the lack of unity and organization appeared as both problem and cause. It really is all that: problem, cause, and the way toward a solution.

Ideas on where to go came next:

1) Raise the people's consciousness, show the truth. That's in their words. It strikes me that I've never seen a simpler definition of conscientization: showing the truth (injustices, rights, etc.).

2) Help the people get organized in communities, unions, and associations. The question of organization as the solution came back in here.

The great priority today is precisely to fortify efforts to organize groupings. That's where the greatest efforts of the local church are headed now, as was decided in the pastoral council in June.

Along with organization comes conscientization, liberation from fear, mobilization for struggle, and the winning of rights. These things are interrelated in a circular way.

It's also important that everything be done in the sphere of faith: *ex fide in fidem:* starting out from faith and ending up there.

The Church and Social Liberation

As these trainees discuss things, I'm thinking about what the church is doing to further their liberation.

What the church as such is doing is an initial "priming." In the area of conscientization, it provides an initial critical access to social reality. In the area of organization, it creates a whole mystique of unity. In BCCs it gets initial organizing efforts going.

The rest of the job has to be the work of persons in areas that are extra-church—but not extra-kingdom—that is, in profane or societal (but not extra-faith) areas.

It's impossible for the church, as institution, to carry forward the whole task of organizing the oppressed.

Nevertheless, its pastoral work alongside them must of necessity lead toward, and reach fulfillment in, a movement of the people, made up of unions, associations, and political parties that belong to the popular classes.

In this area the only pastoral question remaining is how to make sure that those Christians who are active in the movement keep up an *ecclesial relationship* (faith, sacraments, family spirit) with the community of the institutional church.

In any case, persons doing pastoral work feel that what the present situation demands is that pastoral work lead to nonpastoral organizing activity, and that pastoral work must open up in that direction.

In this perspective, the solution is not so much to free up pastoral ministers so they can become grassroots organizers in unions, etc., but rather that pastoral workers discover such grassroots organizers and prepare them for these new tasks. Creating doesn't mean stepping in and replacing. Opening up new positions doesn't mean changing your own position.

My brother Leonardo is always repeating the notion that the greatness of a Christian community is shown when it produces persons capable of dying for others. And that's really true. Faith in the gospel creates in believers an unbelievable openness to total commitment. Faith mobilizes morally before it mobilizes politically. So a lay leader was saying these days, "Folks, why be afraid? If we die struggling, our place is assured. We either lose our life or it will be taken from us."

Death by Overwork

During breaks I chatted with one leader or another at random. I took my plate and sat down on a bench near *Dona* Cecília.

She's a peaceful woman with an attractive, marvelously transparent face. Bright eyes and a quiet smile. She talks very little in the meetings, but her attention is unequalled.

She told me she's a catechist in Estrada Velha, four hours from here on foot.

She's from Minas Gerais, but she was working in Paraná, and she came here after being pushed out of there. Money and those who serve it treat the people like cattle.

She has seven children, the youngest being eleven years old. They're all working to support the family.

I asked about her husband and she said she's a widow. She told me how he died a year and a half ago when it got to him. "What?," I asked her. "Working so hard to support the family. He worked from sunup to sundown, without any rest, because he had no other choice. He just gave out."

This story bothered me for the rest of the day. Dying from working so hard in order to sustain your loved ones. . . . The terrible living conditions of the people often lead to this kind of martyrdom. Why do they get old prematurely and die prematurely? Because they literally spend themselves in the great efforts that their hard life demands. A sacrifice, in the theological as well as the moral sense of the term. That experience links them to the passion of the Son of Man, whether or not they want it, and whether or not they even know about it. In that experience they are being saved and are saving others.

I then recalled my own father. He died when he was fifty-four. But he was already old, worn out from so much work in order to support the family and pay for his sons' and daughters' education—eleven of us in all!

When will the day finally come when the idol of capital "will fall with [its] face flat on the ground before . . . the Lord," the way Dagon did (cf. 1 Sam. 5:1–5)?

The Petrine Function in the Church

Dona Luísa, who for five years has been a leader in a very lively community two kilometers from Xapuri, is taking part in this training session, as she always does. She is faithful to her work and carries on despite all obstacles. She carries the community on her back, so to speak. It was she who started the group. There's now a young man who goes along with her and takes over the work when she can't.

I think of her as a cornerstone, like Peter, on whom the universal church was founded. Her function is the same, except of course that it's at her own level. The Petrine mission of setting up and maintaining also continues to some extent here with these lay leaders.

Dona Luísa has brought her 14-year-old daughter to learn the songs so she can teach them to their group. Luísa herself doesn't have an ear for music. Bursting with pride, she introduces her daughter to me, and says "my greatest pleasure is seeing my children following the gospel and working in the community."

She then shows me photos of a first communion that took place in their community. There were about ten boys and girls, all decked out, because the community members enjoy fiestas and special events. In the photos I can see that their community center is big and has a grass roof. It's open on all four sides, and it stands right next to her house. "It was the people who built it," she explains.

Who's afraid of this "popular church"? "Only the rich and the devils," to use the words of a prophet of our time, Léon Bloy.

Tuesday, November 1

HOW TO IMPROVE COMMUNITY ORGANIZATION?

Today we had a visit from Sister Luísa, who is on the prelature team for pastoral coordination, and Francisca Marinheiro, a lay woman who works full-time in pastoral work and is part of the same team.

Sister explained the conclusions of the last pastoral council meeting. She is a competent woman: calm, mature, and even-tempered. When things get stirred up in these council meetings with a hundred or more persons involved, she keeps a firm hand on the rudder so the boat will head straight. And gradually she steers it toward calmer waters. She does that even when all the priests and sisters get worked up, and struggling with them isn't easy at all.

Next, Francisca led a discussion on how to apply these guidelines to the local situation and how to improve the work of the BCCs.

Group discussion among the leaders led to a series of proposals—more like suggestions than directions—which emphasized the following points:

1) There should be visits between groups, especially on feast days, commemorations, and at outdoor celebrations. That way one group encourages the other, greater unity is created, members come closer together, and they overcome the dispersion that hampers groups in the jungle.

2) The parish coordinating team should visit the groups as often as possible.

3) In each community there should be a coordinating group to lead meetings and the whole community process. Instead of having the lay leader do all the leading, more members should be involved. And so between now and the end of the year, the leader should find and appoint new ministers, among whom there could be a prayer leader, someone to lead music, a minister for the sick, someone to handle collecting the money, a catechist, someone to visit other groups, an auxiliary leader, etc.

4) They should improve the way they treat others, especially those who are more shy. They should strive to be more receptive and sensitive to everyone in the community.

5) Each community should create its own community center, choosing a site for it by consensus. It will be the "House of the Community."

6) The lay leaders should meet once a month in the parish. Those who miss three months without an excuse should be relieved of their responsibility.

These conclusions emerged from group discussion and then a plenary session. But it took a lot of struggle to get to something that clear. Francisca led the discussion and moved the proposals along with the firmness of a schoolteacher.

Always objective, she didn't let the trainees get bogged down in pettiness or personal problems. She brought the group along firmly to a conclusion or decision that everyone was satisfied with.

On the other hand, she didn't let things roll on forever, letting the trainees get tired. Her way of conducting a vote was novel: "Anyone in agreement, stand up," or "Clap your hands," or "Anyone opposed, raise your foot," and the like.

Father Luciano: Pastor of His Flock

As the training session went on, Father Aurélio, recently arrived from Italy, and Father Luciano, the pastor, moved around among the participants. They weren't speaking or leading groups or discussions. But they were in the middle of their people, helping the whole thing move along, and supervising the general process of the meeting to make sure everything was working well.

Actually they were just where they should be: in the midst of the church—*in medio Ecclesiae*—like the heart in the body.

Father Luciano is a typical pastor among the people, in the new sense of that term. It's his style to be simple and open and to eliminate any barriers in the way he presents himself, the way he dresses, talks, and relates to the people. Always kidding, he pokes one in the ribs and calls him "lazy," and tugs on someone else's shirt and asks, "How're you doing, wise guy?" and so forth. The people are used to his style and kid him back.

He's firm and generous, and dedicated to his work, and he doesn't tolerate any injustice. When it comes to defending the weak, he's strict.

Seeing how husky he is in body and even more in spirit, I think to myself, "This priest must give the landowners, the rich, and all the enemies of the people a lot of trouble!"

In fact, he's never been given a permanent visa. He has to renew it each year, going through all that running around and endless red tape each time.

This burly man is enchanted at the sight of children. He shows me some photos he took of children on rubber plantations. Marvelous! They make the butterflies and flowers we saw look dull and pale.

The Prayer of the Poor Is Always Heard

We hold a going-away ceremony, a Eucharist with a good deal of participation.

At the moment of the Our Father, I look around at these fifty pastoral workers, with their hands raised, interconnected as they pray, some with eyes closed and others looking up.

Suddenly, I'm filled deep down with a sensation that snaps me out of the inertia of my habitual way of praying the Our Father. No, this isn't a common, ordinary prayer! The ones praying have been chosen by God. The poor are the object of God's preferential love. This prayer has to be pleasing to the Father, the protector and defender of the lowly. If God doesn't hear this prayer, then what prayer at all? For it is the poor who are crying out for justice, with all their faith.

"Will not God then do justice to his chosen who call out to him day and night? Will he delay long over them, do you suppose? I tell you, he will give them swift justice" (Luke 18:7–8).

V

A Community Walking
on Its Own Two Feet

Friday, November 4: Brasiléia

COORDINATORS: AXLES OF THE COMMUNITIES

There's no priest in the parish of Brasiléia. A community of sisters is leading it. Hence the parish has to live more on its own, and walk on its own two feet.

Today we spent the day in discussion with more than twenty coordinators, going over their functions within the local church. Evangelization groups link up to form small local communities. Four, five, or more of these small communities form a base community. It is led by a team of coordinators, and develops a program of activities in common.

The whole day was devoted to analyzing the function of coordinators.

As always, the first step was to bring out the problems. Here are some that emerged as coordinators made their presentations:

1) Individualism: the coordinating team doesn't work together. Everything falls on the shoulders of just one coordinator.

2) Many are coordinators in name only: they don't assume responsibility for their function.

3) Some coordinators are overburdened with work and don't have time to keep an eye on the different groups as they go in their own particular directions.

4) There are groups that don't accept the coordinators and don't value the work they do, etc.

From that point we went on to discuss what the role of the coordinator should be. That role is really to *coordinate*—that is, bring together, unite persons and groups. In a word, to encourage community members and link them together.

The discussion group came up with the following comparison. The groups are like wheels: they can roll. But if they are to move a cart, there has to be an axle connecting them to each other. Now that's what a coordinator is supposed to be: an axle between the different groups. An axle to articulate the movement of each individual into unified forward movement.

Participatory Church

They asked me to make a presentation on how a community should be organized in order to work well.

I laid out the new model of church: participatory church (democratic, comradely) and liberating church (transformative, prophetic).

I took Ephesians 4:1–6 as my starting point. There Paul speaks of the basic charism of all Christians—baptism, the gift of faith. That is the common foundation of the church, grounding its basic unity.

Other charisms arise over this foundation: the gifts and graces of the Spirit who gives rise to different ministries within the community.

These charisms, the basis for all ministries, are distributed in different areas: the area of the word, the area of celebration, the area of Christian life, and in the center of it all, the area of coordination, as depicted in Diagram 1.

Diagram 1

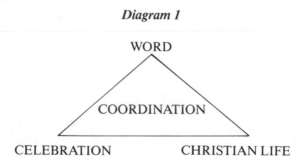

It's clear where the function of coordination fits in. There are many levels of it: on the level of the universal church the coordinator is the pope, with his advisory bodies (synod of bishops, Roman Curia, etc.); on the level of the diocese the coordinator is the bishop, with his advisors (presbytery, pastoral council, chancery, etc.); at the parish level the coordinator is the pastor, aided by the parish council, etc.; and at the community level coordination is done by a team of coordinators.

The main task of coordination is not to replace other functions but to unify, encourage, and stimulate those who perform them. Unification and encouragement are the two main functions in all coordination.

But it should never be forgotten that all this organization is meant for the service of the church and its mission to all humankind: salvation and liberation. In other words, a participatory church exists for the sake of a liberating church—and that always means the whole range of liberation.

Guidelines for Good Coordination

The coordinators met in groups to draw up some rules to guide them in their work of being the "axle between the groups."

These were the rules that resulted, practical guidelines for good coordination:

1) Coordinators should work *together with* the other coordinators. After all, if they don't themselves work in coordination, how are they going to coordinate others?

2) Coordinators should prepare a *program* of activities, something that will distribute the tasks to be done and set out times for meetings to evaluate work already done and prepare for what has yet to be done.

3) Coordinators should not in any way replace the community leaders or other ministers in their own work, but should *show respect and appreciation* for each one's work.

4) Coordinators should *pay particular attention to weaker groups* or those that fall apart, striving to give them more life or to bring them back to life.

5) Coordinators should *bring together different groups* in the community from time to time: feast days, meetings for prayer, meetings to discuss common problems (such as threats made on their land), etc.

6) Coordinators should especially *bring together local community leaders* in order to discuss difficult or tricky situations (quarreling in the groups, etc.).

7) Coordinators should *warn of dangers* threatening the community, such as proselytizing Evangelicals or the threat of expulsion from land holdings. They can't be like "dumb dogs"—the term Isaiah used to criticize fearful leaders who see danger but remain silent (Isa. 56:10).

8) Coordinators should *communicate* to the groups anything important that happens on the level of the parish or of the universal church (persecutions, positive developments, etc.).

9) Coordinators should help local lay leaders awaken groups to social questions.

10) Finally, coordinators deserve to be recognized and respected by the various groups.

This all had to be written on sheets of paper and arranged on the floor because it wouldn't fit on the blackboard. It took a lot of effort to come up with this sort of "decalogue." There was writing all over the floor. Then I put it all together and wrote up a clean version. So we got done what we had set out to do. The coordinators could view their situation in these guidelines, which they carried back home on a sheet of paper.

Saturday, November 5

A PEOPLE VANQUISHED BUT NOT COWARDLY

This morning the customary meeting of parish lay leaders took place. Counting the coordinators who were already here, some sixty persons were assembled.

Some came quite a distance. One woman came twelve hours on foot with her 12-year-old son, whose birthday was today. Others got up at dawn to get here by 9 A.M., the start of the meeting. The whole day was devoted to the "work of the gospel," as they like to put it here.

There they are, all in a circle. I look at them and I see the church of the *poor.* They are workers, rubber-gatherers, small merchants, washerwomen, domestic servants, etc.

I see the church of the laity: baptized persons who take on their faith and their church as something that belongs to them. The division of labor is not as rigid as what you see in the clergy. There are ministers among them: of the sick, for collecting funds, catechesis, the word, singing, prayer, human rights, etc. But these aren't lifelong functions, and they're not very institutionalized; there is a deep unity among them (no vertical hierarchy).

Finally, I see there a church of those who have been *defeated,* the vanquished; but they are not cowards or opportunists. It is a church of resistance, of constancy, of hope, like the church in the book of Revelation. It is a church that doesn't give up, that dies standing up.

Obviously, there are failures and weaknesses, for the church is sinful; but taken as a whole, it is a church that is holy, faithful, invincible, "and the jaws of death shall not prevail against it" (Matt. 16:18)—that is, they will not prevail in the end. This church has the promise of final victory, even if it has to go through many partial defeats.

You can feel another sort of resonance when you apply the whole of ecclesiology to a base-level church like this one. To tell these Christians brought together in faith that they are the spouse of Christ, the people of God, the Mystical Body, the temple of the Spirit, etc., at first produces a feeling of surprise and almost disbelief: "No, that can't be true!" But then they have to come around to see that all these titles bespeak the truest truth, the truth of faith, God's truth. For it is indeed God who looks at them that way.

And that leads me to see that it's one thing to do ecclesiology starting from an abstract and general vision of the church, and another to do it with the whole phenomenon of church taking place right before your eyes. Even though it's true that this isn't the whole church, it does nevertheless have the wholeness of the church: one, holy, catholic, and apostolic (*Lumen Gentium,* nos. 23 and 26).

Sunday, November 6

LEADERS OF LITURGICAL CELEBRATION

We've spent this whole Sunday training fourteen persons—the liturgical team—for leading Sunday worship.

The priest comes here once a month. On Sundays it's the sisters who lead the celebration with the people. But now there's a good liturgical team in place, and the idea is to put this pastoral task in the hands of the community as well.

It was a day of intensive work. In the morning there was reflection on the meaning of the liturgy and the Sunday celebration. That was so that a theological sense of the liturgy would underlie the team's practical work.

In the afternoon there was a rehearsal of how to lead Sunday worship with the people. Evaluation and suggestions came from the team itself.

As far as the laity is concerned, there's little difference between the "sisters' Mass" and the "priests' Mass." The fact is that lay persons are coming closer to the altar: there they speak their word, sing, lead prayer, and sometimes even administer sacraments: baptism and matrimony. You can't help thinking about a more popular kind of "altar ministry"—the presbyterate. There is movement from both sides: as the priesthood comes down toward the heart of the laity, lay persons move toward taking on the priesthood.

Thursday, November 10

VISITING SETTLERS RECENTLY ARRIVED FROM THE SOUTH

Today we visited two camps of families that INCRA (Institute for Colonization and Agrarian Reform) has brought from the south. They're living on a little road that runs off the highway between Brasiléia and Assis Brasil. Those who went were Sister Anna Maria, *Dona* Zeli, Francisca, the driver, and myself.

I had seen some of them wandering around the city "looking for help," as they said, when they came here to the sisters' house. They were sweaty and had a strong smell about them, and anxiety on their faces. They looked like hardworking men and women ready for anything.

At kilometer 13 we turned off the road to Assis Brasil. Soon we came to the first camp. It was a big shed built by INCRA. It's providing shelter for about ten families. The newcomers themselves had divided up the house and closed off sections. INCRA had provided a tin roof, which was high, wide, and well constructed.

Some other families were living around the shed, in little huts. We left some basic supplies: oil, flour, rice, beans, etc., donated by persons in the city.

The settlers got here three months ago. The men have already cleared the lands INCRA set aside for them (some seventy hectares). "The corn and rice are growing beautifully!" they tell us happily. It's thirty kilometers or more from the shed to their clearing. They go there on foot and it takes them almost all day. It's hard for them because they're not used to long distances, unlike our rubber-gatherers who can go for three whole days, from 6 A.M. to 6 P.M., without complaining.

They go out to the field for several days and return only to see how their families are doing.

You can see a lot of children running all over the place and they're of all colors and races. A kaleidoscope of beautiful children, and as dirty as can be. . . .

The toughest thing for the settlers is getting enough to eat. They haven't taken in their first harvest and until they do, they've got to manage however they can.

INCRA lends the group 30,600 cruzeiros a month (approx. $204). "That only lasts the first ten days," they say.

The plantation workers and rubber-gatherers from around here are welcoming these newcomers very openly. They're showing the most noble kind of hospitality and friendship. The settlers from the south acknowledge it and praise them for it. Many rubber-gatherers have offered some of the land they've already cleared for the southerners to plant. Besides that, they've taught them some of their own skills for living in the jungle: how to hunt, how to find water, how to take advantage of the resources in the forest, etc.

Despite all the hardships, these newcomers are happy with their land. The fact that it solves their problems for only a generation doesn't matter. What's going to happen to their children when they grow up? They aren't thinking about that angle yet. The urgency of the present shuts out any kind of future, near or remote.

Even the children prefer things here to the south. "At least here there's land and work," they say quite seriously. They share their country's fate in all respects. When they're just eight or ten they go out to help their parents in the field.

We ran into four children who were coming back after working several days on their crops. They were carrying big sacks with cooking pots inside. They shifted them back and forth between their heads, their shoulders, and their backs. They're not familiar with the *paineiro* in which the rubber-gatherers handily carry all their belongings. These children talked about work just like grown-ups. Their accent is typical of the south, open and clear. They must have been ten or twelve years old. I like them. They were charming and respectful, as their parents had taught them to be toward grown-ups.

The second camp we visited was a more disheartening sight. The families live in makeshift low huts, covered with a sheet of black plastic that they brought from the south. It makes the hut burning hot—"hotter than hell," they say. The hut doesn't have any walls and the floor is bare dirt.

They sleep in low beds made out of sticks. A whole family of seven, eight, or ten members will arrange themselves on two of these beds. Some families sleep on the ground. The stove is made of adobe.

We saw one family that was in particularly bad shape. They were living under a roof of straw that went from a point on top down to the ground. That was the whole house. The couple, their four children, and all their belongings (there weren't many) had to fit in. I don't know how they managed at night.

The oldest daughter was blonde and pretty. She must have been about twelve years old. She was taking care of her three younger brothers and sisters.

Under this cramped low roof we prayed an Our Father with our hands joined, along with all the children who had seen us and come along for the tour, bringing a swarm of flies as well. The way the children prayed showed they were quite familiar with the prayer. Some even raced ahead of the others.

They were happy and laughed at anything we said. Some children were swinging on the liana vines hanging from the trees all around. Others were playing in a nearby creek. In the midst of that misery they were like a banner of hope unfurled in the wind.

The mother arrives, a blonde woman of German descent. She's coming back from the fields, dirty and so poorly dressed you feel sorry for her. Her blouse is loose, revealing her sagging, dried-up breasts. She is the image of the oppressed mother of the oppressed poor, but she's full of great courage and a drive to live. Seeing her so rundown brings to my mind the image of the Pietà. And suddenly it makes me sick to think of all the beautified bodies, all the faces covered with makeup, that are an insult to the Holy Face on the sacred countenance of these poor persons.

Without saying anything, she puts a piece of wood in the stove. She seems embarrassed by her poverty. What should cause embarrassment is our relative prosperity. It's not poverty that's shameful but wealth. That's what produces shame and shames others. Wealth humiliates those who have been disfigured, and humiliates their God!

In all the families we visited the situation is the same. It always tears your heart. But they're happy to have the piece of land they've never been able to have before. So they proudly endure it all.

"When food begins to get scarce," says one young man, "you get up and go anywhere at all until you manage to get something to eat. You can get by with just about anything. But what about the children . . . ?"

Thank God, we haven't found cases of malaria. It's not hitting very hard. But still, some people are wasting away. One man showed us his son, sitting naked on the ground, and said, "He was like a little drum, healthy as a lion. Now look at him," picking him up off the ground and showing him to us. What you could hear in his voice wasn't bitterness—just pain.

His wife and sister-in-law weren't there. They had gone to Brasiléia with the younger children who were sick. The men had come back to their homes at noon, after being away in the field for a week. Lonesome for their wives, they had decided to go to meet them. As we were leaving, we saw the wives on their way back.

We visited a Protestant family, the only one around. The women had told us, "Don't go there, Father, they're Protestants." But we went, to avoid discriminating among God's children. All the more so because they all endure the same suffering.

We noticed that the settlers, all of them, have little critical awareness or class consciousness. They've always been exploited and pushed from one place to another, living isolated from one another, like "sheep without a shepherd."

For most of them this is the umpteenth stop on their migratory journey. They hope it's the last, just as the Israelites did when they got to the promised land.

They came trusting in the assurances of INCRA that they would have help with everything: building a home, a road, a clinic, a school, medicine, seeds, and so forth. None of this is happening. They're used to planting by the sackful but all they got when they came was eight or ten kilos of corn and some rice. . . .

"We were dumped here by the roadside like animals," they say. They have to fend for themselves. They got here at night—perhaps that was on purpose. The government promised them more land than they actually received.

And they've come here from different areas. It's only here that they've come to know each other and acquire a common spirit. But it's hard for them to work together to claim their rights. If someone proposes that a few men get up the nerve to form a commission to go to INCRA and ask that the monthly loan be increased from 30,000 to 600,000 cruzeiros, they sit there looking blank, unconvinced. One of them manages to say, "And what if they chew us out?"

But there's no doubt about it: they are explorers and pioneers. They're setting up a new society here. Only later, a century from now, will their valor be recognized.

There's no point in talking to them about agrarian reform, let alone social revolution, the way intellectuals in Rio Branco do in their endless, and fruitless, seminars.

What the settlers have to do is simply take whatever step possible, but that's on their feet, not in the heads of intellectuals. The step that's possible is to demand that the government give what it can give. What this means is that it not be so cynical and that it provide specific resources for settlers: financing on easy terms, technical assistance, etc. And that's where work should begin, always with the people and based on the de facto needs of the people. What kind of follow-up to do and what direction to head toward—those questions come later on.

With the parishes as bases of support and with help from the CPT (Land Pastoral Commission), the church here is increasingly taking up this challenge.

In addition to the families connected with official colonization projects, hundreds of buses keep coming up from the south bringing more and more families to Acre. These newcomers can be a ferment and a constructive and transformative social force only with the help of the church, inasmuch as unionization is quite weak in this area.

On the way back in the jeep, we were talking about how to take the first step that could set in motion a whole process. The CPT staffers, who had experience in other colonization projects, were with us. They were talking about getting the lay leaders, who will be meeting for their next training session in early December, to do contacting and organizing.

The people had been asking to have children baptized and young couples married in the church. The CPT had been speaking to them of community, meetings, group discussions, etc. I turned around and let loose. "Hey, folks, for the love of God, let's not put a heavier load on the shoulders of these poor persons than what they've already got. Go out there some Sunday, celebrate the Eucharist, with a procession out to the fields. Then baptize and marry everyone who comes forward. After all, if the church isn't with them, who will be? The sacraments are for the people, as it's always been taught in good theology. Later on, of course, you can start talking about community and gospel. But let's not start out making new demands on top of those they've already got. More than anything else we've got to show them that God is on their side—and ours too. Everything else can come later." The CPT men and women all agreed. I seemed to be replaying Peter's speech at the Council of Jerusalem (cf. Acts 15:7–12).

A Pastoral Worker Filled with the Fire of the Spirit

Dona Zeli went along with us on our trip to see the immigrants from the south. As we were going in the car we were talking about them as "victims" (*flagelados*, "scourged," a term of pity for migrant colonists). She broke in, in her own sensitive and self-assured way, and said, "People are speaking of them as 'victims,' but I think that's humiliating. What they are is immigrants or colonists."

As we were visiting the families in the camps, I admired her sensitivity and the way she could give encouragement to poor women, offering advice, and telling them how to fix food for children and the sick.

She's married and has several children. Besides being active in the teachers' association (she's a teacher) and also in the Workers' Party, she's deeply involved in pastoral work. She does everything: she's a local community leader, a coordinator, and she's on the liturgical team. It's too much work for one person. But she's always happy, open, and ready for more. With all her gifts, she throws herself, body and soul, into working with the people.

It's always comforting for your faith to meet persons like Zeli. In these communities you always find one person or another who's completely exceptional and is a living sign of the presence of the Spirit in this church of ours.

They're beautiful spirits and fiery hearts!

VI

The "Four Great Fidelities"

Saturday, November 12

PAIN IS PAIN, DESPITE ANY IDEOLOGY

I got here from Brasiléia in the early morning on the bus—the "night owl." I took a bath, read the paper, and went to bed. It was 3 A.M.

Then in the afternoon I took a very crowded boat to the town of Catuaba, about an hour from Rio Branco. I got to the port, found Ivanilde, the lay leader, and we left. The boat was packed, because few boats were running, due to the shortage of gasoline.

One young man had been waiting in the endless line at the gas station from 4 A.M. until 3 P.M. Eleven hours in line! Only then could he get a gallon of diesel fuel, and that was what we were using.

He didn't make a fuss about his long wait. He scarcely mentioned it. And others weren't surprised. But I was very impressed: waiting a whole day for a gallon of fuel! "You didn't eat?," I asked him. He said, "No—otherwise I'd lose my place in line." He didn't talk like someone who thought he'd been wronged.

No question about it, what the ordinary people have to suffer goes unheard. They don't have anyone to complain to—unlike the upper classes who, at the least inconvenience, have the public media to blare out their complaints.

Poverty and suffering go together like twins. And the poor suffer not only from the nonsatisfaction of biological needs, but also from moral injustices: humiliation, pressure, oppression, persecution.

Ideology may mystify poverty as much as it wants: it can't do away with the pain of poverty. The only thing it can do is anesthetize it, make it less unbearable. But hunger is hunger, illness is illness, and death is death. It's all painful and the poor suffer it. Ideology, as an effective system of mystification, doesn't do away with anything. It doesn't act on the objective state of things, outside the spirit. It just acts on the spirit and on its relationship to the world (although this objectively enters into the objective world). That's why reality always threatens ideology. Reality can be masked but not destroyed. That would be like destroying the face that's wearing the mask. Anesthesia is not a cure.

The Lay Leader: Nourishing the Flame of Life in the Community

Ivanilde and her husband Zé (short for José) are both teachers in the primary school here in Catuaba. They work together, in both the school and the community. They have five children and Ivanilde is expecting her sixth.

She's full of life and very sharp intellectually. She's the soul of Catuaba, the center for dozens of families living in settlements around it. They all have a lot of respect for her.

The community has been in existence here for eight years. All that time, Ivanilde, along with her husband, has been like a vestal virgin maintaining the flame of life in Catuaba.

Her husband ran for the city council on the Workers' Party ticket, but he got less than a hundred votes. "That's the way it is," he says with resignation. "Oppression knocks people over, and won't let them get up." They go on from defeat to defeat, but toward victory—as a famous revolutionary put it.

Enough Order for the Basic Things in Life

Ivanilde and Zé have an old, roomy house. It used to be the center of a rubber plantation.

The kind of order here—in the house, the school, the health clinic, and the community center—goes along with the style of the area: enough order for what is vital and essential, but skipping anything superfluous. Things are hastily piled up, and roughly sorted out, enough to function. Beyond that, it's impossible to completely overcome the savage aggressiveness of nature, which stands ready to challenge any more refined or polished way of doing things.

Delicacy and grace aren't to be found in this part of the world—except in children, flowers, and butterflies. And interpersonal relationships.

The First Christian Community: An Example for Every Community

Today we had an all-day meeting. We started at 9 A.M. with about thirty persons. By noon there were more than fifty. And for Mass in the afternoon, there were some seventy-five or eighty adults, plus children, of whom there are always a lot.

As Ivanilde, Zé, and I had agreed, I made a presentation on the community of the apostles, the first BCC in history. Of course I used the Acts of the Apostles as the basis for what I said, especially the well-known passages in chapters 2 and 4. I especially emphasized the "four great fidelities":
1) fidelity to the *word of God* (the "teaching of the apostles");

2) fidelity to *community of goods*, understood here as mutual aid and pulling together to struggle for justice;

3) fidelity to the *breaking of bread* or the Mass, and here we discussed the priest shortage and the need for the community to deal with this issue, not just by furnishing vocations, but more and more taking on responsibility for standing on their own as church in all respects;

4) fidelity to *prayer* (novenas, the rosary, processions, family prayer, etc.).

I rounded out this picture with two more characteristics of the church of the apostles:

5) *difficulties* both internal (conflicts) and external (persecutions);

6) and *joy*, despite everything else, even in the midst of contradictions.

Eating with and like the People

We were very hungry by noon, but lunch was delayed due to the unexpected number of persons who had come. While we waited we snacked on cookies, *abacaxi* nuts, and mangos. There were lots of mangos; they're in season. And they're "sweet as honey," as Homer might say.

During lunch I ate like they do here: off the same plate with a 6-year-old girl, who stuffed the meal down with an astounding appetite.

Afterward, the children got me to play games. "Tag me!" they shouted behind my back. I fooled around a bit, and immediately gained their confidence. "Wasting time with kids" is one of the clearest signs of grace. That's what God does and what Jesus did too. The child is a straightforward protest against our exaggerated seriousness in political and pastoral activity.

There were also a dozen young adults there. They participated well, especially in the singing. I liked them.

The heat was suffocating. The air was still and the sky overcast. Really awful. Thank God, in the middle of Mass there was a refreshing shower! An undisguised blessing!

Conflict: To Be Found in Every Community

At 2 P.M. we went back to the meeting. Together we compared the BCC in Catuaba with the Apostles' BCC. It fitted point by point, as neatly as a school drill.

The point that the Catuabans stressed most was number five: difficulties, conflicts, and persecutions. They left all fired up to keep struggling.

In short, with different methods we kept repeating the six characteristic points of the Apostles' BCC that had been written on the blackboard and were the subject of reflection during the day. They were read out loud, recited all together, sung, etc.

In consultation with Ivanilde, I had intended to also take up Paul's speech in Ephesus for those who were in charge of communities. Of course, that would be for the local lay leaders. But I forgot. Besides, it wouldn't have been a good idea, because the comparison with the early church filled out the time perfectly.

Enlightening Others and Setting Their Hearts on Fire

We started the Mass at 3:30. At the offertory the children came up carrying their offering of flowers, picked in the jungle. The adults offered intentions along with each bouquet. Some of them referred to today as "a great day."

At the moment of the kiss of peace, I went from person to person, congratulating everyone. This gesture really breaks psychological barriers and opens up a space of trust and freedom. And then the Mass flows better. So it might have been a good idea to have had this gesture at the beginning in order to break the ice, loosen inhibitions, and free up hearts.

At the end of the Mass, I congratulated the community, and the lay leaders and ministers, and I spent some time encouraging them to keep moving forward, holding firmly onto the "four great fidelities."

I'm more and more convinced that, alongside our work of conscientization, it's important that we encourage and stimulate the people. The head needs light, but the heart needs fire. It's not enough to make things clear; we have to fire persons up—like God, who gives us revelation, but especially grace.

Fidelity: More Important than Enthusiasm

After Mass a woman told me she had drifted away from the community but that now she was going to begin attending meetings again. What I was intending to do here was to reinspire persons to continue their journey in faith and unity. Ivanilde was saying that they were going through a discouraging period and needed a strong injection of encouragement.

Actually, discouragement is part of the life rhythm of any community. It's no reason to be surprised or to lose heart. There's always a time when spirits are low. But that's just where *fidelity* comes in. The community doesn't always have to be excited and enthusiastic, but it must always remain faithful. That's the essential thing.

It's true that all communities go through phases of discouragement and weariness. That's natural in the life of the church. So the church fathers used to speak of the "mystery of the moon," referring to this rhythm of a "new moon" and "old moon" in the life of the church. I said this to the community, and especially to Ivanilde, so they could revive their spirits in their work. You have to take on the role of Second Isaiah and "console" the people in its affliction.

As a matter of fact, even as I was giving this all-day training session, my psychological state wasn't what you would call enthusiasm or excitement. But that's not the important thing; what's important is faith and patience—and the joy of the Spirit, which is like a deep current in the ocean, quite different from the waves thrashing about on the surface.

A Weakness in the BCCs

I'm overwhelmed by a sensation of weakness whenever I'm around BCCs. They're always poised between "making it" and "not making it," as someone here put it. And as far as I've been able to find out, that same feeling of weakness affects all BCCs in Brazil, and probably elsewhere.

Is this a temporary situation, one that is yet to be overcome? Will this turn out to be an indication that they are still in their infancy, a sign of immaturity—and thus a stage to be gone beyond?

Or is this not rather part of the makeup of the true church of Christ: the truer it is, the poorer it is, and of course, the poorer it is, the weaker it is? "God . . . singled out the weak of this world to shame the strong" (1 Cor. 1:27). The ideal of strength, and that there should be "strong communities"—is that a gospel ideal?

In any case, there's matter for reflection and discernment here. This weakness, fragility, the almost ephemeral quality of BCCs, is something ambiguous. Perhaps their weakness derives from the fact that BCCs are new, and that leaders aren't trained and experienced. That kind of weakness should be regarded as a passing phase and should be overcome and surpassed as we all make progress. But there is a gospel weakness that comes from the fact that BCCs are made up of persons who are poor, semi-illiterate, oppressed, and alienated, and yet, despite all that—even because of it—they are the bearers of the church's mission and of the promises of the kingdom. "Do not live in fear, little flock" (Luke 12:32).

BCCs must find their center of gravity in faith, never in fear; in a clear consciousness, never in alienation; in courage, never in cowardice.

Sunday, November 13: On the Acre River

GOING BACK BY BOAT

It's 6 A.M. I'm going up the Acre River toward Rio Branco. The trip will take more than two hours.

I look around. On both sides there are clusters of houses that belong to wealthy families from the capital. They have everything. It strikes me even more because my experience this past week has left me with countless impressions of how abandoned and needy the settlers in Brasiléia are.

The Story of a Lay Leader

Last night at supper Ivanilde told me her story as a lay leader, and the story of the community as well.

She said she got married fifteen years ago. The first six years she lived far away from the church and the gospel. In her house there were always parties and drinking, as well as beatings and fights every two weeks or so.

She had a niece who was closer to the church and who listened to the radio broadcast of the Mass early Sunday morning. One Sunday Ivanilde also felt like listening to the Mass. That's how it all began. She heard Bishop Moacyr say, "The harvest is great but the laborers are few." And the bishop invited listeners to become involved in the communities, anyone who wanted to.

The word "community" sounded strange to her. But that call echoed in her heart. She kept thinking that whole Sunday morning. She experienced remorse for the empty kind of life she had been leading. She cried. She wanted to respond to the bishop's call, but she didn't have any contact with church persons. She then went to her mother-in-law, who lived nearby (a woman I've gotten to know, full of faith, a tough faith like they have in Pernumbuco, in northeastern Brazil. She said to Ivanilde, "Daughter, it's God who's calling you. Follow his voice."

She went to the city to speak with the bishop. They met. Dom Moacyr told her how to start a catechetics group, because that's how she wanted to begin. And he said that when children were ready for first communion, he would go himself.

And that's what happened. It was a big celebration. Men, women, and children came from all over. It had been eight years since any priest had been there.

The Story of a Community

"Next," continued Ivanilde, "there was a training session for lay leaders. Father Pacífico led the meeting. For four days we studied the life of the early Christians. When the training session finished, the trainees felt they were leaving paradise. That's the way they all put it.

"That's how the community got started. There were periods of intense participation, not just in the numbers of participants but in the quality of what they did. There were Holy Weeks when the Way of the Cross was dramatized, and Christmases when the nativity scene was acted out, etc.

"Today there are five groups that belong to the community, and one minister of baptism.

"By its struggle the community has gotten the school, the health center, and soon there will be electricity.

"My husband and I take part in the union struggle, in the teachers' association, and also in the PT [Workers' Party]." (I can see PT slogans painted on the walls of houses.)

"The community," she continued, "has an informal coordination team made up of all the lay leaders and other ministers. It meets once a month to plan activities.

"Would you believe it? A year after the community began, backbiting had stopped? Now everyone around here lives peacefully and we're all friends."

On my own I was able to verify that there is a high degree of good community life in Catuaba. However, Ivanilde was clearly somewhat discouraged, and said to me, "The community is going through a period of spiritual 'recession.' " She was quite insistent about this, and that was what she prayed about at the Mass yesterday afternoon.

Still, I think a good deal of this comes from her psychological state: she's in her last month of pregnancy and her nerves are exhausted. All this makes her supersensitive to whatever happens around her and to anything that's said about it. That's what I found out in a conversation later that night.

"You work too hard, Ivanilde," I told her as a bit of criticism. She answered, "The community won't let you rest." That's how it is when you're a mother serving the life of your children and the faith of your people!

Tensions in a Marriage of Lay Leaders

Last night Ivanilde asked me to have a talk, she and her husband, with me. It was about the kind of problems that affect all married couples.

She complained that her husband wasn't being very sensitive to her situation as a woman who was pregnant and exhausted besides. In their own relationship she thought he was being too introverted, too closed in.

I have to admit that this speech caught me a bit by surprise. Knowing husbands in this area and how much machismo there is I had been impressed by how dedicated Zé was. I had seen him handling pots and pans in the kitchen and fixing our supper the night before last. The next morning I saw him pick up a broom and sweep the floor. Besides, weren't both of them working together in the school, in the party, in the teachers' union, and in the community? A couple like that is quite exceptional. I said so to Ivanilde to lower the tension and put things in perspective.

Zé didn't say much. He just listened, and then finally said that the whole thing didn't seem like such a problem to him, that that's the way he was, that it should be kept within the family, etc.

I thought, "What husbands have said from time immemorial." I could see he had been somewhat affected, and he was paying attention and showing good will.

I gave them a few words of encouragement. I told Zé that I supported his wife, and urged him to show more attention and care because she's so sensitive, especially now when she's about to have a baby. I also told Ivanilde she should understand her husband's temperament, and try to pick up the signs of attention he showed her, even if they were low-key.

This all helped me understand why Ivanilde's eyes had been red when she came into the room Friday when we arrived, and also Saturday morning. She had been with friends venting her hurt feelings.

I found her frankness and openness with her husband courageous and beautiful. It was one more proof of her strong personality and spirit, of her own self-initiative, all of which makes her quite different from her husband. But that's just why these tensions are there. They have to be dealt with rather than avoided.

Basically, they're a very fine couple—a gospel couple.

Early this morning, as we were saying goodbye, Ivanilde gave me some messages for Dom Moacyr, and said if her child is a boy she's going to have the bishop serve as godfather. "He's the one who taught me the Billings Method, and it didn't work," she laughs. She didn't want an abortion, for that would have been against her conscience. Her youngest child, Diana, isn't even a year old and she's about to have another baby!

But she keeps going on, borne by the strong but gentle breath of the Spirit.

The Wiles of Poverty

An old man about sixty-five or seventy just got on our boat. He staggered on barefoot. He says he's dying for something to eat; he hasn't eaten for five days. He says he's a widower and lives alone and that he's going to the city to get some "grub," that he's got a daughter there, etc.

His eyes have a dull look. His stomach is drawn in. That's hunger, I think to myself. However, I can't understand how that can happen when he lives in an area that provides everything. It could only be due to some strange combination of circumstances.

I go to talk with two women on the boat and with the boat pilot. They tell me that this story of going without eating for five days is just meant to take advantage of someone's naivety. "With so many mangos and sweet potatoes on the beaches, and bananas everywhere, no one could possibly go hungry that long," they say, skeptically. The boat pilot adds, "There are so many people living around here near him, how could he go hungry like that? What he really wants to do is go to the city and have a good time." He ends the subject with a laugh.

Too bad I've felt so sorry for him and given the crafty old guy 1,000 cruzeiros (approx. $7). I had thought of giving him even more but now I'm sorry for having given even 1,000.

The poor can be wily. . . .

Work and Religion in the Life of the People

Friday, on the way down to Catuaba, I was talking with an old man who had been born in the area, had worked gathering rubber, had run a canoe on the Acre River for fifteen years, and was now living in a settlement near Catuaba with his wife. He continued to work in the fields even though he was seventy-five. His lifestyle is simple and his needs modest. Dignified poverty.

I think to myself that an old man like this, who has been working his whole life, still has to work in order to stay alive. . . . A lot of other persons must have gotten fat on what he did out there. He stands for many, many thousands of rubber-gatherers who have spent their lives working for others who could sit back and enjoy life. But they knew nothing of the kind of self-giving that comes from freedom, fulfillment, and love; they engaged in exploitation, violent and hateful.

So I'm quite surprised to hear the old man say, "It's a pleasure for me to go out and hack at the jungle with my machete. I observe Sundays only because it's God's commandment. If it were up to me, I'd be out in the field. Even when it rains I go out." I ask him whether he has pains in his back from bending over so much (recalling my own experience). He says he doesn't, that he's been used to it since he was a kid.

I tell him, "It's time for you to rest and take it easy, because you've already produced so much wealth for the world." His laugh indicates he doesn't understand. I go on, "What you've already done should entitle you to live in a golden palace." I joke with him like that, but he goes back to talking about the field, the beauty of his corn, cassava, and rice, how they're all growing. "I'd like you to come out to my field and see," he invites me, contentedly.

He tells me his wife is a catechist, though she's now quite old. I think to myself, "She still has some life to give the people."

As for himself, he says he's religious but not closely linked with the community. But I find it hard to believe: his face, his eyes, and his voice reveal someone who's "pure of heart," one of those whom the gospel calls blessed or happy.

I ask him about the dangers he's run into during his life in the jungle and on the river. He says there haven't been many. He's always been "protected by the powers of God and the Virgin Mary." Every time he says the name of God—too often to count—he raises his eyes to heaven and touches his cap. Such amazing respect for the divine! The Jews in Jesus' time would have appreciated such a fine gesture.

I ask him, "What kind of prayer do you say?" He tells me a prayer he says whenever he goes into the jungle. "It's a powerful prayer," he explains, "and defends you from any kind of animal." In front of him I jot down the prayer he recites for me:

> Saint Benedict, holy cattle herder
> of the Blessed Sacrament,
> Deliver me from cobras,
> And from all toothed and venomed animals.

He goes on, "Afterward, you have to say an Our Father and a Hail Mary in honor of St. Benedict."

I ask him what "venomed" means. He doesn't know. But he explains that St. Benedict raised animals and that's why he's a "holy cattle herder."

In return I tell him another powerful prayer to St. Benedict that I learned from a young woman who entered the religious life. "This one is to protect you from dog bites," I tell him. "It goes like this":

> Saint Benedict, holy water, and
> Jesus Christ on the altar,
> Enable me to get by this dog
> And go on my way.

The old man thinks I believe in this kind of prayer with the same piety as his. And he's happy he's been able to share his prayer with me. Seeing me write it on a scrap of paper, he emphasizes it again, "You're going to see how powerful it is!"

I believe that these prayers, rather than changing the state of things in the world, bring about a positive change in the spirit, enabling persons to carry on a successful struggle with the way things are. If it changes something in the world, it's through the spirit, and perhaps through some sort of procedure whose psycho-physical logic mostly escapes us.

However, I don't think God is beyond such means. God's power can go through these human mechanisms. But I don't think such prayers act physically on the physical world. That would be magic.

As I get off the boat, I tell the old man, "I expect to see you tomorrow in Catuaba." He says he will. (And he shows up with his wife, the catechist.)

The Gospel: Ferment for the Whole of Life

Writing on the boat, I recall how Ivanilde would speak: "Before getting to know the gospel . . ."; "we've gotten everything: a school, health post, and other things like that, starting out with the gospel"; "you try to live in your home the way it is in the gospel," etc.

How marvelous! Persons like that really take the gospel seriously. It's the law for their life, the law of freedom, the law of love. It's leaven within the person, the family, the community, and society.

Is that because there's no other competing reference point, no other vision of the world? Whatever the reason, the gospel penetrates into the whole of life with its fermenting action. And life is like delicious leavened bread.

The Political Capital of the People

I'm noting down a strong question that hit me when I was coming back to Zé and Ivanilde's house, tired from the meeting at the end of the day. Not thinking anything in particular, I was trudging along the edge of a high cliff that runs along the Acre River. This thought came to me, sneaking up like a cat on a rooftop, "To what extent are these persons really protagonists of change in our society?" The question made me smile. But I'm thinking about it again. No matter what else, it's always worthwhile to do any kind of work with the poor and the oppressed. Yes, it is worth it to love those who are politically weak. Even if it doesn't make much sense for Marx, for Christ it does make sense, a lot of sense. *Sub lumine Regni Dei*, working with those who are the least among the least of this world is something essential: it builds up the eschatological kingdom, even if it doesn't build the historical kingdom. And what would the historical kingdom be as measured against the eschatological kingdom? By putting its emphasis on the working classes, Marxism comes to the point of scorning "those who are least"—the *Lumpen*—and peasants, because it has only human history in view. But that can never happen with a person of faith who reads another meaning in this history, one that is transhistorical.

Still, the question remains: Where is all this work heading? Is it possible that we can't get a picture of where it's all heading, or a sketch of the new society? Is it possible that we're clearsightedly preparing persons for radical fidelity of faith within history, so they will be able to follow things out to their ultimate consequences, including martyrdom? That's what Jesus did with utter realism, foresight, and vigor. I recall that Catherine of Siena, who was quite *popolana* (close to the people), thought the possibility of martyrdom went right along with faith: any faithful Christian is headed toward martyrdom.

Are we ready for martyrdom ourselves? To be baptized in blood like the Master?

"To desire martyrdom as you desire paradise," said Léon Bloy, "is a grace." "It's a grace that the Father keeps for the children he loves most," as our own great Dom Hélder Câmara has said.

VII

The *Diakonia* of Liberation

BUILDING UP THE BODY OF CHRIST

A meeting of the Council of Sector Representatives is going on here in the Training Center today and tomorrow. We're going over the various sectors in which the local church provides services: land, Indian work, catechesis, ministries, etc.

Those responsible for each sector have come here: lay persons, sisters, priests, and the bishop—around fifty persons altogether. The term "sectors" refers to important areas of work—not this or that community or parish, but the local church as a whole. They are like the "ligaments," mentioned in the letter to the Ephesians, that enable the "whole body . . . with the proper functioning of the members joined firmly together . . . [to] grow [and to] build itself up in love" (4:16).

I'm jotting down some thoughts that this evaluation has triggered in my own mind.

Ministers to the Sick or Health Promoters?

Here's how the question is being posed at the pastoral level: Should ministers to the sick, who are also ministers of communion, get involved in the social side of health: promoting conscientization and helping communities to organize around their right to health care? Should the ministerial responsibility include that of being health promoters?

Not necessarily. The two functions are different, though interconnected. It's obvious that the minister to the sick is important and necessary, because there should be a Christian and church presence among the sick, to pray for them and with them, and to give them encouragement in their trials. Such a minister should at the same time encourage them to get the medical treatment they need, whether in the form of home remedies or medicine. The two should never be

95

separated: prayer and medicine, blessing and health professionals, consolation of the spirit and cure of the body.

There are many sick among us and it's important to show God's love toward them. Protestants hold "divine healing sessions" and the poor come in droves. It meets a real need on their part, and it should stimulate communities to include the sick in their charity. A further reason is the healing power of prayer, something that can scarcely be denied. The sacrament of the sick was intended for the bodily health of the sick person and it still is. Psychosomatic medicine is showing how the spirit plays a role in the physical restoration of a patient. "Uneducated" persons have known about this for centuries, out of their experience with their own healers and prayers for healing.

The health promoter, however, takes on the problem from a social angle and from within a healthy community. In dealing with sick persons there's no point in discussing the social and even economic roots of illness and involving them in working out structural solutions.

The two levels of love musn't be confused: the interpersonal level (micro-charity) and the social or political level (macro-charity).

Priests and Presbyters

It's important that the work done in this sector be provided with a theological basis that is broad and firm, as some of the priests in the meeting have insisted.

For example, it's important to reflect theologically on the mission of the priest and his role, and not remain stuck within the existing ecclesiastical discipline, which demands that the priest receive a particular philosophical/ theological formation, observe celibacy, etc.

If there is no such thing as an adult community without the Eucharist, how are we to keep pace with communities that are becoming adult, unless we allow them to have the ministers they need, such as the minister of the Lord's Supper?

The big issue here isn't the priest, but the community. In other words, the real problem isn't "turning out priests," but enabling communities to celebrate the Lord's Supper. It's certainly possible to conceive of a kind of figure who would preside over the Lord's Supper without necessarily being a priest—that is, not the type we know today. He would be of another kind: he would be the "presbyter" of his own community, which would certainly be small, and there he would preside at the eucharistic liturgy in a manner that would be appropriate, but different from the official way.

If the BCCs are a "new way of being church," they also imply a "new way of being priest (presbyter)."

Theology and Ministries

The Council of Sector Representatives has requested that there be a stronger linkage between these two sectors. The issue could be formulated like this:

1) communities sending members to theology courses so they can get the training they need to be well-qualified ministers;

2) professors and students trained in theology acting as in the different sectors, including the area of ministries.

"Penitential Silence" vis-à-vis Indians

Generally speaking, CIMI (Indigenous Mission Council) has done good work among indigenous peoples.

Nevertheless, the "mission" aspect in CIMI should be subject to discussion: What has it done specifically with regard to mission? Very little. What gets done, whether within CIMI or independently, is in the area of general pastoral work, by priests as they make their customary rounds, and other activities.

Lori, a Lutheran minister who works among the Marinawa, along with her husband Roberto, who is also a minister, raises the issue of the evangelization of the Indians in a theology thesis she wrote as an ordination requirement. She brings up some excellent points. For example, she says that for a period of time evangelization of Indians should be limited to the minimum program that Bonhoeffer outlined in 1944 when he was in a Third Reich prison: "pray and struggle for justice." Should there be explicit evangelization? None, for the time being, she answers. In such a case, pastoral strategy would amount to a "penitential silence" that would enable the church to purge the sins it has committed in the name of evangelization. Gradually, it would regain its right to speak in the name of the gospel and be heard. Only after, and out of, this extended "penitential silence" would the words of faith once again take on their own inherent clarity and strength. This was, in fact, what the "death of God" theologians proposed in the 1960s.

I think this is especially valid for those Amerindian groups that were destroyed—culturally and physically—in the name of the Christian faith. In such a case the credibility of the faith must be won back through a twofold approach: prayer and the pursuit of justice. Both are essential, not justice alone. Bonhoeffer's proposal could become an alibi for not doing anything along pastoral lines. Actually the tension toward later evangelization can be maintained only if there really is prayer. Prayer holds the word of the faith the way the earth holds the seed until it sprouts.

On the other hand, there is the real issue of tribes that ask for the priest and the sacraments. They shouldn't be put off.

What about tribes that don't ask for anything? Why deprive them of the "fullness of human life" that the faith is meant to bring them? Obviously if Indians show opposition and direct resistance, the only thing to do is to respect the signal they're sending. In such a case there are probably good reasons for applying Bonhoeffer's formula. But if there isn't, why not evangelize? Is someone going to claim that it's "cultural colonization," "an ideological occupation force"?

The issue here is not the thing in itself, but the *way* it's done. In fact, you can make a reasonable case for preaching your faith to others simply by the fact that cultures are enriched by dialogue and exchange. Besides, it can no longer be prevented today in a world that has become a "global village." Besides all that, preaching one's religious convictions is a "human right" recognized by the United Nations.

Moreover, Christian faith can be set within the context of human expectations, and that is what it seeks. It doesn't contradict those expectations at all, but propels them forward, purifies them, and fulfills them without limit. At this point we are in the area of *how* evangelization is to be carried out. It can be done authentically only if whatever is part of true Amerindian culture is assumed, and that includes religious expressions. And this is a point that the church should analyze in order to reexamine its missionary pastoral work. The *intrinsic* demands of faith and the gospel are one thing; the *cultural* demands, always relative, of the community of faith—the local church—are something else.

Subjects and Objects of Agape

Here also the activities in question are almost exclusively social, although pastors always add the dimension of faith, both in training sessions and in the work of the CPT in the field.

Agencies like the CPT express Christian *agape* toward the oppressed. Nevertheless, being satisfied with the practice of *agape* and not moving toward the soul of *agape,* which is faith itself, amounts to once more treating others as an object—the object of our *agape.* They are not being motivated toward becoming a subject of *agape;* that can happen only when they have faith—the root of *agape.*

True, liberating action doesn't necessarily have to be *agape* in the sense of evangelical praxis, praxis consciously motivated in and by explicit faith. But liberation reaches fullness only in *agape*—that is, in faith. That's the way God wanted it and that's the way of God's plan of salvation. And that's the way the human being is constituted.

Finances and the People

With regard to this sector, some raised the point that decisions are made in an individualistic way, bypassing the body whose job it is, the economic council.

However, I think we have to be more radical: administration must be democratized. That kind of democratization takes place at the level of policy making—the level of overall guidelines—whereas the technical level (execution and specific procedures) is left up to a technical commission. Hence Pericles used to say, "Although not everyone can carry out political activity, everyone knows how to judge it."

What the priests have in mind is the presentation of the annual budget to the pastoral council and discussion of it, as well as the annual financial report. But isn't this largely just a report and a mere formality? To what extent is the community really involved in these questions?

Perhaps what's involved here is an even more basic and also more obvious fact: the resources of the local church don't come from it and its own efforts. And it's only natural not to be concerned with something that doesn't cost anything.

This is where the whole issue of the prelature's resources should be raised. Those resources sustain an economic infrastructure set up for the prelature's pastoral superstructure. But does this provide the appropriate foundation for pastoral work that is really gospel-oriented?

Shouldn't the church perhaps be poorer, even in the means it uses? Wouldn't this bring us closer to the people and wouldn't it force us to put more trust in the people and the resources of the people?

In Innocent III's dream it wasn't the rich and powerful pope who was bearing on his shoulders the church, which was in ruins, but rather the Poverello.

St. Anthony Pucci, a Servite, used to say, "Without poverty, there's no prosperity." That's the logic of the gospel, a logic that runs directly against the logic of capital.

In our pastoral work is there perhaps a contradiction between having an economic foundation that is strong and solid, and the building of a "poor church" and a "church of the poor"?

In any case, such questioning should be gospel questioning, not legalistic questioning. Its setting is the freedom of the gospel and the profound inspiration of the Spirit, not that of a dominion governed by imperial decree. Such questioning points toward the prophetically radical stance of Jesus of Nazareth and doesn't fall into the radicalism of imposition. The church is the community of the offspring of God, offspring who are free—and free both to use this world as though they weren't using it, and to "unuse" it as though they were using it.

Adult Catechesis?

Is it necessary or not? That's the issue. There were two answers. On the one hand, the gospel reflection in BCCs is already a "catechesis for adults." After all, isn't the gospel the oldest catechism book in the church?

On the other hand, lay persons feel the need for a systematic overview of the faith. In this respect, the little booklet *Abre a porta* ["open the door"] is doing a good job of meeting the need. On the national level, the idea of a "popular catechism for adults" is being discussed.

Otherwise, it's like "wasting a candle on a dead scoundrel," muttered the bishop at my elbow.

Sunday, November 27

SPIRITUALITY AND IDEOLOGY

In the plenary session the question came up: How is it that persons active in the church end up switching sides, going over to the government side? For example, almost all the members of a certain governmental board in Acre have come out of the church context and now they're aligned with government policies. When pastoral agents leave the framework of church *activity,* why do they also leave the framework of church *life?* When they cease being active pastorally, why do they cease to have any sacramental connection? The question is important, although the problem still isn't terribly serious.

I have the impression that some see the value of the faith only in its political potential; apart from that, or without it, faith loses its human relevance or meaning.

Political commitment does have its own relative *autonomy:* to some extent it is self-validating and doesn't need any reference to faith. One can devote oneself to work with the people and to activity in favor of justice simply with a humanitarian or ethico-political sensitivity, such as may be found in Marxism.

But that autonomy is *relative:* radically and ultimately, it must be based on a transcendent or "religious" view of the world and of history. Unless it is open to the transcendent (not necessarily revealed or Christian transcendence), politics doesn't have sure enough foundations, and it is prey to perversions and manipulations on the part of human beings. That is what Paul VI saw clearly, both in *Populorum Progressio* (humanism closed off, without God, ends up turning against humans, recalling Henri de Lubac), and in *Evangelii Nuntiandi* (chapter 3: liberation that doesn't have a transcendent perspective ends up becoming enslavement).

Hence it is clear that faith is a power that prevents politics from becoming alienated.

What should be done to ensure that faith be ferment, not only for action, but for the whole of life; that it be salt not only for society but also for the individual; that it be revolution and conviction as well?

Without this personal rootedness, Christian liberation becomes empty and it easily turns into ideology: Marxism or liberalism. A faith that doesn't mean anything beyond the "option for the poor," and a theology that simply takes over for an ideology, whether it be liberal or Marxist, ends up self-destructing and giving way to what it replaced.

What should be done? We should make it possible for pastoral workers, especially those most qualified, to receive *specific training in the faith.* They should be helped to develop a serious theological background, by reading, discussion, celebrations designed specifically for them, retreats, the discipline of personal prayer, etc. The idea is to create a whole *Christian spirituality* to meet the needs of our situation.

Studying and organizing our work is no longer enough. There has to be a deepening in the faith as such—training and nourishment in Christian mysticism, in other words.

Christians in Popular Organizations

Grassroots associations of persons living in a given area, which are spreading rapidly today, do not have to have a confessional nature. They can be guided by an ethic of human rights. Christians should be there as responsible citizens, either as individuals or as groups but not *institutionally*—that is, as ferment, with their faith, but not as church.

We have to think this through some more, and draw all the pastoral and political consequences (making sure they get tested). That will take both time and thought.

Revolutionism

Several times today, during the plenary session, there were statements that could be called radical or even leftist. Someone said: "When INCRA gives land, it's not agrarian reform. Down with it!—let's move on to real agrarian reform, the kind the people carry out." Or: "Holding a direct election for president is a bourgeois solution. Down with it! What we want is another kind of power: people's power." Or again: "The issue of the colonists who have come up from the south won't be solved with commissions and improvements. Those are just band-aids. Land has to be divided up equitably, and we have to carry out a social revolution." Admittedly, those who express such sentiments represent isolated voices, and they aren't taken very seriously because they don't show much common sense.

In every large meeting you always run across these idealists of revolution—the revolutionists. They don't see all the steps, the different moments, that have to be part of the overall process of social change. They can't recognize that INCRA land may be a step in the direction of real agrarian reform, or that direct elections of a president may contribute to the realization of people's power—that it might begin there. Revolutionism confuses the overall process of revolution with just one of its moments, the moment of the break.

That's why this revolutionary immediatism—Revolution Now!—leads to very negative consequences: "vanguardism," that seeks to drag a people along by the yoke, the way you pull a draft animal; and "coupism" or "conspiracy-ism," meaning those for whom "preparing the conditions for revolution amounts to preparing a conspiracy," as Marx puts it.

What this reflects is the inability to relate the overall project to strategies and tactics that go part way, and to relate long-term (historic) proposals to short- and medium-term (conjunctural, transitory) proposals.

They say, "The solution is revolution!" and think they've discovered the road, when they've only found out what the final destination is.

During the discussion of how to help the colonists from the south, the proposal was to take concrete steps, because the problem is concrete: to demand of the system what it could give—as opposed to the rhetoric of those calling for "Agrarian Reform Now!" and "Social Revolution Now!" After the meeting one of them came by and sniped at me, "You're a reformist!"

So there it stands. The only thing left for this kind of revolutionary imme-diatism is conspiracy, if they have the courage to get beyond their idealist kind of verbiage.

Reform isn't always reformism. Small measures, single steps, are revolutionary in content and meaning if:

1) they are *assumed by the oppressed themselves* as subjects, possibly themselves acting as protagonists in the matter;

2) they *head in the right direction*—that is, with a view toward transforming the social system, as one moment in a whole process; in other words, they question the existing order as a whole.

Revolutionary immediatism is a malady of the petty bourgeoisie, whose stomach and mouth are full, and whose head and hands are empty. Project and process aren't the same thing! The only cure for this disease is sinking deep roots—and working for a long time with the people, in the school of the poor.

Localized and Nationwide Work

Questions like the present campaign of agrarian reform and direct election of the president are very much under discussion.

No doubt these things demand that grassroots works be carried out with the people. But that isn't enough. There also has to be nationwide work, the kind that will move the population as a whole, including large sectors of the petty bourgeoisie and sizeable segments of the bourgeoisie.

But to do that you have to use the mass media so as to get mass participation. Hence the importance of solidarity from professionals, students, and politicians, even if they're not from the popular classes.

If we want to stir up society, we have to stir up the masses. And in order to stir up the masses, it's not enough to stir up groups at the grassroots level; we have to use the mass media, demonstrations, etc.

Two Spheres and Two Kinds of Work

This brings us to a very important point. What kind of presence should Christians have in official spheres—within the institutions of the prevailing system: radio, newspapers, schools, university, and the government itself?

It's one thing to do liberating pastoral work in the people's own sphere, where the rules are laid down by the people, and something else again to do it in the official sphere, where the dominant classes set the rules. How do "official space" and "popular space" relate to each other?

To simply carry a popular strategy into the official sphere shows a lack of political acumen. Prophetically attacking the system in a classroom is tantamount to repeating what happens in Amos 7, without the same sort of mandate. It means changing the professor's chair into the revolutionary's platform—as Max Weber said, showing how much it horrified him. The same thing could be said of radio stations, which we sometimes want to change into church pulpits. However, in church we're on our own turf, whereas on the radio we're on foreign, and sometimes hostile, terrain.

It's important to have a correct theory on this question, and to have deepened our vision of it. Here are some elements that may serve to shed some light on the matter.

We often have a simplistic idea of official or public institutions: schools, courts, newspapers, police, radio, and especially the government. We lump them all together and regard them as "instruments of the dominant class," and see them as "on the other side."

The error we fall into is thus the opposite of the naive vision that leads some persons to believe that all these institutions promote order, progress, and the welfare of the people. To say that they're simply an ideological mask is more than half the truth, but not the whole truth.

It's important to realize that the official sphere isn't monolithic. It's full of contradictions, and there are cracks in it.

True, it's dominated or controlled by the dominant classes and it serves them: the police, the school system, government, etc. But domination does not mean exclusivity. Dominant power isn't all-inclusive power. There's not just one team playing and always winning—there's another team, even though it's weaker.

And so in the official sphere there are cracks that the oppressed can get into and that they can expand. Those seeking the liberation of the people can't be limited to one area: working only in the area of the people or only in the official area. The people and its cause (justice) are to be found in both areas. The issue of the common people is posed everywhere: in the government, in the universities, in research centers, in the churches, etc. The issue of the people is found on all sides.

Therefore, the confrontation or battle isn't between two *blocs* of monolithic institutions, but between two *forces* that run throughout institutions and are struggling over them. The forces of liberation are present in the official sphere, just as the forces of oppression are present in the popular sphere (by means of their representatives and their ideology). Social classes don't stand facing each other; they're *intertwined* with one another.

Hence, it's important to do both kinds of work, combining them, and making sure that they're combined correctly.

1) Work in the people's sphere, making this the priority area, means creating autonomous bodies, where the people can be in charge. Here you have a chance to go quite far because it's a relatively untouched space. The germs of a new society, a new kind of power, a new economy, a new kind of knowledge, and also a new way of being church, can all be created and developed in this space. This is where the decisive break takes place, where the dominant system is dealt a lethal blow.

2) Work in the official sphere means getting in there and augmenting the slice of power the oppressed have. True, work is harder here, because the struggle is being waged on someone else's turf, someone who is often an enemy, and it's under the control of dominators. You have to be cunning and know how to feint and dodge. This kind of work doesn't aim at destroying the power of domination but weakening it, not at bringing about the overthrow but

paving the way for it. Hence, the point is *not to diminish but to extend* the role played by the people in the realm of this dominant power.

The big question is how to articulate, or combine, the liberating forces acting outside official institutions with the liberating forces acting within them. They both have the same *objective:* to liberate the oppressed. But their *strategy* has to be different: a strategy of penetration into official space, and a strategy of creation within the people's space.

Those who work inside can advance only when they're supported by those who are working outside. And those working outside are aided by the information and resources supplied by those who work inside.

This way of looking at things is fruitful for dealing with several problems:

1) How to relate to the government and its official bodies, especially now during the phase of liberalization.

2) How can a Catholic school make its "option for the poor."

3) How the "church of the people" can best relate to the institutional church as a whole (its internal configuration as a result of its history).

These thoughts came to me after I happened to get hold of and read a discussion between N. Poulantzas and H. Weber that came out in the review *Teoria e Política,* No. 4, 1982, pp. 129–47.

In any case, we have to go a lot deeper into this issue, which is more and more important in our work with the people.

VIII

Retreat: Toward an Incarnate Spirituality

Monday, November 28: Rio Branco

THE NEW LIBERATING SPIRITUALITY

All of us in the presbytery of this church, including Dom Moacyr, the bishop, have gathered for four days of retreat. Not a single priest is missing: all sixteen are here. We're meeting in the Training Center outside the city.

In our meeting last night we laid out the purpose of the retreat: to deepen our faith convictions, to nourish our mission once again at its roots, and to be ever more converted to the gospel and what it demands today.

The dynamics of the meeting were worked out in the group: some observations by Dom Moacyr and myself, then silence or conversation in twos or threes (but done so as not to disturb the climate of recollection) and sharing in common.

We opened the retreat with an exposition of an article by Gustavo Gutiérrez, "Beber en su propio pozo" (English translation, "We Drink from Our Own Wells," *Concilium,* no. 159, 1982, pp. 38–45). The article deals with the kind of spirituality now emerging in Latin America, a spirituality of our own, the "well" we're now drinking from.

This spirituality has two characteristic aspects:

1) It's a community spirituality, one that's *collective* and, hence, not privatized or closed within the confines of the individual "soul"; it's something experienced by a whole church, a whole people taking its own route through history: the route toward liberation. The fact that it's collective doesn't make it less personal.

2) It's an *incarnate* spirituality, one that's concrete, historical, political and, in a word, open to the "material" life of the people and linked with the real struggle of the people. Hence, it's a spirituality that's not closed off in one's inner depths, focused on one's "spiritual" experiences, in the Greek sense of spiritual: as opposed to what is outside, matter. Being incarnate doesn't make it less spiritual.

To sum it up, it's a spirituality that is certainly *rooted* in what is deepest in human nature, in the heart, in the spirit, but *open* to the people and to the people's ongoing history.

One meets the Lord, therefore, in meeting the poor, in approaching their world, even if one never fully gets there.

Tuesday, November 29: Rio Branco

MEETING THE POOR: A SPIRITUAL EXPERIENCE

At the end of the morning we met to share our thinking and experiences. Here are a few statements I jotted down, condensing them in my own way.

1) Father José, pastor of the Immaculate Conception church (Rio Branco):

"The poor are oppressed, but they have hope. Despite the conditions of death they have to live under, they always hold onto a hope for life. To realize this you just have to observe them at Sunday Mass. They suffer from extreme poverty, but they still sing out strong. That's always very impressive to me. I don't see that as alienation or running away, but as being firmly set right at the heart of things, and that means life and freedom."

2) Father Paolino, pastor in Sena Madureira:

"Contact with the people increases a priest's faith. Visits to the faithful are real retreats for me, and it's they who do the preaching.

"They enable me to find joy and fulfillment in life and in my priestly and religious life. They always confirm my sense of consecration and my mission. If I'm unfaithful to that mission, I betray my people. Trips through the jungle to visit them don't drain me, but enrich me.

"The peace you feel in the jungle at the end of a day of intense work is worth more than all the gold in the world. A few minutes of that true interior peace will nourish your spirit for twenty years of apostolic work. And your heart keeps returning there, calling that contact to mind, in order to sustain you and keep you going."

Father Paolino has been a missionary in Acre for a long time. He's a combination of St. Paul, with his long apostolic journeys, St. Francis, with his poverty and gospel spirit, and Padre Cícero, with the way he's become incarnate right there with the people of the jungle. He speaks of the power of the people's faith. He tells how several times it has happened that the people's steadfast prayer has brought down rain from heaven at a time of terrible drought. The connection between prayer and rain (cause-and-effect, chance, hindsight) doesn't concern him. He relates the fact and bears witness to it.

3) Father Luciano, from the parish in Xapuri:

"I've often had the same experience as Father José. I've gone off on a journey feeling very low and pessimistic. Being with the communities has raised my spirits and enabled me to feel hopeful again. The power we find in their lives is contagious."

4) Father Mássimo, pastor in the church of Santa Inês (Rio Branco):

"The poor really are a whole universe in themselves. It's important for us to appreciate the positive values they show, no matter how poor they may look. Jesus, the Servant of Yahweh, knew how to appreciate the mustard seeds of faith, life, and liberation he saw in the lowly. That's why our church does well when it shows its appreciation for popular culture: letters, poems, songs, and even books, like the ones by Bacurau, *À margem da vida* ["on the edge of life"] and Maria Lúcia, *A coragem de viver* ["the courage to live"], both of them lepers, and both books published by Vozes, the Franciscan publishing house in Petrópolis.

"The poor evangelize us, us priests, especially with their willingness to really share what they have." At this point Mássimo mentioned a poor woman whom he met after she had come to the city looking for something for her many children, and had just gotten three bananas, which she was clutching tightly in her hand. That's all she had. Still, she took a banana and offered it to the priest. "The very image of the widow in the gospel, who gave out of her poverty," he said.

5) Father Paolino recalled another experience:

"One time I arrived at a settlement drenched by the rain. The woman of the house hadn't expected me. All she had was a pair of scrawny chickens. She grabbed one of them and started to make supper for me. I said, *'Dona,* why are you doing that? You're going to finish everything off. A year from now you could have a whole flock of young chickens!' No use! The poor don't look at things that way. Their generosity is unlimited."

6) Father Roberto, pastor in Boca do Acre (Amazonas):

"I always feel very mixed up when I have to refuse someone a sacrament because of the regulations the church lays down, that they have to participate in the communities, and so forth. How can we combine love for the poor, hearing their cry, and these regulations, whose purpose is to help persons get beyond a childish form of faith that foments dependency? How can we really love the poor?"

7) Father Sírio, from the parish of Santa Inês, made some observations on the basis of his own experience of life elsewhere. He has recently arrived from Italy and is over sixty years old:

"Simple persons like to pray together in a simple way. Only the rich like to pray alone and with an elitist kind of jargon.

"In East-bloc countries, which I've gotten to know reasonably well, you don't see the joy and hope that you see in Latin America. I think that's the saddest experience I had there. The only time I found a glimmer of hope was when I talked to a journalist in the Yugoslav Communist Party.

"The danger for us is that we'll go spend a little time with the poor, and then go back to our more comfortable world. That will be a loss for us, both pastorally and spiritually."

A Spirituality That Measures up to History

There was a discussion about whether Latin American spirituality (of liberation) will turn out to be a short-lived phenomenon.

To my mind, it's not a spirituality for a particular moment, an interim period, that might run out in a few years. Nor is it a spirituality that's timeless, everlasting, transtemporal. It is rather a spirituality that's valid for a particular *period in history*. And periods in history tend to be long, covering centuries.

When this period is over, the spirituality of liberation will form part of the accumulated experience of faith. Later on it may be taken up again and put to use. The results it has produced are to some extent definitive—for example, in its sounding out social, historical, and political dimensions of faith. And that is common to all spiritualities.

Putting an End to Poverty

How would the church look if the scourge of poverty were eliminated? Certainly, the figure of the "poor person" is permanent in the life of faith. That's everyone in need, who suffers, who is needy. What varies is the *shape* that the poor assume in history. Today the prevailing shape of the poor is of a *collective* and *conflictive* nature: the poor are the exploited and marginalized masses. Although we shall "always have the poor among us" in a general sense, the poor may and should disappear as masses and classes. And that should come about in the name of the gospel, which commands that we "give food to the hungry."

So the question of poverty in its present form isn't just a question of a particular moment (it's not just a hunger crisis that will go away) and it's not a perennial problem that goes back to "the beginning of the world." It's primarily an issue in history. It arose in history, and it will go away in history. And as long as there is poverty that's social in nature, there is going to be a faith and a mystique of liberation that's social in nature.

The Way Jesus of Nazareth Lived

Starting from the infancy accounts, Dom Moacyr made a short presentation, highlighting aspects of Jesus' life that can challenge us today:

1) Jesus is born *poor* and lives out his childhood in the midst of poverty. And he carries that poverty with him to the end: he dies naked, rejected by his own, by his "church," by his people, by his friends, and even by his Father.

2) Jesus lives in *anonymity*. He is subject to the Law. Until his "public life," he doesn't stand out in any way. He shares in the situation of those who have no history, who have no privileges, and aren't in charge of anything. He's like the ones we find in emergency wards, whose life has no value at all in the eyes of those who are important. He doesn't have any honorary titles and he certainly can't say, "Don't you know who you're talking with?" He's like those three million persons in northeastern Brazil who are going to die in next year's drought—none of them will be a bishop, priest, or sister.

3) Jesus is *persecuted* from his childhood to his death by those who hold political and religious power.

When he finished Dom Moacyr raised the challenge: Like the pope, who, when he got to Brazil, stepped off the runway and knelt down to kiss the ground, are we ready to leave aside our privileges in order to embrace the reality of the people?

Sharing the Life of the People

During a discussion period I managed to get down some statements. Here they are:

1) Father Asfury, pastor of Cristo Resucitado parish on the outskirts of Rio Branco:

"We priests are always running around, loaded with meetings, evaluations, and so forth, so that we don't have time for anything else. The poor are less frenzied and less preoccupied. And so they're happier."

2) Father Luciano, from the parish of Xapuri:

"I'm always happy on Sunday when I can be with parishioners after Mass. But then comes the problem: an old woman comes over, draws me aside and asks for a little rice because she has only beans at home. And there are endless cases of needy persons like that. There is a neverending line of people asking for something, those who are sick, hungry, and so forth. What can we do?"

3) Father Manoel, from the parish in Boca do Acre (Amazonas):

"There's no justification for cases of real misery (I'm not speaking just of poverty) in a land that's as rich as our Amazonia. I believe in the value of little actions for getting out of this situation—the kind of action that opens the way or that launches a liberating process. For example: overcoming superstition about one kind of food or another, or about combining certain fruits, etc."

4) Bishop Moacyr:

"I don't put much stock in having rubber-gatherers demand their rights from the government. That looks like idealism to me: it just isn't realistic to encourage them to come to the city and expect the government to perform to their satisfaction. It's more important to start with *things they can do on their own* than to be making demands on others. That means encouraging them to do what they can on their own; to take their lives in their own hands, and stop turning to anyone else to solve their problems."

5) Father Aurélio, from the parish of Xapuri:

"The communities have to be educated to the point where they will take on their own problems; they have to get used to it. Otherwise, we're creating and encouraging an atmosphere of accommodation and dependency."

6) I, pastoral advisor to this local church, spoke not as an advisor but simply as another member of the presbytery:

"Normally, you have to work-with. But in cases of extreme need, you have to work-for. If a man has fainted and fallen to the ground (not just fallen asleep), there's no point in yelling 'Get up!' You have to take hold of him and pull him up.

"The poor come to us because we have things and we can do things. If we ever became like them, then we wouldn't get this kind of request. Perhaps the poor are asking us to be like them. Or perhaps the effect of what they're asking for, if we responded, would be the same: we would become poor like them.

"We have an 'uneasy conscience' and it pursues us obsessively, especially when we can travel and enjoy certain comforts. So we're always asking ourselves whether it isn't time to 'move out' to go to live among the poor once and for all.

"In view of all that the masses suffer, you end up becoming defensive and shielding yourself: you close your eyes and go forward. Behind this there is a painful confession of impotence in the face of the enormity of the dire poverty of the masses. Why is there a separation between the nurse's love (compassionate) and the doctor's love (cold)? It's important for us to avoid the indifference and cynicism of those who become accustomed to the suffering of others, to have the heart of Christ: 'At the sight of the crowds, his heart was moved with pity. They were lying prostrate from exhaustion, like sheep without a shepherd' (Matt. 9:36)."

Wednesday, November 30

JESUS' UTOPIA: THE KINGDOM AS RADICAL AND TOTAL LIBERATION

With the priests I go over a reflection on the kingdom of God, developing these points:

1) The kingdom is Jesus' utopia or ultimate ideal. That utopia means *absolute revolution,* overthrowing everything that crushes human beings and fulfilling their highest hopes (pleroma). In this sense the scope of the kingdom is immense, transcendent. It is a "mystery" that can only be evoked, never described. That's why the language of the kingdom is the language of parables and signs (miracles).

2) The kingdom is rescue, rehabilitation, justice. It comes into an evil world. That's why it is those who are *lost,* the oppressed and the poor, who are open to it. The kingdom is destined for them.

3) There are three dimensions to the kingdom: the *personal* dimension (grace), the *historical* dimension (social justice), and the *eschatological* dimension (the resurrection of the dead). In other words, liberation from personal *sin* (initial phase), liberation from social *oppressions* (middle phase), and liberation from *death* (final phase). Jesus is Messiah in the fullest sense: suffering Servant, Son of David, and Son of Man.

Demands of the Kingdom in Our Pastoral Work

1) Father Mário, from Sena Madureira:
"Our education has been aimed at the personal dimension of the kingdom,

complemented by the eschatological dimension. But we ignored the historical dimension, even though that's an integral part of the kingdom in its fullness. I feel there's room for conversion in this area."

2) Father Mássimo, pastor of Santa Inês (Rio Branco): "The personal and historical dimensions are full of failures. There are times when only the eschatological dimension sustains and nourishes the struggle. That's theological hope, divine hope.

"We can feel this especially on certain missionary trips: we travel for hours and hours only to find that, after years of work, everything has fallen apart. Sometimes we don't even find the same persons there: they've moved away. At that point only the perspective of the death and the resurrection of Jesus sustains our spirituality.

"I find it admirable the way atheistic revolutionary movements can struggle and keep giving themselves to the very end. What sort of hope sustains them? What do they find that's worth so much effort?"

3) Father Manoel, from Boca do Acre (Amazonas):

"The general idea of kingdom is associated with the idea of power. But the kingdom of God is *of God*. When we become aware of this, we're freed of the will to power. That doesn't free us from struggle, but it pours into us, right in the midst of our struggle, an immense confidence in God, who *gives* the kingdom as grace."

4) Dom Moacyr:

"What I see is that there are Protestants who are very serious about the way they live out the here-and-now, personal dimension of the kingdom, and their life is upright, and exemplary, but they forget the political or historical dimension. On the other hand, I observe many Catholics who are active politically and struggling for a new society, but their religious life is weak. In fact, I am aware of pastoral workers who focus on social struggle and sometimes lose all reference to the personal dimension: faith, conversion, and so forth."

5) Father Aurélio, from Xapuri:

"Perhaps the problem Dom Moacyr brings up, pastoral workers ignoring the personal demands of the kingdom, is due to their not being connected with a community where there's real sharing, developing the faith, etc. Priests and other officially recognized pastoral workers should live in community, following a gospel lifestyle and perhaps even sharing the life of the people."

The Original Kerygma of Jesus: The Kingdom

Father Asfury brought up a pertinent question. He said that ordinary persons don't use the *language* of the kingdom. But the letters they send to the newsletter *Nos Irmãos* ["we brothers"] are full of *signs* of the kingdom: how they're moving ahead with a group, how they deal with injustice, etc.

Even priests, he said, scarcely use the word "kingdom," or the language that grew up around it. Is that language only for intellectuals, theologians?

I answered his question along these lines. It's true, there's no need to cling to the words, but rather to the realities themselves. St. John and St. Paul don't use the language of kingdom much. They translated it into life, grace, forgiveness, justification, etc. What counts is the message, not the language.

However, we should keep in mind that kingdom is the *matrix metaphor* associated with the original kerygma of Jesus of Nazareth. So we always have to come back to this source and reference point when we want to translate the idea and to evaluate translations already made.

Secondly, the idea of kingdom has a *theoretical breadth* greater than that of any other idea in the teaching of Jesus. It succeeds in relating the different dimensions of the faith, and can sustain an effort to deal with a whole range of issues today, especially with the overall question of society or politics. If we lose sight of the theological scope of the idea of kingdom, we run the risk of limiting ourselves to the two other categories that translate it: grace or life (personal dimension) and eternal salvation or resurrection (eschatological dimension). However, today "integral liberation" fits well with the New Testament concept of the kingdom, as Gutiérrez has defined it from the start, and as can be seen in the Puebla Document and in *Evangelii Nuntiandi.*

Personal Communion with Christ: The "4 P.M. Experience"

In the afternoon Dom Moacyr took up a sensitive point: our personal commitment to Jesus Christ. Far from doing away with the need to have a deep personal relationship with that Person-Mystery, a spirituality that is open to the people and to political struggle cries out for it.

Certainly when we get into this realm we should maintain the sense of modesty that the highest and most precious things in our faith demand. When we speak of these experiences—which Gutiérrez calls "4 P.M." encounters, alluding to the moment when Andrew and John first came into contact with Jesus (John 1:35-39)—we can't use whatever sort of language occurs to us, even if devoid of any reserve, "like bedroom language," as a friend of mine put it. "Holy things should be treated in a holy manner."

The bishop based his presentation on several New Testament texts, and sought to show the importance of personal commitment to the risen Christ: Romans 14:7-8; Galatians 2:20, etc.

He linked this commitment to the commitment we have with the poor. He pointed out Jesus' love for the poorest among the poor, for the least among the lowly:

1) *Women,* who in Jesus' time had no public standing whatsoever. In Matthew he performs one of his first miracles for an old woman. "And yet many of us don't want to have anything to do with old women, those old women who think so much of us and do so much work in the communities," said Dom Moacyr.

2) *Children,* who were regarded as nonpersons in Jewish society.

3) *Lepers,* who were on the bottom of the social pyramid at the time of

Christ. In Matthew 8, Jesus' first miracle is performed for a leper.

"The church's credibility depends on our love for the poor," said the bishop. "Christ pointed to the fact that the poor were being evangelized as a sign that the Messiah had arrived." He then related that when a commission went to the Argentine government with a list of names of persons who had "disappeared," the government wouldn't meet them. Someone suggested that the church mediate. But at that point the people shouted out, "Not the priests! Not the priests!" The church had lost all credibility in the eyes of the people: it couldn't serve as a mediator, because of its complicity with the military dictatorship.

At the end of his meditation, Dom Moacyr raised some questions about commitment to Christ and to the poor:

1) Regarding the *breviary.* There's no longer any juridical obligation here, but the church wants us to be faithful to the new "book of the hours." The question is whether we correspond to the signs of the time, whether the content (biblical, patristic, etc.) and rhythm of our life is truly ecclesial.

2) Regarding the celebration of the *Eucharist.* If we can't always celebrate it, do we devote an equivalent amount of time to prayer, the word, or adoration?

3) Regarding *care of the poor.* The bishop said he was edified (and shamed) by how much each of his priests does. "On this point I have nothing to teach and everything to learn from you," he concluded.

The Revolution Should Be Even More Revolutionary

During the afternoon break I struck up a conversation with Father Sírio about Eastern Europe and its socialism. I know he's been there, and can talk about it.

He told me about how power is concentrated and how all social life is controlled, about the privileges of bureaucrats, the general climate of suspicion, the unbearable level of boredom and tedium found in the social realm and, in a word, the suffocating atmosphere in these so-called communist countries.

Still he acknowledged that there you don't see the kind of abject poverty you find in Latin America, but rather a shared and dignified poverty.

All this has deep implications for our dreams regarding our struggle alongside the oppressed. Actually the material basis (meeting basic needs: food, water, housing, clothing, literacy, etc.) is just the *precondition* for something greater. Basic needs are *means,* not ends. The purpose of the whole realm of economics is the full realization of the humanity of human beings in terms of culture, interpersonal relationships, and religion. To sacrifice all this for the realm of economics is to exchange means for ends.

That's why the revolution in Latin America has to be much more radical than Marxist revolution.

In the first place it must be a revolution that is *thoroughly social* and not just economic. It has to involve all realms: politics, family, culture, religion—in short, *everything social.*

Secondly, the process of change observable in Latin America today, especially within the church, is headed in this direction. The banner of "integral liberation" is being raised. It is in the people as a whole, at all levels and in all sectors, that the ferment is taking place. What's underway is a "molecular revolution." It is the cells of society that are renewing themselves, heading toward the formation of a new body. Perhaps religion can totalize in a human manner the process of revolution (always understood as social transformation). The revolution should course through human hearts, and through families, schools, neighborhoods, factories, and parish communities, bringing with it skilled workers, day laborers, women, youth, the unemployed, the handicapped, children, etc. The idea is "integral revolution."

Of course, there still remains the whole huge question of connecting all the different levels and aspects of the process; how to organize this massive undertaking into fronts, support groups, dominant sectors, etc. But that mustn't obscure the overall aim of the revolution, which is to give birth to a greater measure of humanity. And more humanity means more freedom and participation, more unity and creativity. "I'm not interested in revolution unless it's about changing human beings" (Ché Guevara).

That's why the revolution we're aiming at can't simply deliver more bread, but has to mean participation—equality and freedom indissolubly linked. Bread first, for sure, but not at the sacrifice of faith. If things came to the absurd point of having to choose one or the other, the people would probably be ready to sacrifice bread, given a free choice.

In his book *O Tempo da Ação* ["the time for action"] José Comblin says that many persons see socialism not just as an alternative to capitalism but as the alternative for a wholly different society. It means a new culture, a *new way of life,* and not just an economic system. It bears traces of utopia, in the best sense of the term.

The de facto socialism of Eastern Europe no longer represents a true alternative to capitalism, because it includes many of the same defects: authoritarianism, industrialism, consumerism—in short, materialism.

Who knows whether the peoples of Latin America, precisely because of their Christian tradition, might not be destined to inaugurate a model of a new society, one that would really be new, a valid alternative to the two other models, chained as they are to their patterns of gross materialism and truncated humanism. This is something Pope John Paul II seems to have intuited in his own way.

Christians on the Firing Line of History

Fathers Cláudio, Asfury, and I met under the large mango tree in the patio of the Training Center and we began to discuss the church's commitment to the poor in the name of faith. At a certain point the discussion got polarized.

Cláudio was saying, "When you analyze the great fronts of political struggle in the world today, where the future is opening up and moving forward, you see that almost always Christians aren't there. Movements on those battlefronts bear the imprint of Marxism, not of the faith."

Asfury replied that, on the contrary, "religion" seems to be giving a powerful thrust to peoples in their struggle for liberation. That's been the case in Poland, Iran, and in Latin America in general. There's a new sun on the horizon of history just coming into view, whereas the old Marxist sun seems to be setting quickly.

In any case, we can ask whether the faith is or is not pushing Christians (not the institutional church) toward the "firing line," toward the battlefront, where the danger is greater. Isn't prophecy, and martyrdom, and the giving of oneself to one's brothers and sisters part of the very vocation of Christians? And isn't that true in the political arena as well?

Is the institutional church today perhaps holding Christians back from this impulse, by delegitimizing their initiatives in history? To some extent, that is what's happening. To get around this situation, there are two tasks that must be carried out:

1) A theological critique that will enable Christians to perceive the possibilities or potentialities of the gospel in the urgent tasks of our moment in history (being at the vanguard of history, certainly not to dominate but to serve, and to offer one's own life if necessary, etc.).

2) Making workable the institutional possibilities of the church, in the sense of evaluating the degree of commitment the church establishment can take on specifically in terms of social transformation.

By bringing these two aspects together we can free up more "salt for the earth," more "light for the world."

Theological Chauvinism

Today in some places, including here in this retreat, there's a lot of talk about a "theology that takes Latin America as its starting point," "Latin American spirituality," "liberating pastoral work," etc.

Given our history and present situation, this accent is understandable and even necessary. However, it mustn't deteriorate into chauvinism, whether theological, pastoral, or spiritual. It doesn't do any good if your outlook is limited to your own home—if it's *casalingo,* as the Italians put it—especially for theology. It just leads you into a closed, stuffy room.

Latin America also has a great need for universality and dialogue with other cultures. We have to broaden our horizons—obviously not to be subjected to domination once more, but to be enriched. And we are now mature enough in the church to do that.

Of course we have to be deeply rooted in our own soil, but those roots lead to branches: let the leaves, flowers, and fruits be exposed to the great winds of the world and of ongoing history!

Certainly, any theology is *set* in a particular place, but it doesn't always have to be *organized* in terms of that place. A Latin American theology is legitimate only as a development and "application" of Christian theology, which is universal or catholic by nature. The relationship between "first theology" and "second theology," which I tried to describe and justify in my book *Teologia e Prática* (Petrópolis, Vozes, 1978; Engl. trans., *Theology and Praxis,* Maryknoll, N.Y.: Orbis Books, 1987), seems more and more relevant to me.

First theology, which is always elaborated in a particular place, looks toward universality. It speaks of all human beings as called to conversion, to faith, and to the kingdom of God. For its part, second theology is contextual, situational, involved in ongoing history. It has a conscious and programatic socio-historical thrust. But by that very fact it presupposes first theology and builds on it.

This relationship also exists in the pastoral realm. There is "first pastoral theology," which studies the basic mysteries of the faith: Christ, kingdom, grace, sin, sacraments, church, etc. Obviously all this has to take on specific cultural forms, but they always retain a core of universality. "Second pastoral theology" looks to the whole range of cultural and socio-historical problems of a particular people.

To line up *all* pastoral work, or *all* theology, in the "Latin American perspective" would be to close oneself into a church that is sectarian and no longer catholic. Even deeper down, it would mean that one has not understood the nature and power of the human spirit, which means openness and transcendence aimed at wholeness.

Latin America should certainly be there at the roots, but the branches should be open to the great gusts of history and of the Spirit!

A few days ago I was looking over a little booklet of "liberative catechesis." I thought it put the accent too much on the side of the social commitment of faith. The language gets overloaded with so much talk of "liberation" and then the horizon is shortened to a perspective that's simply pragmatic or moralistic. This kind of "second catechesis" may be making an impact today but it doesn't create much of a problem yet because it's still nourished by the theology that's been accumulated in the past and stored up. This "second pastoral theology" is supported by, and nourishes itself from, a kind of "pastoral accumulation." But unless there's an effort to nourish the hidden sources of this theology and pastoral work, the sources that make up what used to be called "Christian doctrine" (suitably updated, of course), "liberative pastoral action" itself will gradually wither and disappear.

It's always important to return to the biblical sources of faith, not only for the sake of "liberative pastoral action," but also to subject that action to criticism and improve on it.

What I've said applies only to "liberative pastoral work" and not to that kind of pastoral work where Christians haven't even discovered the political dimension of the faith. Although it resembles a thesis, synthesis comes only after antithesis.

Thursday, December 1

THE JOY OF SERVING

One more meditation. This time on service. Dom Moacyr stressed our inborn tendency to dominate. The same thing happened among the apostles, and Jesus had to take a firm stand against the yearning for power that existed among them (cf. Mark 10:41–45).

Another point the bishop emphasized was the joy of serving. The New Testament connects joy and service in several passages. John 13:17: "Once you know all these things [mutual service], blessed will you be if you put them into practice." Hebrews 13:17: "Preside [in itself a service] with joy and without complaining." Romans 12:8: "He who rules should exercise his authority with diligence." Acts 10:35: "There is more happiness in giving than in receiving."

Dom Moacyr finished by saying, "It is joy that gives and giving that brings joy."

Living with Joy by Serving the People

A little before noon we got together under a huge mango tree to talk over the theme for today: the joy of serving. The conversation flowed freely and living experience of the highest quality came out. Here's the gist of what was said:

1) Father José, pastor of Immaculate Conception parish (Rio Branco):

"I wonder if a priest is meant only to serve. Doesn't he have a right to personal self-fulfillment? Why can't he pursue his own interests?

"Really, though, I've realized that personal self-fulfillment is never the aim, but a result. It's one of those things that you get without striving for it, that comes in addition. When we make others happy, then we feel happy.

"A priest feels most frustrated when he doesn't find happiness and fulfillment in his work with the people. If that doesn't happen, a priest can regard himself as the biggest failure in the world."

2) Father Paolino, pastor in Sena Madureira:

"You feel happy only after you've done your work. That's what I feel after a training session or a novena I've been worrying about. I feel a great relief, a restful, peaceful feeling that easily repays any previous effort and concern."

3) Myself:

"But there is also the joy of expectation—the kind you feel on the eve of a feast, or while waiting for a friend, or on Saturday evening. That's *ante festum* joy; the other kind is *post bellum*.

"Actually you don't feel the joy of service or serving, for it often demands sacrifice and self-denial. What you feel is the joy of having served, of a service done. That's like the joy of childbearing that Jesus spoke about: there's the time of pain and then of joy (John 16:21)."

4) Bishop Moacyr:

"But according to the New Testament, there is a joy in the midst of suffering, persecution, and poverty. This is a deep feeling, deeper than that of pain. It's a joy that denies sadness and despair, but not pain. It can even be present with pain. It's the joy of the beatitudes. It's paschal joy. It's the 'true joy' of St. Francis. It's the sick person's gaze, full of hope. It's the transfigured smile of St Thérèse of Lisieux or of Charles de Foucauld."

5) Father Heitor, from Sena Madureira:

"Yes, there is joy in serving, the joy of being able to serve. If you can't serve, if you feel useless, if you can't carry out a good piece of work, it pains and depresses you, and makes you unhappy. That's the situation of so many invalids and older persons.

"Being able to help makes you happy then and there. I could sense this in young persons in Fortaleza who used to work with me in a shantytown."

Serving of Course, but How?

After a half hour the topic of discussion shifted. The question became that of how to serve. We shared with one another the problems involved in genuine service and seeking out the criteria for it.

1) Father Heitor started the ball rolling:

"Sometimes you feel exploited when you serve. You're assaulted with requests and you help out here, and go running off there. You have the impression you're being devoured by the people. Isn't this perhaps the wrong kind of service, a paternalistic way to serve? But if you withdrew and kept to yourself, wouldn't that be running away? What does true service mean?"

2) Father Asfury, from the parish of the Risen Christ (Rio Branco):

"Sometimes when the people ask for services it only creates dependence. For example, a few days ago I got a call asking me to take someone to the hospital. I refused, and asked, 'Does it have to be the priest who takes someone to the hospital? Can't the community get going and do something?' I hung up. Then I began to feel sorry. I couldn't hold back. I hopped in my car and went to the home of the person who had called me and said I was sorry for the way I had talked on the phone.

"I think the question of 'genuine service' isn't so much a matter of accepting or refusing a request from the people. That's part of it, but it's mainly *how* you accept or reject it. It's the manner—the charity, the sensitivity. Service is more in the way it's done than in the thing itself."

3) Father Sírio, recently arrived from Lucca, Italy, now in the parish of Santa Inês:

"What's the root of our difficulty in serving? It's our attachment to what we have. It's our lack of freedom with regard to things. Deep down, it's our possessiveness, our bourgeois spirit, our spirit of *harpagão,* our 'pirate' spirit—making a Portuguese word out of the Greek word used by Paul in Philippians 2:6, *'arpagmon.* There Paul says that Christ became a servant in a radical way; he didn't hold onto his divine condition as plunder.

"Perhaps only in death will we achieve the radical experience of being detached from everything. That will be our greatest act of total poverty and decisive freedom."

4) Father Cláudio, pastor in Xapuri:

"True serving is always *serving-with*. That was how Christ served. He affirmed others and always awakened their energies by demanding faith.

"We're often still *serving-for*. And that's what causes different kinds of dependencies."

5) Dom Moacyr:

"But when you 'aid,' how do you involve those being 'aided'? After all, there are cases where what's required is immediate emergency involvement. That is *service-for*. If you don't step in, someone is going to die. These are situations that don't allow for any delay, where the effects are irreversible or irreparable. In that case, how do you involve the one 'aided'? It's like someone lying half-dead on the roadside, as in the parable of the Samaritan. Or like a wounded soldier who has to be carried away in a stretcher."

6) Father Luís, pastor in Plácido de Castro:

"For me one of the rules for helping in the right way is always to help alongside others, in a community manner, asking advice and help from others so as to be able to discern correctly."

7) Myself:

"Given the complex situation in which we live today, service, especially in the social field, demands a very serious discernment process. Simply following our intuition or the impulse of our feelings may lead to a service of slavery rather than of liberation. That's why this effort here, to deepen our awareness, is so important.

"I've never forgotten what Mother Teresa of Calcutta told me last year when we flew together from Salvador to Brasilia. I asked her how she viewed the question of the evangelization of the rich. She answered, 'We have to serve the wealthy, not their wealth.' I would round that out, 'And we have to serve the poor, not their poverty.' "

The Group in Dialogue: The "Collective Intellectual"

I can see that my role here among these priests is not that of a consultant, but simply that of a traveling companion. When I speak it's not as an advisor (stimulating or leading the discussion, gathering up conclusions, deepening the matter, etc.) but just to contribute to the collective discussion, although of necessity I speak out of my own specialization.

The presbytery as a whole is functioning as a "collective intellectual." They go over an issue starting from the experience each one has lived through and reflected upon. What's going on here is a kind of homemade theology. Their thinking moves forward through shifts and changes that are small, sometimes very small, but always significant.

And this work has a greater impact in really changing things than many "discoveries" and theoretical "revolutions" trumpeted by theoreticians.

The Gospel of Power/Service

In the afternoon it was my turn to lead the meditation. It seemed appropriate to deepen the topic of service and relate it to the present. I followed a paper I had done for the Brazilian Conference of Religious and presented in the general assembly in July. This study is going to be published, but for the retreat I just wanted to stress a few points:

1) As set forth in the gospel, power/service means, more than anything else, *encouraging*. It is consolation and encouragement aiming at participation. *Parakaleo* (to comfort, encourage) is in fact the word most used in the New Testament to describe the kind of relationship that exists or should exist between the community and those responsible for it.

2) However, personal experience and human history show that power left to itself leads to *domination*. That's the idea of the satanic aspect of power, as it appears in the Bible (Daniel, Revelation, etc.) and also in the popular mentality ("Politics is dirty").

3) The satanic aspect of power, domination, appears not only in authoritarianism, but also, somewhat camouflaged, in *paternalism*. That's especially true in the area of religion. Paternalism dominates the other not through force but through *dependence* (moral, psychological, religious, etc.). By contrast, power/service affirms others and encourages them to act autonomously.

4) If power/service (aimed at encouragement) is not to become ideology and is to keep going with a dynamic of permanent conversion, it has to be subjected to an *ongoing vigilance* through self-criticism (examination of conscience); criticism from others (peer correction); and established mechanisms, such as elections by those at the base, rotating responsibilities, having regular control over those in power, recognition of pluralism, sharing responsibilities, eliminating privileges, etc.

I left two questions for personal meditation:

1) How do we react when we are challenged or criticized or others show signs of discontent or opposition to our authority and the way we exercise it?

2) Do we encourage criticism from others in a family spirit, or do we make it hard for them to bring it up? Is it hard for us to listen to criticism?

Doing Things for the Poor or Letting Them Act on Their Own?

The evening sharing session was a lot of work. For a half hour the group got bogged down. Nothing seemed to fit together or to focus attention and interest. The group was just taking random shots until the conversation moved to the perennial question of popular education, and it became a critique of the kind of paternalism that creates dependency.

Here are a few statements:

1) Father Manoel, from the parish of Boca do Acre (Amazonas):

"The poor are already carrying in their bodies and spirits hundreds of years of dependence. It's impossible to get them to participate all of a sudden. It's useless to force them. That would just be oppressing them once more, under the pretext of liberating them.

"The important thing is to discern whether to let them be or to prod them."

2) Dom Moacyr:

"I think it's a mistake to leave everything in the hands of the poor. Experience shows that sometimes you have to push things, that it sometimes works, even though it might seem authoritarian."

3) Myself:

"The alternative is not between letting the poor alone and forcing them, but rather *going along with them until you can let them act on their own*. That's what I see as a good pedagogical relationship. Among equals, of course, the only way to operate is to allow others to act.

" 'Pushing them to move' is a tricky way to proceed, though experience shows it sometimes works. Sometimes it's necessary to jolt them a little, to awaken them, especially at the beginning. Many lay leaders say they started because they were pushed a little to get involved in the process taking place in the communities. And they're thankful they were pushed.

"Anyway, pedagogy always means going through trial-and-error. There's no way of knowing ahead of time which kind of procedure is more appropriate. You have to take chances. Experience and thinking things through help a lot but they don't solve all problems."

4) Father José, of Immaculate Conception parish (Rio Branco):

"I think it's important that we check with our co-workers to see how genuinely we're serving the people. We have to ask their opinion and see what critical observations they may offer us. Actually it's sometimes more important to simply be present than it is to be involved in direct action with the people. That runs against our own constant rushing around. In order to get over that kind of activism, I meet with my immediate co-workers and we all go over our agendas and criticize each other."

5) Father Paolino, from the parish in Sena Madureira:

"Yes, it's okay to push things a bit, in order to get some results. That's been my experience with Indians. However, you've got to have the *touch* and you've got to work *alongside* them. Pushing things is okay, but you've got to be sensitive and work with the people.

"Here's one experience I've had like that among the Maronawa Indians. They were in bad shape. They hadn't cleared and planted any fields and they were hungry. I went there and by using all kinds of devices, even joking around, I got them to go out to the field. Of course I also went out to work with them. I hacked away with a machete until both my hands were raw.

"That was so successful that later on a group of twenty Kulinas came and asked me to go out and work with them in their fields.

"I don't think that's a gesture of domination but one of liberation. You can see it in its fruits."

Friday, December 2

SACRAMENTAL BONDING OF PRIESTS

This morning I made a short presentation on priestly unity. My intention was to help the group reflect a bit on mutual relationships among priests. I laid out the following points:

1) "The twelve" are the model for the priesthood, the clergy. They constitute a community built around Christ.

The community of "the twelve" has a twofold dimension, as can be seen in Mark 3:14: "being with Jesus" and "being sent by him." "The twelve" are simultaneously "disciples" and "apostles." They are a community of life (brothers) and a working group (companions).

What is called the "apostolic life" includes both aspects. That's also how it was in the early community. "The twelve" made up a tightly-knit group. What counted was not so much individual personalities (there are apostles about whom we know nothing, or next to nothing), but membership in the group.

2) By the same token, it is not individual priests who are responsible for the church community but the clergy. It is a collegial power. Outside the presbytery the priest is null. Together priests make up an "apostolic senate"—as St. Ignatius of Antioch and St. Jerome put it (see "Decree on the Ministry and Life of Priests," 8; also note 98, in Walter M. Abbott, ed., *The Documents of Vatican II* [New York: Guild Press, 1966]).

Ordination means insertion into a collegial body, entering into an "order," being incorporated into the presbyteral corporation. That's why the sacrament of orders is a sacrament of bonding. It creates a "sacramental fellowship." Priests are really always "co-priests."

This unity can be seen in the ordination of a priest at the moment when all the priests present impose their hands on the ordained. It can also be seen when Mass is concelebrated.

Hence, it is clear that fellowship among priests is not simply a matter of convenience, not even for pastoral reasons, and not just a matter of sentiment, but rather an *inherent demand* of the sacrament of orders.

3) Practical consequences:

In the area of *attitude:* We should realize that the local church isn't entrusted to the bishop alone, nor is the parish the responsibility of the pastor alone—both have to be led collegially. It's not a matter of "my church," but "our church"; nor of "my parish," but rather "our parish."

In the area of *witness:* Priestly fraternity is "already an evangelizing reality" (Puebla, 663), an "element of evangelization" (John Paul II, Opening Address at Puebla). "That all may be one . . . so the world may believe" (John 17:21 and 23). It was the practice in the early church to have two apostles preach together as a sign of unity (Paul and Barnabas, Paul and Silas, Paul and Titus, Peter and John, the two prophets in Revelation 11). "He sent them out to preach two by two" (Luke 10:1 and Mark 6:7).

In the area of *common life:* Vatican II (Decree on the Ministry and Life of

Priests, 8) calls for "some kind or other of community life," in terms of a place to live, meals, meetings, etc., with a view toward pastoral work, study, prayer, friendship, and leisure (cf. Mark 6:31). Puebla 705 recommends bringing together "priests living in remote regions." "Community life" is valuable in itself and is not limited to religious orders; it has validity for all Christians.

In the area of *pastoral work:* Systematic pastoral work together, as manifested in priests' senates and pastoral councils, is a very obvious outgrowth of the sacrament of orders.

Starting from the above points, we could think about these two probing questions:

1) How do the faithful see the way we priests relate among ourselves? How does our unity or disunity have an impact on the people and how is it reflected in the community?

2) How can we create or improve ways to bring priests closer together, in everyday life and in pastoral work?

Withdrawing in order to Jump back in

The retreat is over. We celebrated the Eucharist at the end of the morning. The afternoon had been set aside for dealing with concrete problems and for making a short evaluation.

Negative points: topics shouldn't simply be left up to those speaking, but everyone should be able to take part in choosing them; at night, instead of discussion there should be a meeting for adoration or for the word.

Positive points: the climate of silence; very rich sharing sessions; celebration of the liturgy.

The liturgy has enabled the group to assimilate and experience in a deeper and more communal way the meditation topics. It was varied and unfolded with a rhythm that was free and spontaneous. And so it had a decisive influence.

This retreat has been like a "breather" along the way, where the experiences and problems of day-to-day life were gathered together. But it has also been a new takeoff point for the life of faith and missionary tasks.

If it *withdrew* us from the daily struggle, ultimately that was to *throw us back in* with more energy. That's the way the dialectic of this incarnate spirituality works, as it did with Jesus. His moments of withdrawal were followed by greater advance (Mark 1:12–15 and 35–39).

A good retreat dedicates and confirms our life for the service of the gospel.

An Incarnate Spirituality?

I've felt that this retreat has really fortified all the priests, and the bishop. And yet it's been a simple retreat, firmly on the ground, stripped down, appropriately incarnate (in poverty), as it was intended to be. It all took place naturally, without anything artificial and with no effort to be different or novel.

Still, as I look back over the experience, it's clear that it was a deeply spiritual retreat, but spiritual in the sense that the gospel is spiritual—permanent newness. We spoke of prayer, meeting the Lord, mission, suffering, brotherliness, etc. We had prayer, adoration, confession, silence, meditation—in a word, all the marks of a retreat.

What is "incarnate" or "liberating" spirituality? It's the only true kind. If it's not incarnate, can a spirituality still be Christian? It might be Buddhist, Hindu, Greek, spiritist, Zen, or anything else, but not a biblical and evangelical spirituality.

Hence, from a Christian viewpoint it's redundant to speak of "incarnate" or "liberating" spirituality. Such terms are useful only insofar as they point out the proper nature of Christian spirituality, something that has been ignored or covered over. It's simply a return to the legitimate origins of Christian mysticism, which never meant fleeing the world but taking it on and saving it.

The effort had not been so much one of making spirituality incarnate as of living the dynamism of the Spirit of God, of the word of God, which has to lead to life, liberation, conversion, *agape.*

Even the very specific issues Dom Moacyr raised (the breviary, daily Mass, etc.) were raised in a very serious way and within a broad, open, and free spirit—*modo evangelico,* after the manner of Jesus Christ, and not *modo pharisaico,* in a legalistic fashion.

Who is afraid of this kind of mystique and this kind of church? Obviously the devil and worldly persons. And also those whose tradition goes back only to the Middle Ages and not to the early church—the church of the fathers and of the apostles of Jesus Christ.

Saturday, December 3: Rio Branco

FATHER PAOLINO: *VIR EVANGELICUS ET APOSTOLICUS*

Early this morning I said goodbye to Father Paolino, with some feeling. There he was as always, small and skinny, in the same threadbare cassock he always wears.

He spends months and months in the jungle moving back and forth between rubber-gatherers and Indians. He's had malaria more than eighty times but that doesn't stop him at all. In words and gestures he's like something growing wild, a true child of the jungle, which is his whole universe, his natural habitat, as it were. He's like a tall tree hosting vines and parasites, and birds singing their songs.

His face radiates with such friendliness and human goodness that it's just not enough to say he's likeable—you think rather of the *philanthropia* of Titus 2:11: the sense of human concern shown by Jesus of Nazareth.

Behind and through his rustic features there shines a soul full of sunlight, the heart of a child, the secret radiance of a man who is overflowing with human goodness. Father Paolino is one of those rare beings in whom it's not the body that envelops the soul, but the soul that embraces the body and conceals it. His roughness, smallness, and weakness is all illuminated and transfigured by a magnificent, noble, and intrepid spirit. The result is that his physical features become an expression of the goodness and beauty within him.

His very presence at the retreat these past few days left a definite mark. Everyone was impressed whenever he spoke, showing both his realism and a clearsightedness that was moving. He shared many of his experiences with us. They were all very genuine, earthy, and concrete: different kinds of work in the field, long and difficult journeys, dramatic encounters, etc. You got a sense of a whole life moving along, full of drive, expressed with no embellishment or interpretation, almost without language. Life seemed to be there as a whole, like the solid trunk of a *cumaru-ferro* tree.

He works alone, without any other priest, although he always makes sure someone goes along with him on his pastoral trips. But that doesn't mean any individualism on his part. It's a solitude that's hungry for communion, a solitude in which his brothers and sisters in the faith travel along in his heart, in his recollection, in his prayer, in his yearning.

He told us of how happy it made him to listen, in the middle of the jungle, to the radio broadcast of the bishop's Sunday morning Mass, or to hear the voice of priests speaking over the radio during the week, and of how good he felt during the few precious meetings during the year when he could get together with his brethren.

And how he enjoys it when he can see his fellow missionaries and greet them with an embrace after such a long time apart! He's the priest who spends the longest time hidden in the jungle, like the good shepherd seeking his wandering sheep, yet he's perhaps the one who feels and experiences community most deeply, both as a priest and as a religious. Even though he's not a community man, in the sense of living under the same roof, he's certainly a man of communion, and that's what really counts. In that sense he's a *vir fraternus*. He knows how to subject what he does to his fellows for evaluation, just as he's able to acknowledge that he has some authoritarian traits, due to his own training under fascism.

But he is unconditionally committed to the people and there's no turning back. His own life is as poor and austere as that of the rubber-gatherers.

In the little booklet *Abre a porta,* a kind of textbook for Christians, he found popular songs and folksongs. He wanted to learn them so he could teach them to his communities in the jungle. He especially liked the one about Saint Lucy ("Blessed and praised be Lady Saint Lucy"), so I had to teach it to him and even write down the music so he wouldn't forget it.

In Father Paolino you can see the gospel in living and concrete expression, to the point where there's no need for words. Those who know him come to the conclusion that the stock of *viri evangelici et apostolici* is still with us!

IX

Community and the Lord's Supper
as Described in the Acts of the Apostles

Saturday, December 3: Vila Capixaba

A MARRIED COUPLE WELL OFF AND YET COMMITTED

I've come here to visit the local community. Eleutério and Nilza, husband and wife, brought me in their VW mini-bus along with some sacks of seeds. Bumps along the way shook the vehicle so severely that the doors would fly open and some of the sacks fell out on the road.

Vila Capixaba is 68 kilometers from Rio Branco and 120 from Xapuri. More than 300 families live here. Most of them have come up from the south, especially from the state of Espírito Santo. Hence the name of the place, *Capixaba* being a nickname for someone born in Espírito Santo.

Nilza and her husband are sharp and very socially aware. *Seu* Eleutério—everyone calls him "the gaucho"—does everything with a flair. He owns a plantation called Campo Grande. It's around 300 hectares (740 acres) and on it he has 250 head of cattle, 4,000 coffee bushes, 20,000 rubber trees (planted, not wild), and dozens of hectares of rice, which yielded more than a thousand sacks last year. He and Nilza process their coffee and rice themselves and then sell it in the city. Our community house in Rio Branco is stocked with their pure and aromatic coffee.

The "gaucho's" house is spacious and open. It is surrounded by big trees, some with fruit, which provide shade all day long.

I spot different kinds of farm machines under an open shed: a tractor, a coffee-roasting machine, and even a threshing machine, the kind of machines for threshing rice and wheat I used to see as a kid in the *planalto* of Santa Catarina.

Eleutério and Nilza can be considered in the category of medium-range farmers. They're doing well and are on the rise. They have only one child, a son they adopted. Right now they're thinking of adopting another.

Normally, persons in this kind of socio-economic situation feel impelled to adopt a conservative, or even reactionary, position. This couple, however, is deeply committed to the struggles of the community, and in fact they are one of the most dynamic elements in that struggle. And the faith has a lot to do with their stance.

Nilza: A Scrapper

Nilza is the prime mover of the Christian community in Vila Capixaba. Her role here is like Ivanilde's in Catuaba. In both cases, their husbands are their number one co-workers and helpers. In this respect, it's not Eve being given "as a helpmate" to Adam, as the Bible relates, but the opposite: it's Adam who's serving as a helper to Eve.

In fact, Nilza and Ivanilde are very good friends. One day they came together to the training center to invite me to come visit each of their communities. They are among the strongest lay leaders in Immaculate Conception parish (Rio Branco), to which both their communities belong.

Nilza is rather young, somewhere around thirty. She's quite aggressive. She gets the community together and discusses ways to improve things. Then they organize delegations to go to Rio Branco to present their demands to the authorities.

Coming here in the van today, Nilza told me how she went along with a delegation of eight women as they went from one government agency to another: the Sanitation Department for the state of Acre, the Department of Health, and the Department of Education, asking for measures to benefit the whole Vila Capixaba area. In the end they did get water delivery, but because the back roads were being neglected, they went to get the service extended.

She is involved in struggle through the BCCs and the Union of Rural Workers, and also through the Workers' Party. She was a candidate for the town council in the last elections. Even though she wasn't elected she is undaunted and keeps on struggling.

Southerners Bring Their Customs with Them

Today I had lunch in the house of a young couple. He's from Espírito Santo and she's from Acre. They have three daughters. The food was good and also quite varied.

They told me there's a lot of mixed blood in Vila Capixaba. This place is like a microcosm of Brazil in terms of both racial mixture and the states that residents come from.

Those who have come from other places, especially from the south, have brought with them their attitude toward work, the way they keep their houses, their penchant for keeping things neat and clean, honesty in business dealings, love for their families, and especially their deep religious and Catholic sense.

Evangelicals don't get very far here, although they do have their place for worship, as they do everywhere else.

Strong Women in a Strong People

During the afternoon Nilza took me visiting several families around here. As always, there were lots of children. In one case, besides the six that belonged to the woman of the house, there were seven children belonging to another woman who was staying there.

We went to the house of *Dona* Chiquinha. She's active in the gospel group that Nilza leads. A poor woman, but one with a great deal of wisdom. She's quite self-assured, and shows a great sense of her own dignity. I could see that in the way she spoke, with such assurance and firmness, clarity and frankness. At moments like this I have to wonder where uneducated persons get all their moral and spiritual riches.

I said to her, "You're still strong, even at your age. May God watch over you and grant you many more years of life."

She answered, "I'm sixty-seven now. But I want to live a while more, so I can take care of my grandchildren." There were a whole bunch of them there around her, happy, playing and running around, but quite dirty and not well dressed—poor, in other words. But, the liveliness of these children is always more amazing than their poverty.

I asked her if she had a husband. She told me he had died, and that another man "came along" in her life. "But," she went on, "thank God, he went on his way." And she ended, "It's God who does all this. When God wants to give you peace, you get peace. I never felt more at rest than after that man left. It was like a dark cloud passing over and then going on. Now I feel relieved, thank God."

These are the *anawim* the Bible talks about: they draw their life from God!

Work and Family

In the evening I had supper at the house of *Seu* Caboclo, whose family also came from the south, from Mato Grosso do Sul. He owns a very busy sawmill where he employs a half dozen workers.

He also has a farm. Every morning without fail he, along with one of his sons, milks his forty cows. He sells the milk to CILA, the company that furnishes milk for Rio Branco and other cities.

He's presently building a big house, which his children and grandchildren call "Noah's Ark."

I can see that this is a "middle-class" family, and they're doing well. All the relatives work together in their economic activities. The traditional family in the patriarchal mold is still a productive unit here.

The house was really swarming with family members. Including the kids, there were more than twenty persons at supper. They're simple persons with rural customs and an austere way of life—and very hardworking.

They play an active role in the community, especially *Seu* Caboclo, an energetic man whose words are full of wisdom.

Model for BCCs: The Church of the Apostles

After supper, around 7 P.M., we all went over to the training center. It was too small to hold all those who came pouring out of their houses. That's why they're putting up a new church right alongside it. The whole community has been involved in the work, and the walls and roof are up. That's the main thing.

The old center was filled for my talk—more than a hundred persons. Nilza and Eleutério suggested I talk to them about how the first Christians lived. There's a lot of interest in that topic in these communities, perhaps because they feel very closely identified with the early church, in their simplicity, poverty, equality, persecutions, etc.

So I reached for the Acts of the Apostles and developed these four points, trying to be pedagogical:

1) The first Christians remained *steadfast* in these things: listening to the word of God, celebrating the Lord's Supper, meeting for prayer and worship (cf. Acts 2:42). I emphasized how important their meetings were and illustrated the point by referring to the meeting of the community at Troas, where they all heard and deepened their awareness of the word of God and then celebrated the Lord's Supper. That was one of the Apostle Paul's BCCs. Our situation was so similar to that of Acts, with the simplicity and poverty of the people, the plain, newly-born faith (and even some pointed details: persons sitting on windowsills . . .), that I felt I had been swept back to the time of the Apostles.

2) Among the first Christians *"everything* was held *in common"* (cf. Acts 4:32f.). Here I stressed our overall aim of creating a society of brothers and sisters, the need for us to put what we have in common even now—especially putting our energy into social struggle. "Having our goods in common" is part of our faith now and in the future.

3) The first Christians also had their *failings:* there's the case of Ananias and Sapphira who wanted to deceive the community (Acts 5:1ff.); the disagreement over the way different groups of widows were cared for (cf. Acts 6:1ff.); and the conflict over Christians converted from Judaism who were still attached to their old ways (cf. Acts 15:1f.); the fight between Paul and Barnabas over Mark, whom one wanted to take with him on his journey and the other didn't (cf. Acts 15:36), etc.

4) The first Christians suffered *persecutions* (cf. Acts 4:1ff.; 5:17ff.; 6:8ff.; 8:1ff.; 9:1ff.; 11:12, etc.).

I made comparisons with the situation of the church today, especially with the BCC movement. This "new way of being church" is really not so new. It's not something that bishops and priests have invented out of their own heads. It's like the BCCs the first Christians had. It's turning back to the Acts of the Apostles. It means being an apostolic church.

I was in my element, speaking freely and uninhibited. My hearers paid complete attention right up to the end (around 10 P.M.).

It seemed very worthwhile to me. I had a very strong sense that today the BCCs really represent a way of returning to the early church, the church of Peter and the other Apostles, the church of the Virgin Mary and the other holy women. That means a church that's plain, made up of ordinary persons, austere, and poor. A church that's human and yet full of the Holy Spirit. A church that's primarily lay, where priests are the ones most ready to serve. A church that's missionary and persecuted, and yet joyful.

This *forma Ecclesiae* ("way of being church") is a kind of paradigm for the whole church, just as the *forma Sancti Evangelii* is for being a Christian—as St. Francis put it.

At the end of the meeting we stood up to pray. In the spontaneous intentions that came out in great profusion, the group especially thanked God for the "kind of church" that was arising, one so close to that of the apostles, and prayed that the local community would follow the example of the first Christian community, especially with regard to "putting their goods and energies in common," and with regard to courage in the face of persecutions.

After the meeting *Seu* Caboclo came up to me and said, "We were ready to keep going on all night, the way they did with St. Paul in the story you read us!"

That's fine, but still. . . .

Going out into the Cool Air on a Saturday Night . . .

There were about seven or eight of us: my host couple, Nilza and Eleutério, *Seu* Caboclo and his wife, and a few other community leaders.

We went to a little bar to get something cool to drink. As always on Saturday night, there were a lot of persons outside. They were gathered everywhere in small groups, in their front yards, or walking in the street, in lively conversation, laughing, and some of them singing.

The whole atmosphere seemed free and wholesome, and in keeping with popular culture. Everyone knows everyone else here and they respect each other.

Above our heads the sky was full of stars and the night was utterly serene. Nilza tugged at my arm, pointed up to the sky and said, "Clodovis, that's our sky in Vila Capixaba!" And the way she accented "that's" was half proud and half kidding.

An atmosphere of peace and reconciliation, of persons who work hard all week and then on Saturday night turn to leisure and enjoying one another's company.

The spirit is turned loose in the body: the world is good and deserves to exist!

Sunday, December 4: Still in Vila Capixaba

HUMAN LIFE AS FRIENDSHIP, NOT DOG-EAT-DOG

Early in the morning when I was still in bed, I heard Nilza talking with a man who had come to see her. I could make out that he was asking her for information and help for going to Rio Branco.

I could also figure that Nilza had offered him a cup of coffee and was reassuring him, "Don't worry, it's going to be all right." I couldn't make out the whole conversation but I could detect in the tone of the visitor's voice a great deal of respect and trust in Nilza. That's no doubt because she's the natural leader in this community.

As he was leaving she tried to assure him once more that everything was going to go okay. When he had already gone outside she added, raising her voice a little, "Send word if there's any problem."

I admired Nilza's readiness to help out, as well as her tact and sensitivity. I immediately thought of what the Samaritan said, thinking ahead, "Look after him, and if there is any further expense I will repay you on my way back" (Luke 10:35). And of course the words of Paul, "Help carry one another's burdens; in that way you will fulfill the law of Christ" (Gal. 6:2).

I began thinking about what the gospel can do, and actually does, with regard to humanizing persons and their interrelationships. Only faith can unite human beings in what is interior, in their innermost depths. I doubt that Marxism can do that. In order to change the dog-eat-dog aspect of human life, you also have to reflect on St. Francis.

No mode of production in itself can replace the task of working out human relationships in terms that are really human. It might facilitate it, and encourage it, but it can't bring it about. That's the work of freedom. And of the Spirit.

The Gaucho

After our morning coffee *Seu* Eleutério took me out to have a look at his farm. We went through the coffee grove, through the rows of rubber trees, past jittery calves, and out to the field where he is going to plant rice.

It all has the look of something done with zest, intelligence, and hard work. "The gaucho" tells me about his experiences and the lessons he's drawn from them. He criticizes EMATER [government land agency] for how little its officials understand the characteristics and potentiality of land in that area, and for how slack they are in supplying technical aid to local farmers.

For example, he explained that planting coffee bushes between rows of rubber trees is beneficial for both plants. Nevertheless, EMATER doesn't approve of that method and doesn't provide any financing for it.

Something else he does is to put young calves out to graze on the grass growing between the rows of rubber trees, so the animals help keep the area clear, and yet they don't harm the rubber trees, because by this time, when they're four years old, they're quite tough. He showed me other things like that.

Like everyone else I see around here, "the gaucho" has brought with him his southern customs and his inclination for doing things in a rational way. And of course that contributes toward economic development.

The rubber-gatherers, by contrast, are used to another style of life and work. They don't have the same rational approach as persons from the south, but no one can match them in toughness and courage. But their methods and techniques for extracting rubber have scarcely changed since the beginning of the century. As far as the rest of their life goes, the jungle itself provides most of what they need. It's their pantry, refrigerator, and store, all in one. That's why they're relatively unconcerned about the future and don't have very technical minds.

I was talking over these things with "the gaucho." He said that he got on very well with the local people. In fact, his wife Nilza is from Acre. Still, he tells me, they tend to just let things happen, and then they adjust to problems that arise, figuring out a "trick," getting along "by hook or by crook."

In fact I do notice how persons around here find a way to deal with the contingencies of life: loading a pack animal or a car, getting a car through roads that are all torn up or nothing but mud, finding a place to sleep and managing to get to sleep at night. Everything seems to be unplanned, unforeseen, and every solution is makeshift. But things do get worked out, whether easily or by force, and everyone keeps going. Why be concerned about problems that haven't yet arisen, or doing things the "right" way, or using the right tools? Anything can be used for anything. And life sails along.

Southerners, whose cultural tradition has roots going back to the Old World with its rationalism, smile condescendingly if not disdainfully at a lifestyle where everything is improvised. Yet they were the ones who invented the proverb: "The bouncing cart settles the potatoes."

The Lord's Supper Like That of St. Paul in Troas

At around ten in the morning we all went to the community center to celebrate Mass.

When I got there I realized that I had completely forgotten things needed for the Eucharist. And there I was in the community center, filled with persons waiting for Mass to begin!

I quickly got together with the leaders, and they all agreed that we had to have Mass. We would do it as best we could.

One person went running in one direction and another somewhere else to get what was essential: bread and wine. For a chalice, someone brought out the nicest cup in the house, with three bands of gold running around it.

I explained to the community that we were going to have a celebration of the Lord's Supper a little like the way St. Paul had done it in Troas, as I had explained the night before. The style was going to be very simple and natural, even in the bread and wine.

The lay leaders themselves took charge of the first part of the service, just as they're used to doing here in their Sunday worship. That way the people would respect and appreciate what they've been doing.

Dona Rosária proved to be a very good leader. Everyone participated as usual. I remained quietly on the side, letting things take their normal course. Individuals spoke up about the readings. The theme was preparation for the coming of the Messiah, because today is the second Sunday of Advent. I remember that someone said something like this: "We pressure the government about the terrible bumps and holes in the road. But today it's St. John the Baptist who's coming to us and asking us to repair all the bumps and holes in the road of our lives, so that when the Messiah gets here, he can come in on a road that's flat, smooth, and well cared for."

Toward the end, I came in to pull together this first part, discussing with the community the "holes" that would have to be filled in order to smooth the road. These "holes" were the same as always: the fact that participation in meeting and in common struggles is weak, and so forth.

Dona Rosária continued leading for the creed and the prayer of the faithful. I came in to preside only at the offertory. They brought up the local bread and wine. I explained what they signified: God's acceptance of the work of our hands. The "our" seemed more packed with meaning at that point, even though the wheat bread and grape wine weren't as much "ours" as, for example, cassava bread and palm wine might have been. In any case, they were more genuinely "ours" than the round white hosts and the sweet wine that the priest brings in his bag and, from the viewpoint of the people's own culture, must seem to come from some mysterious far-off place.

The eucharistic prayer followed the leaflet used by the community in its Sunday worship, but there were many exclamatory prayers and some moments of silence.

At the moment for distributing communion, I motioned to *Dona* Nilza and *Dona* Rosária to help, for they had already shared the bread of the word with the community.

More than forty communicants shared the consecrated bread, dipping it in the sacred wine. It all took place with the greatest respect and awareness. It was a great sight to see those humble persons come up, hold out their calloused hands, take the bread with great veneration, and carefully dip it in the cup, keeping one hand open beneath the other to catch any drop that might fall.

There was a deep seriousness about it all, except for a tiny incident such as might occur in any Mass. At communion time Marcinha, *Seu* Caboclo's 4-year-old granddaughter who's as quick as they come, walked up to me and said "Father, give me some bread and juice!" The little episode was more cute than funny.

The Lord's Supper took little more than an hour. The whole community was at worship, and no one was around to wonder what was going on.

In its format, this celebration was something of a mixture of the Sunday worship that the community was used to having and the canonical Mass that priests celebrate on Sundays. The way we carried it out validated what the community was already doing, especially by the fact that the lay leaders took charge during the first part. Putting the Eucharist into that setting brought it closer to the community and its own particular world.

Perhaps the church ought to envision different ways of celebrating the Lord's Supper, ranging from Mass with the people of God, the traditional formula and still practically the only one in use today, to the "breaking of the bread" as it was celebrated in the early Christian communities, such as the one at Troas. The document put out by the Brazilian Bishops' Conference in 1977, "Directory for Masses with Popular Groups," seems to move in this direction. It's still being studied in Rome.

Liturgical pluralism, which has been accepted for certain rites, is an exigency that parallels the notion of pluralism in the "ways of being church." For if the church is to start from the bottom and grow upwards, if it desires to take on popular culture in a catholic way so as to be incarnate in that culture and thus be a participatory church, how can the Eucharist not express what the church is and what it wants to be: a "church of the poor," a "church that is the people of God," and in that sense, a "popular church"?

Only a "popular church" can carry out a "popular Eucharist"—just as only a "popular Eucharist" can nourish a "popular church."

X

Evangelicals and Justice

Monday, December 5: Brasiléia

THE FURIOUS CRY OF THE POOR

Four of us have come here to help with a training session for lay leaders in the area of Brasiléia: Sister Sandra, a novice in the Servants of Mary; Isaías, a theology student and candidate for the priesthood; Father Asfury, pastor of the parish of the Risen Christ in Rio Branco; and I.

The people of the area had asked that the topic be the Evangelicals. They're everywhere and they proselytize very actively. The relationship between lay leaders and Evangelicals is always quite problematic. And that's why there's a need for a training session devoted to this topic.

Naturally, the meeting, which will last five days, began with a moment of prayer. When you see these fifty, sixty, or seventy lay leaders, raising their hands up to the heavens and praying the Our Father, you get to imagining how God must react, listening to them. Present in their voices is the very reality of life itself. This is the "cry that is ever more insistent," the "cry of a suffering people." It is their cry that is "loud and clear, increasing in volume and intensity, and at times full of menace"—as Puebla put it in one of its most moving passages (87–89).

We can be sure that the ears of Yahweh, the Father, are attuned to the poor, who are suffering and crying out for help. How could God not hear them (cf. Luke 18:7–8)?

The value of this prayer isn't measured by the state of mind or the feelings of this group, and in fact they might even be very tired and their minds might be blank. It derives rather from their overall attitude toward life, the spirit with which they confront the objective conditions of their downtrodden existence.

We can be certain that, when the poor pray, their prayer is heard. "When the afflicted man called out, the Lord heard, and from all his distress he saved him" (Ps. 34:7).

135

Lay Leaders Introduce Themselves

I took some notes. Here are some of the things I observed:

1) There are persons here from every state of Brazil. Many of them have been pushed here like cattle by capital. They've opened up roads, cleared fields, made the soil produce, and left lands opened up, tilled and planted for others to take. They're the new pioneers, the real *bandeirantes* [members of official expeditions sent to explore the Brazilian hinterlands during colonial times] but they're oppressed, not oppressors.

2) They are well-mannered when they introduce themselves. Their bearing and language become somewhat ceremonial. Everything is quite sincere, respectful, and modest. Some still retain the deferential formula, "I, So-and-so, your humble servant. . . ."

3) Many of them said, "I'm very happy to be here with you." It's not just a cliché but reflects what they really feel. One woman said, "I was sick for more than a week, and I was very worried and afraid that I wouldn't be able to make it for this training session. But, thank God, I got better and I'm very happy to be here."

4) Another woman said she had come to take her husband's place at the course, because he was sick and couldn't come. She ended by saying, "I ask the Divine Holy Spirit to give me a good memory, because I don't know hardly anything, but I'm going to make a real effort to pass on to my husband as much as I can."

5) Many leaders said they have an assistant to work with them. That's a very good idea. I recalled this text: "Two are better than one: they get a good wage for their labor. If the one falls, the other will lift up his companion. Woe to the solitary man! For if he should fall, he has no one to lift him up. So also, if two sleep together, they keep each other warm. How can one alone keep warm? Where a lone man may be overcome, two together can resist. A three-ply cord is not easily broken" (Eccl. 4:9–12). This limpid passage, written in language close to the people, always has a real impact in group reflection.

6) There are two women there, mother and daughter, from among a group that had come up from the south a few months ago, colonizers. Both of them had worked as lay leaders in Paraná (there they call them "coordinators"). The mother is thirty-six and her daughter sixteen. Both seem eager to learn.

7) It's great to see young persons as lay leaders or helpers! All the more so when you see a large group of husky guys playing soccer on Saturday afternoons and Sundays when the community is meeting for the gospel, worship, or Mass. Is their apparent indifference a passing phase, due to their age? Life tends to force us to deal with Mystery sooner or later.

8) Just about the only ones who can take part in this kind of training, spending a whole week in study, are persons from the country and self-employed workers in the city. That's why the lay leaders come from these sectors. There are very few wage-earning workers. And yet we advisors, out of

habit and without thinking, keep talking about low wages, when most of the people here don't get their income from wages.

9) The proportion of men and women among the lay leaders is more or less equal, even though there are more women than men participating in groups at the local level. That's a sign that there's still a certain amount of machismo at work in the BCCs.

Lay Leaders and Evangelicals?

BCC methodology is inductive: its starting point is always an observation stage, carried out by the people. So Father Asfury put together the results of a brainstorming session focused on what is commonly believed about Evangelicals. Here are some of the observations:

1) Evangelicals go to houses of the poor and first try to win over the women in order to then bring the whole family over to Evangelicalism. Sometimes they even break up a Catholic evangelization group.

2) They talk a lot about the Holy Spirit, and think they're the only ones who have received the Holy Spirit.

3) They say things would be better if there weren't any sisters or priests.

4) For them a procession is idolatry.

5) They say the church's work of conscientization is really the work of the world, and that all these matters of liberation don't have anything to do with religion.

6) They think sickness is like a current that seizes persons because they aren't Evangelicals.

7) When Catholics have processions, they pass out leaflets with titles like, "The Crowd Is Wrong."

8) They criticize lay leaders for not reading the whole Bible, only the New Testament.

9) They don't believe in Mary as Our Lady, the Virgin Mother of God, and say she had other children besides Jesus Christ.

10) They say lay leaders are the blind leading the blind.

11) They don't believe in infant baptism.

12) They believe only in baptism by immersion.

13) They say they're the only ones who are saved, because only they have accepted Jesus Christ and entrusted themselves to him.

14) They despise reverence for the cross and the way Catholics bless themselves, make the sign of the cross, and also light candles. For them the sign of the cross is the sign of the Wild Beast.

15) They come up to the bedside of dying Catholics and try to convince them, telling them they'll be condemned unless they become Evangelicals.

16) They try to intimidate Catholics, instilling fear, by saying that the Wild Beast is coming to put a mark on the foreheads of those who don't have the sign of Evangelicals on them. (A lay leader tells how he calmed down a woman who had been tormented by this kind of fear, explaining to her the true meaning of

the number 666, using the mimeographed sheet from a training session on Revelation.)

17) They say priests and sisters should be married.

18) For them the pope is the Wild Beast, and priests and bishops have the number 666 written on their cassocks.

19) They say the Catholic Church is a religion that accepts any and all kinds of persons.

20) They think only they have the power to cure the sick, cast out demons, and speak in tongues.

21) They use magnetism to impress the people.

22) They do cures, or say they do, but they can't prevent death, and those who go to them crippled leave the same way.

23) What they're interested in is money.

Observations

1) *Confrontation between Catholics and Evangelicals has reached down to the local level.* Lay leaders experience confrontation with Evangelicals as a serious problem because they're rivals competing for the same religious space. Not long ago it was the priest who had to face the minister, but today it is the lay leader. Lay leaders feel they are responsible for their communities, and so they feel they're up against it when Evangelicals try to convert their members. The conflict doesn't prove that Evangelicals are any more aggressive, but simply that they are finding more Catholic resistance at the grassroots level. Bourdieu would reduce all this to simply a "fight over the religious market," but a theologian has to inquire about the quality of both "products."

2) *A strategy that is meant to counter an ideology.* A good deal of the Evangelical missionary methodology—not to simply call it proselytizing—is really the same kind of strategy used by any counterideology. The aim is to demoralize one's competition or adversary so as to come out on top oneself. That's the way it is with ideologies, political parties, governments, companies, soccer teams, etc.

3) *The main issue is theological.* Do these sects function as means of salvation as mentioned in paragraph 3 of the Vatican II Decree on Ecumenism? Despite the faults we see there, are they ways of coming to Christ? Is what Paul said of Judeo-Christians perhaps valid for them: "Some preach Christ from motives of envy and rivalry. . . . What of it? All that matters is that . . . Christ is being proclaimed!" (Phil. 1:15–18).

Are the Evangelicals a means God uses to console, draw together, encourage, and save the people, dispersed and confused, like sheep without enough shepherds (cf. Matt. 9:36)? Are Evangelicals our companions in the harvest of the Lord, or are they our rivals, or perhaps worse, our adversaries? Are they gathering with us or scattering what we gather?

Perhaps there's something of both, the proportions varying from case to case.

Yet, there's no denying that at the theological level the Christ of the Evangelicals is not the one who fully liberates the human condition. Paul's Christ, yes, but not the Jesus of the synoptics, the poor man, the worker, the friend of the oppressed, the prophet who denounces oppressors and defends the weak, who is persecuted by the powerful and murdered by the leaders of his time. The Evangelical churches are resurrection without incarnation.

In this regard, it's better to be silent about Christ than to preach him in a distorted way (cf. 2 Cor. 2:17 and 4:2). Ultimately, however, it's better to preach a partial Christ than no Christ—and this is to the credit of the Evangelicals.

The Poor Don't Live Life, They Battle It

This afternoon ten more lay leaders arrived, all men. Some were held up by problems on the way, and others because they first had to get food so their families could make it through the week.

They're young—twenty, thirty, or thirty-five years old—most of them married. They have children, and some have a lot, like *Seu* Evaristo, who's only a little over thirty but has eleven children.

Sister Ana Maria took the floor to say that some lay leaders had already left the training session because they felt ashamed that they hadn't brought anything to it, no contribution in food, as is the custom. She calmed everyone down, saying that no one should go away or feel ashamed for that reason. Everyone should stay and eat heartily. If someone can contribute, fine—but if not, that's okay too. I noticed heads nodding in agreement.

It was impressive to see these ten men lined up in front of everyone and introducing themselves one by one. "This is a tough kind of Christianity," said Isaías, standing next to me. Yes, it's a Christianity that has rediscovered its power to be a ferment in history and a fire that can purify society.

These men were a moving sight, with their withered bodies, punished by the heat, the sweat, and the buffeting of nature, their faces wrinkled by battling an adverse kind of life (they battle for their life, they don't just live it; it's a struggle, rather than something they can enjoy; a never-ending conquest, not something in the present). Yet they have a way of smiling that is both open and yet restrained, revealing their missing teeth—which is why they cover their mouths with their hands when they laugh.

Who can pay enough honor to such men, sacrificing themselves, struggling forgotten in the jungles, who live on the underside of history, on the far edge of the world? They bear their share of the weight of humanity on their shoulders through their work and the food their work produces, food needed for the lives of so many others who never recognize that fact, and are oblivious of it.

But God has honored them by becoming one of them—the Savior of the world!

Humans Ranked below Animals

Édison, at whose marriage I officiated some years back on a ranch named Santa Clara, called me aside during a snack break and told me, "On the ranch where I'm working one of the hands got on this unbroken horse and had a run-in with another horse, which threw him to the ground, stomped on him, and left him battered. The horse kicked away at the untamed one, broke its hindquarters, and left it lying there.

"So the owner came over with some of the other hands. They all stood around the injured horse lying on the ground, and ignored the poor guy who was all beat up. One of the hands even said, 'A horse like this is worth several million cruzeiros.' "

And Édison said, "Isn't that being a false prophet?"

I reminded him of Psalm 72 where it is said of the Messiah, "precious shall their blood [that of the poor] be in his sight." But for the powerful of this world, the life of the lowly isn't worth anything.

Later I thought of several gospel passages where Jesus criticizes systems that set human beings below animals. For example:

1) "You are worth more than an entire flock of sparrows" (Matt. 10:31; in Luke 12:24 the reference is to ravens).

2) "Which of you does not let his ox or ass out of the stall. . . . Should not this daughter of Abraham . . . have been released from her shackles?" (Luke 13:15–16; a similar comparison is made in the case of a man with dropsy in Luke 14:5).

In our society it would be a good idea if the laws protecting animals were applied to human beings.

It's capitalism that turns things upside down like this, to the extent that—contrary to the great law laid down by John Paul II in *Laborem Exercens*—it places things (and animals) above persons, and specifically, capital over labor.

Capitalism not only treats human beings like animals—it treats them like things.

"They Came from Our Group but They Hadn't Really Belonged"

The president of the union in Brasiléia used to be a lay leader. Three years ago when I gave a training session here, he took part and looked very dynamic.

Now they say he's "sold out," gone over to the government side. He gave up his connection with the base communities. But is he perhaps still connected to the people in some real and organic way? In a society like this where the church is the main, if not the only, institution that has a fermenting influence at the grassroots level, it's hard not to be within the radius of the church's influence if you're involved with the people.

This morning I ran into another former lay leader, who had also seemed very promising. I asked him whether he was coming to the training session. He said he couldn't, because he was going to Rio Branco for the union in order to prepare a demonstration for next Friday, to protest the murder of Jesus Mathias, a union member (about whom I'll have more to say). He's far removed from the work of the gospel. Members of Libelu [small, radical, left-wing organization], some of them ex-seminarians, have gotten to him.

It's important to draw conclusions from unexpected changes in church members. The church should take some interest in this, because the problem has come up a number of times.

As far as the Bible is concerned, we've lost some lay leaders to the Evangelicals. As far as the struggle for justice is concerned, we've lost others to the system, and a few to tiny, radical groups.

However, such things have been happening since the beginning: "If they had belonged to us, they would have stayed with us" (1 John 2:19).

Experience and Religion

There's no getting around it: there's no shortcut to experience. That's especially true in practical matters like this whole issue of the Evangelicals.

Books can be of some help, and so can serious reflection. But the most important thing is personal, living, direct knowledge of what the Evangelicals are all about. Otherwise you can't really think through and assess the issue adequately. Everything remains bookish and abstract (removed from living reality) and rather irrelevant. And the experience of these things has to be personal. It's not enough to pull together the experience of others and reflect on it. The learned medieval scholars said long ago: experience in itself is incommunicable. It's one thing to hear someone else's experience and something else to go through it yourself. There's an unbridgeable gap between experience as described and as lived.

That's even true when you're dealing with an issue academically. But when you're taking it up in terms of practical pastoral work, experience is indispensable. However, none of the four of us in the group of advisors really measures up in this respect, and I even less than the other three. I can see that my colleagues are well prepared, they're well read and well informed. What's lacking is lived personal experience.

That's also why our answers to the specific and realistic questions of the lay leaders (who live right alongside the Evangelicals and are always contending with them) are unsatisfactory. They're completely orthodox, but they're also quite abstract.

I recently reread the "pastoral guidelines" I put down in a manuscript for a training session for the lay leaders in Santa Inês on the topic of the Evangelicals in January 1982. These notes were part of the background material we brought with us. I had given them to Father Mássimo, the pastor there, to make copies of and pass out to the lay leaders. Thank God, his pastoral sense prevailed over my presumptions.

Not that there was anything doctrinally wrong with what I had done. It was correct, but pastorally deficient. What was wrong were the things I chose to stress, and especially the basic thrust. These pretentious "pastoral guidelines" laid out the relationship with Evangelicals along the lines of Vatican II ecumenism. That's applicable in Europe, but not in the situation of the Evangelicals here who are so unecumenical. What use is all the ecumenism in the world (dialogue, joint prayer, collaboration, the "providential" value of these churches, etc.) if your interlocutor doesn't accept it, either in theory or in practice? Such a mistaken position on my part could be traced to one basic fault: what I knew about Evangelicals didn't come from experience.

I can now understand why at that training session in Santa Inês the lay leaders turned a deaf ear to the steadfast position of the group of advisors and resisted with an equal unanimity. It all came to a head during the evaluation on the last day, when there was a strong overall feeling of dissatisfaction. I recall how one woman snapped out with bitter irony, "Sure, this training session has been helpful—more to help lay leaders join the Evangelicals than to defend themselves from them." As advisors we were unanimous—a disgusting consensus!—in interpreting this as "natural resistance" and "understandable dissatisfaction," sitting above it all, with our all-embracing reason.

However, even to understand religion theoretically, you need experience, because religion is inherently more a matter of experience than ideas. Emile Durkheim said that even from a sociological viewpoint a religion should be understood on the basis of its faith—that is, from within.

That's the source of the basic philosophical or epistemological error in Marx's critique of religion: he thought he had found the essence of religion in the social and economic conditions surrounding it, not in its own irreducible experience. In doing so, Marx thought he had grasped the kernel of religion when he had scarcely touched the shell. And he came to the conclusion that religion was like an onion—it's all outer peel; there's no inner core. If you keep peeling, it comes apart and there's nothing else.

But when did Marx have a true religious experience or even study one? In this area, Engels wasn't so precipitous, and his critique of religion was more serious.

If this is valid for understanding religion in theoretical terms, how much more so must it be the case for understanding it in practical terms, as it has to be understood for pastoral activity?

Isn't that what the old epistemologists of theology were saying when they held that you must believe first in order to understand?

It's true for almost anything, but especially for the things of God, that experience comes first and understanding follows.

The Central Issue: Commitment

The sisters pointed out that despite the fact that seventy-some lay leaders are here, a number of others are missing. There are several reasons given, and some strike me as worth noting.

Some didn't come because they're watching over the equipment and crews opening a road near Assis Brazil. They got the equipment by pressuring the mayor. But to make sure that work comes out right, the lay leaders around there have been taking turns carrying out a "people's surveillance" over the work of the local administration.

Another group didn't come because they went to Rio Branco to put pressure on the governor to fix the road leading to the area where they live (I don't remember where it is). They had made some effort with the mayor there, but without any result. That's why they went to the governor's palace in the state capital.

Sister Ana Maria said there should have been a baptism ceremony in that group a few weeks back. But the coordinating team there thought the time wasn't ripe, because the community hadn't united around the struggle for the road. They explained the delay, saying, "In order to be baptized and be a Christian, it's not enough just to take part in community meetings. You also have to take part in community struggles."

It's good that this was said to the lay leaders assembled here, not so much to excuse those who weren't present but to "justify" them, in the sense of backing up their decision.

After all, training is for faith commitment, and not the other way around.

Tuesday, December 6: Brasiléia

THE MURDER OF JESUS MATHIAS

Since our arrival here on Sunday, the atmosphere in the city has been heavy and foreboding. Last Friday, Jesus Mathias, a member of the Union of Farm Workers in Brasiléia, was murdered. Back in July 1980 another leader was killed here, Wilson de Souza Pinheiros, and the repercussions at that time extended to the national level.

This recent case seems connected to the earlier one. Rumors and suspicions are running wild, and the cloud hovering over the city is becoming thicker and darker. They say that it was a plantation owner who had Jesus killed, and that his death represents the revenge of the area landholders over the death of one of their own named Nilo, who was killed by workers because they thought he had been responsible for the murder of Wilson. There are rumors that the landowners have drawn up a list of workers who were involved in killing Nilo. Jesus Mathias was the first name on it. Moreover, there are fears that the rubber-gatherers and plantation workers will take matters into their own hands in order to get justice for the most recent murder, just as happened before.

It is this charged atmosphere that has brought state security authorities here to the city.

They invited the people to a meeting in the town council building. But then we had one of those funny incidents that can take place only out here in the far reaches of Brazil: they couldn't find the key to the council building. So they decided to hold the meeting in the sports club building.

A politician opened the session. First, he set up the head table by calling the secretary for state security, a battalion commander, the commander of the state military police, the federal police commissioner, the municipal commissioner, and other authorities: mayor, deputies, town council members, and so forth.

When they saw I was there, they invited me to join the table. I declined the honor but they insisted. I explained that I was there on my own and not as a representative of the church. I thanked them for their consideration and they acceded.

The secretary for security opened the meeting, saying he had come to launch a campaign to bring peace and take away firearms.

To those present (some fifty persons, almost all men) he emphasized that everyone was responsible for public safety, and should collaborate in giving testimony regarding the murder of Jesus Mathias. He said he had encountered resistance among the local population.

He pulled out campaign posters: a revolver lying on top of blood stains, with the words "Turn In Your Weapons!" written across the top, and in the middle, in bright red, "Violence Provokes Violence."

"Bad taste!," I thought to myself. But the masses don't see it that way. The lay leaders in the training session scrambled to get the dozen he brought.

The secretary explained laws on using and carrying firearms, and then opened the discussion to the public.

A number of persons spoke. In most cases they complained of injustice in particular cases. There was one case where a military officer, apparently drunk, was speeding and killed two children in the city, and yet there's been no sign of any punishment (it was the father of one of the children killed who was speaking). In another case a murderer killed a rubber-gatherer in his bed, with three children right there, then threw the body into the yard and desecrated it. Then he took one of the rubber-gatherer's daughters, eleven years old, and raped her near her father's body. He was jailed but was let out a few months later through the influence of some wealthy persons.

The secretary acknowledged the pressure that wealth can bring to bear on the law, and criticized how faulty our laws are, with enough loopholes to let all kinds of injustice through. He reinforced his point with other examples taken from his own experience as a public prosecutor.

It seemed to me that the discussion was getting off track, and I asked to speak. I began by praising the initiative of the secretary and the other authorities in coming into contact with the people, and I also praised the secretary's explanations of the use of firearms, and I expressed my own support and that of the church for any peacemaking action. Then I came on strong. I took the liberty of observing that the roots of violence go far deeper than simply the carrying of firearms. They belong to the social order (monstrosities in the matter of land tenure) and they are strengthened by the fact that important persons go unpunished for their crimes. I pointed to the experience of the church in the countryside and said that church officials are tired of seeing how the crimes of farm workers are punished, whereas those of plantation owners aren't. I ended by stressing that if the murder of Jesus is punished, it would contribute toward restoring the credibility of public authority, which at present has been quite eroded as far as the general population was concerned.

The secretary acknowledged that the way some can get away with crimes encourages criminal behavior, and he again mentioned how wealth is brought to bear in these matters. That was why he was appealing for the support of the general population. His position struck me as frank and true: he was aware of how justice is conditioned economically, and said so plainly to his hearers, and asked that they help so as to overcome that conditioning.

But his position didn't always seem consistent to me: he made a backhanded slap at class struggle and all those who would like to change society. "We live under capitalism," he stressed, without recognizing that it is precisely capitalism that gives money such power in the maladministration of justice, and in other areas.

Of course, he had the church in mind when he made this attack. On the other hand, he was thereby admitting the church's power among the people. He even said he'd already gotten to know me by attending Masses in the cathedral.

After others had spoken, I took the floor again to ask how far the investigation of the murder of Jesus Mathias had proceeded. Not very sure of himself, he said that the local investigation was in its final phase and that the police were on the trail of someone named Manoel, who is a murderer. But the whole thing was still very much up in the air.

At the beginning of the meeting I noted an atmosphere of tension and concern that everyone present was feeling. After two hours of very open discussion, the atmosphere had cleared up a lot.

Toward the end the number of persons present had risen to about a hundred. There were representatives from the union Jesus Mathias had belonged to. The union president got up and spoke forcefully, but he talked about a number of side issues. He wasted a good opportunity.

When the session ended, I went over to pay my respects to Jesus's father and to his young widow. She was standing there petrified in her sorrow, like a statue portraying suffering.

The authorities then came over and we shook hands. With a good deal of deference, we exchanged a few words. I stressed how important it was that the guilty party be found, so as to restore the credibility of public authority among the population, which was now quite skeptical of the police and the system of justice. A colonel pointed out what a difficult situation the secretary of security was in, despite all his good will. "This is a bomb ready to explode," he said to me, spitting out the words. I took him to mean that the case probably could not be brought to a successful conclusion.

This same colonel asked me if I were the pastor there. I said I worked half the year in the church in Acre and taught theology at the Catholic university in Rio the other half. When another local authority came by he introduced me as a "professor at the Catholic university in Rio," with the implication, "Did you realize . . . ?"

All things considered, it seems to me the meeting worked out well. It's always a good idea to keep up an appropriate relationship with any authority figure. Respect without subservience, firmness without arrogance: that's what St. Gregory the Great recommended for dealing with authorities.

A prophet doesn't have to be disruptive, disrespectful, or bad mannered. You can be courteous without being a courtier. Prophecy isn't in how loud your voice is, but in truth. It's satyagraha.

Wednesday, December 7: Brasiléia

OFFICIAL CHRISTIANITY AND POPULAR CHRISTIANITY

In the morning I go into church and kneel down before the Blessed Sacrament. As I'm leaving, I can see, over by a side altar, a woman standing in front of the statue of Our Lady of Perpetual Help. She stares at the image and barely moves her lips. I recall old Anna, the mother of Samuel. I can almost hear her prayer; she must be making an urgent appeal to her saint. To get well? To find work?

There are two forms of faith: one more "taken for granted" and the other more "anguished." Christianity is expressed very differently in these two forms. The church clearly means one thing to a people in its oppression and something else to a cleric whose sustenance is guaranteed. The signifiers are all the same: same creed, same sacraments, same prayers, same images, and so forth, but the things signified are very different. With one kind of faith the accent is on the spirit and transcendence: with the other the accent is on the body and this world.

What does all this mean? That although we may be close to terms of signifiers, we're far apart in terms of what is signified, even in the area of religion. It would be profitable for us to come together in order to exchange our religious experiences.

But inasmuch as those experiences are rooted in different conditions of life, blending will occur only when lives are blended. That is, when the church becomes the people and the people becomes the church. And that is already underway.

I've never been so aware of this religious difference, and how urgent it is to overcome it, as I was this morning.

The Humble Work of Planting Seeds

Yesterday there were more than ninety lay leaders present in the training session. I looked at them lined up in a large circle inside the training center.

In all there are four sisters here and they're very low-key, sometimes so much so that they look like they're not doing anything—but that's not the case.

The fact that they've gotten this whole crowd of leaders here for a week means that they have a great deal of drawing power. By the same token it means they've done a great deal of grassroots work in terms of visits, conversations, breaking down resistance, etc. And a lot of work that is like planting seeds—the hardest and humblest kind of work but also the most important.

These lay leaders remind me of a ripening cornfield. Behind it stands the work of these sisters who are responsible for the parish. It's a field that was sown, often with suffering but always with hope, "for one who plows should do so in hope" (1 Cor. 9:10).

Visitors or advisors who come from outside and see all these persons gathered together and full of enthusiasm are encountering the process at an advanced phase. If you don't take into account the preceding phases, which were harder and demanded more sacrifice, you can sometimes get a naive and simplistic picture of work with BCCs.

Jesus was a lot more realistic, and hence more dialectic:

> "One man sows; another reaps."
> I sent you to reap
> what you had not worked for.
> Others have done the labor,
> and you have come into their gain [John 4:37–38].

This is especially applicable to those who just come passing through the communities: bishops, theologians, experts, advisors, all kinds of visitors.

But all have their place and their moment, and God is with all: "I planted the seed and Apollos watered it, but God made it grow" (1 Cor. 3:6).

Struggling in the Communities

Six more lay leaders have arrived, all of them remarkable. When they introduced themselves they spoke in terms like this, "For three years I've been *battling* along this road"; "I'm happy with the *work* of the gospel"; "my *struggle* with the community is going ahead no matter what," and so forth.

It really is both struggle and hard work to lead a group in material and social conditions like the ones these leaders have to face: the distances, how spread out they are, the frailty of their resources, both technical (pamphlets, books, etc.) and cultural (instruction, access to information, etc.).

Among the newly arrived was a young man who was twenty-seven, but who looked a lot younger. He had a delightful personality, smiled a lot, was a good speaker, and played the violin. He said, "No one believes it, but I'm married and have six children." Some young women sighed and couldn't hold back their reactions, in a way that the rest couldn't help but notice, so there was laughing and kidding around the room.

Another lay leader, a wrinkled black woman, said she was married and had five children. She said, "Even though I'm sick, I battle away with my group as much as I can."

You can't help but be moved by such a great spirit of sacrifice among these lay leaders. There is a lot of heroism in this grassroots work, a hidden heroism known only to the Father "who sees in secret" (Matt. 6:4).

Being able to speak about their own struggles gives more encouragement to the lay leaders than does anything else. They get consolation from one another, and they are stimulated to keep going. They fit the description John made of himself at the beginning of Revelation: "I, John, your brother, who share with you the distress and the kingly reign and the endurance we have in Jesus" (1:9).

Sandrinha

Although each one of the advisors is putting out a real effort, I don't think we're meshing very well. Some even slipped away to take a little jaunt over to Bolivia on the other side of the river. And the trainees noticed it.

This was the first time Sandra has been part of the group of advisors, yet she was given a disproportionately heavy work load. We should have worked more closely together at the planning stages. Those who are involved at the beginning should make sure that no one is saddled with tasks that are more than they can handle well, and hence make them run the risk of failure and the blow it might be for them.

That didn't happen in this case because Sandra was flexible and because her two other co-workers were very dedicated.

Bury the Dead and Liberate the Living

A woman leader asked the people to contribute to a collection for the funeral of "Old Chaves, one of our brothers." A thousand cruzeiros were needed. The collection yielded 4,300 cruzeiros.

The poor don't feel any contradiction between this and their work toward liberation. Members of the petite bourgeoisie do, because they think in an abstract manner.

Christians aren't concerned with just liberating the poor, but also with burying the dead. They celebrate the hope for the living and the memory of the dead, with an eye toward their resurrection!

Moses and the People

The time is coming for "the people" to stop being the fetish or idol that it is for those whose relationship to the people in fact hasn't matured.

The romantic image of the people is either purely theoretical or is one of first love. After that, a people comes to be seen in all its greatness and all its contradictions.

That is what Moses experienced: "I cannot carry all this people by myself, for they are too heavy for me" (Num. 11:10–15). This is when a people shows all its faults and someone working with it becomes weary. Just like the people of ex-slaves that was Israel, and that needed to become unalienated by marching forty years in the desert (that's what the book of Deuteronomy sets out to show).

But Moses' greatness lies in the fact that he never moved away from the people. Even when he was placed between Yahweh and the people, he chose to stay with the people. He would rather die with the people than live with God but away from the people (cf. Exod. 32:32).

Only divine faith and love can explain that paradox.

Catholics and Evangelicals: Three Rules

I've never seen a more slippery topic to discuss with the people than this one of the Evangelicals. It's like trying to catch fish with your hands. All the more so because Evangelicals, like the Protestant movement as a whole, can seem to be a bazaar of different doctrines, rites, and customs.

Besides that, all lay leaders have their own questions and experiences to relate. There's no doubt that they all feel the Evangelical issue very strongly and that they feel a certain attraction toward Evangelicalism.

Brazilians have an enormous interest in this issue. They could spend days and days hearing about Evangelicalism. It's about religion, and the people, and especially these leaders, are always interested in religion.

In order to wind up this troublesome topic, I laid out three little general rules that had emerged out of the discussions and might serve as guidelines for the lay leaders in their relationship with Evangelicals.

1) Be well mannered toward everybody, including Evangelicals.

2) Remain firm and serene in your own faith.

3) Don't discuss religion with any Evangelical who is a fanatic.

That isn't especially brilliant. But that's as far as we could get. The rules are simple and practical.

The trainees seem to appreciate them. "That's what we needed," said one of them with relief.

Catholic Good Sense: A Skit

In the prayer at the end of the day, the group of lay leaders who were in charge took up another topic: false prophets. Their idea was to make a connection between the topic of Evangelicalism and that of prophecy, which was being introduced in the training session.

The prayer time opened with a skit. Once more I was impressed by how easily ordinary persons communicate among themselves. The skit portrayed a sick man, whom an Evangelical tries to cure. But he has a relapse. At that point the minister of the sick of a BCC comes on the scene. He prays over the sick man, encourages him in the faith, and sends him to a doctor, who cures the illness. And so the story ends.

The presentation wanted to show that Catholics are more open to reasoning, and in that respect are more practical, than are the Evangelicals. Catholics don't have the same kind of spiritualistic single-mindedness that would lead them to say things like, "Only Jesus cures."

That has always been the "Catholic dialectic": affirming both aspects, both this *and* that! Catholicism's sparing use of the absolute negative has its reverse side: it easily leads to compromises.

Epiphenomena

I note that often within these meetings or alongside them there are epiphenomena in the realm of emotion. Relationships and attachments are formed, especially between young men and women.

There's no way to prevent this in pastoral work. We have to recognize this and neither overdramatize it nor be naive about it. The scene of Jesus and the woman in Luke 7 is not only illustrative, but paradigmatic in this respect.

Thursday, December 8: Brasiléia

POPULAR METHODOLOGY

Six more lay leaders showed up today. One of them said he was late because something had come up that had to take precedence over anything else. And he told how his little grandson had been run over and eventually died. Such things happen all the time in the world of the poor, which is always so full of tragedy.

One young woman said she came "in place" of another, a lay leader who couldn't make it. That meant she had come to learn for the other woman. She's not the only such case. I imagine that what they intended to learn, besides the general ideas put forth here, are the songs, jokes, games, skits, and prayers. They learn primarily with their eyes, and even more with their hands and body—by doing.

Moving around among the trainees during Isaías's talk, I noticed how hard they were struggling to take notes, not so much of what Isaías said, but of what he wrote on the blackboard. They were practically tracing letter by letter what they saw him write down, including charts and drawings. All without any apparent logical order. I have no idea how they would make heads or tails out of it later. Perhaps those isolated words, traced out there, serve them like those small signs they leave in the jungle to keep from getting lost—a slash on a tree trunk, or a branch placed on the ground.

In having the trainees take notes I wonder whether we're not subjecting them to an assault on their culture. It would have been better to have brought mimeographed notes on what was being said, especially because this section was more a question of information (on Evangelicals and prophets) than of leadership training.

It also would have been a good idea to use posters or drawings. The poor catch on more with their eyes than with their ears. That's true of everyone, of course.

How slavishly we stick to our own habits and our own cultural resources, especially writing and concepts! How about metaphor, example, proverb, deed, etc.? Where is the language of Jesus of Nazareth, who used parables to adapt to how the people understood things (cf. Mark 4:33)? There's too much writing! Too many ideas! That can help others to understand but it can't make them feel or make them live!

I've heard that Carlos Brandão is studying the way the poor learn and how they share and spread what they learn. That's what we need. The "popular methodology" we should be aiming at is primarily the one the poor themselves have created and are using.

We're Too Professorial!

I've been thinking about how we advisors give our presentations. Advisors often act more like professors than like prophets or sages. They're more given to teaching others than to stimulating them, more to clarifying than to animating, more to informing than to encouraging. They reach the head rather than the heart.

They raise their voices and go through contortions to explain a concept, communicate an item of information, or pound home an idea. In order to keep their listeners' attention, they use a kind of external coercion by their voice, gestures, writing on the board, eye contact, etc.

With Jesus things were different. I imagine that when he spoke to the people he didn't strain his voice (Matt. 12:19), nor did he need any other techniques. Yet his hearers hung onto his every word. Those words reached deep down inside, into the soul, into the feelings of the heart, and remained engraved there, buried like a seed in the ground. There they went to work, as the parable of the grain sprouting on its own describes (Mark 4). His hearers didn't need to take notes. The impression left by the words was all that was needed. The memory in their hearts functioned like notebooks and blackboards.

Today Carlos Mesters, a priest in Brazil who in teaching and writing has related the Bible to popular culture and experience, has gone back to that style. Anyone watching or listening to him realizes that he is talking more like a sage than a professor. His words come down like rain; not like nails he is trying to pound into heads. The prophet's proclamation and the sage's counsel are quite different from what happens in the professor's classroom.

Each kind of language has its own appropriate time and place. Theology and catechesis belong more to the professorial (doctrinal or magisterial) category. The idea is to teach and learn. In contrast, the homily is of a more prophetic or sapiential nature, and only rarely should it be professorial. But sometimes things get switched around.

I only know that our training procedures are too professorial and hence very doctrinal and cerebral, and scarcely sapiential and prophetic at all.

Professors say what they know. Sages and prophets say what they have to say.

Prophet: Another Name for Lay Leader

On the question of "how to be a prophet today," the groups presented three skits and three large drawings. They did a good job.

What came out clearly was that for them "prophet" means basically *courage* and *encouragement*. And this isn't some incidental function, but is in fact the proper function of being a lay leader. Someone remarked, " 'Prophet' is another term for lay leader." The same person went on, "An Evangelical attacked me by saying that the term 'lay leader' [*monitor,* "monitor," the term used by the church in this area] isn't in the Bible. I was a bit confused, I'll admit it. But now I know that it *is* there, but expressed by another word: prophet!"

A jury that they had chosen rated each presentation, and gave each group a little card showing how it had been rated.

The group that did a large poster showing Our Lady of Aparecida as Queen of the Prophets, with verses from the Magnificat written below, came in third, but that was due not so much to the drawing, which was rather sketchy, as to what it represented. In my opinion, their high ranking was more for the Mother of Jesus than for the artistry of the group.

Anyway, there is a new image of Mary emerging from the heart of the people, one that is more in the spirit of the gospel and more liberating.

Helping Colonizers

Two lay leaders named Isaías and Gérson, representing the CPT, have come from Plácido de Castro, in order to help colonizers get organized here. They've had valuable experience in their work on the colonization project sponsored by INCRA called Pedro Peixoto, over in Plácido.

The lay leaders in the meeting said what they knew about the situation of those who have recently come up from the south. What they said made the picture even grimmer than what I had already known from having been with them myself.

The issue is stark, naked hunger. That's the main problem, no doubt about it. One of the men says he saw families weeping in the corner of a shed with nothing at all to eat.

Another saw at least fifteen men make a lunch out of two packages of cookies and two cans of sardines.

Another says, "Those peoples' insides are all knotted up from all the hunger they've had to suffer." And after talking about something else, he comes back to it again, with amazement: "Their insides are stuck together because they've gone so long without eating."

Another says he saw these poor devils faint from hunger while they were working at clearing the forest. He overdramatizes, it seems to me. "They take a couple hacks at the tree and fall over from hunger. . . . They get up and try again, but they can't keep going."

One lay leader says, "They're exploited in the hardest kinds of work, like clearing weeds from cornfields. It's hotter than hell out there. And they don't make much and don't have much to eat. And what about their families?"

Everyone agrees that, despite it all, the southerners keep their hope alive in the midst of all their troubles. Some of the leaders here think the colonizers are deluded in their expectations. "Their illusions make it hard to work at conscientization," says one group. But others don't agree: "They may suffer hunger, but their hope is even greater!" I wonder whether this hope is so illusory. And even if it is, don't dreams serve a vital function?

When Isaías asks what lay leaders have done for colonizers, he hears:

1) they've provided plots of cleared land for planting;

2) they've visited the southerners and talked with them;

3) they've organized fund-raising events for them in their own community, such as on the feast day of St. Francis;

4) they've tried to get them together in evangelization groups, etc.

But it seemed that Isaías was looking for something more. And he jumped in. "What's this? Aren't you prophets here? Isn't it your function to announce and denounce, as we've been learning these days? So what have you been doing?"

I thought Isaías was going too far. The reaction came right back. The lay leaders felt they were being criticized and they reacted forcefully: "We're here with the best of intentions. But we don't know how to do any more. We didn't invite you here because we didn't have anything else to do!"

The two visitors from the CPT picked up the discussion again. On the basis of their own experience, they explained how lay leaders could direct their own work here toward the colonizers. It was Gérson who began this second approach; Isaías was still recovering from the way the trainees had come back at him.

Gérson told how they had begun with food in Plácido. But they saw that that wasn't enough. So they went on to organize commissions of these homesteaders to pressure INCRA and other government agencies. That's how they got what they needed: food, roads, and so forth.

Isaías came back in, telling how they had brought colonizers together into groups to meet on a regular basis. They stayed in contact with those groups, occasionally injecting a note of encouragement. "The idea is not to leave them isolated," he suggested.

So everyone agreed that they ought to draw up a small commission to work out a proposal for well-organized work and present it the next morning. The plan should involve those leaders who live near a new settlement, and others should be willing to provide support in a broader sense.

Gérson and Isaías would make an initial visit to colonizers, along with lay leaders from the area, and begin the organizing work.

The discussion was good and so was the result. God always accompanies the people through the Egypts of history.

A Community Penance Service

At the end of the afternoon we had a community confession in preparation for Christmas. It began at dusk. We all stood in front of the church to show how sin cuts us off from communion with divine life, here represented by the material church building, and how forgiveness brings us back in.

There was a reading of Luke 3:1–14: the preaching of John the Baptist. Then everyone sat down on the steps outside the church for an examination of conscience. There was a deep silence. Passersby in the street would stop a moment to look at that group of persons sunk in prayer, make the sign of the cross, and go on their way.

A little later everyone got up and went into the church, still observing silence. There they lay down in the aisles, face down on the ground. That was a sign of repentance, humility, and penance. Several minutes went by. The silence in the dark church was impressive. When the lights went on the whole assembly stood up and, raising their hands up high and lifting their voices, they begged the Father for mercy, singing three times, "Forgive your people, O Lord."

Next, two by two, they came up to the minister who put his hands on each one of them and absolved them, tracing a sign of the cross on their foreheads.

At the end, we sang the Lord's Prayer and left the church in a joyful procession with a song that made body and soul sway together: "Our rights will be respected." We kept singing, and some were even dancing, as we came to the front of the training center, and there, with a number of slogans chanted and a good deal of clapping, the penance ceremony ended.

Everyone's face was beaming. "And the grace of those unique days will become everyday," as a beautiful expression by Mounier puts it. This was really an anticipation of a world completely and utterly reconciled.

Lay Leaders: Saints without Knowing It

You're sometimes deeply moved by the gospel spirit of these lay leaders. Some of them, I believe, show great sanctity: their lives are full of goodness, they're ready to respond to any human need, their generosity knows no limits, and they don't make a show of their sacrifice.

Just getting here for this training session is already a struggle. Some of them spent days walking through the jungle and rough roads. They had to leave their families behind for a week in conditions that are almost always precarious. To drop work for a week can easily throw the whole economic situation of the family off balance: they live practically from one day to the next without much in the way of reserves.

That explains why some lay leaders have brought some of their household here, especially children. Two have even brought their whole families. That made one of the sisters point out that this shouldn't become an abuse.

Today, when they were discussing the help that lay leaders might be able to give the homesteaders, it was remarkable to see how generous they were. Some offered to let them come into the area they had planted with rice and beans and let them harvest some for their own use.

Seu Almerindo, who's from Minais Gerais, offered to put his cassava at the disposition of the colonizers from the south. Besides that he said they can take some of his rice. A latter-day Barnabas (cf. Acts 4:36–37).

Evaristo, although he's a young man with eleven children of his own and lives in a precarious situation, still finds time to visit the colonizers every week, to talk with them, just being there, being a friend, in effect, loving them.

At one point he told me, "Last week ten of the thirteen members of my family were flat on their backs. Only three were healthy. It looked like I wouldn't be able to come to the training session, but with God's help and my will power, things got better. So I'm here, thank God."

Evaristo is wonderful. He's got a good head on his shoulders and a rather sharp critical awareness. He is a pure soul. Although he has experienced the evil in the world, he doesn't allow himself to be poisoned with the least taste of bitterness. That's something rare and precious. His life is based on the gospel in a marvelous way: he joins peace with justice, meekness with hope, forgiveness with courage.

I've thought to myself that such a man, if he had had a chance at education, would surpass many intellectuals. "How many Mozarts have been murdered," was Saint-Exupéry's bitter lament when he saw a beautiful baby who had been abandoned and had no future.

These lay leaders are saints without knowing about it. They live the gospel, but aren't aware of it. And isn't that true sanctity? "You are not to let your left hand know what your right hand is doing" (Matt. 6:13).

Today when we asked the lay leaders what they had to do to be prophets, they came back with two or three seemingly banal statements. However, their *lives* are quite prophetic in the effort and courage they display alongside their brothers and sisters, sustaining them in unity, struggle, and hope for a new world.

Vigil for Peace and Justice

Given the murder of Jesus Mathias, we thought of having a public ceremony, a vigil. At first the idea was to focus it on justice, sending forth a cry to heaven, and doing it publicly, demanding that justice be done in the case of this worker. The idea was to get together as many participants as possible to show that the church community was paying attention to this case, and any others like it, because the threat of others hung in the air.

Later on, the idea of peace was added to that of justice. That was to provide a gospel counterweight to the demand for justice, which by itself might risk tilting toward the idea of revenge.

We began with the liturgy of the word. As celebrant, I came in, carrying the Easter candle already lit, while everyone sang, "Pilgrim people, you seek liberation, raise your eyes to your Lord, your forgiveness."

The readings were Genesis 4 (Cain and Abel), and Matthew 5 (the beatitudes). The statue of Mary Immaculate was all decked out alongside the altar, because it was the feast day of the Immaculate Conception.

During the homily I spoke on both readings. I was quite impressed by the atmosphere of both anxiety and courage that the situation had produced. The only lights in the church came from the candles, which created pockets of glowing light and made the faces of the participants stand out against the dark space of the church.

I stressed that Jesus spoke with meekness and peace, and yet spoke of a hunger and thirst for justice and of seeking justice. The beatitudes are inseparable.

We then set out on a procession through the city. That was in order to give public testimony that we were in favor of peace, but also of justice, both of them linked together. The people lit their candles from the flame of the paschal candle. The celebrant carried the candle at the head of the march; the statue of the Immaculate Virgin went along in the middle of the throng.

The whole procession was carried out in silence and recollection. The silence was interrupted only three times, each time to pray the Our Father. The first time was near the union headquarters. We offered the prayer for Jesus and Wilson, and I asked that Nilo, the landowner killed by the workers, also be included. I thought we Christians should demonstrate a breadth and openness not exemplified in the way oppressors act toward us.

We said the second Lord's Prayer in front of the police station. The intention of the prayer was that the authorities would have the strength and courage to do justice and be on the side of the people. As we came up, policemen sitting on the porch stood up with respect. We stated our intention and said the Our Father. Then we continued the march, in complete silence.

Further on, near where Jesus' father and brother live, we prayed for his family and relatives. That was the last Our Father.

When we got to the street that leads to the church, we broke the silence with a song, "Our joy is knowing that one day all the people will be freed." I should say that the fact that people sang out so strongly showed how relieved everyone felt for having gotten through the city safe and sound. That procession, even though (or perhaps because) it was essentially religious, was loaded with real political content—politics in the broad sense. The prevalent psychological and social atmosphere was one of a diffuse uneasiness.

When we came back into the church the lights had come back on (I left wondering how the lights tend to go out at times like this). We continued the Mass with great spirit. Everyone was singing out with gusto.

At the moment of the greeting of peace, I came down from the altar and in the middle of the aisle I gave Jesus's father a long and warm embrace. Then I went to pay my respects to his wife, now a widow, who was in the back of the church, crying and holding a baby in her arms. When I saw her like that, the very image of the *Addolorata,* I felt my heart breaking. I paid my respects without knowing what to say. I think what came out was, *"Senhora,* receive the peace of Jesus."

When the Mass was over everyone had a strong feeling of peace and hope. That was what you could see on all the faces.

When we had been preparing the processions, we were somewhat afraid of the possible repercussions. But it had a very positive demonstration effect. It instilled courage in the lay leaders not to fall back in the face of acts of injustice, and it projected a church that is alert and ready for whatever the future may hold.

Friday, December 9: Brasiléia

BCCs AND MARTYRDOM

Celebrating commitment: that was our morning prayer today on the last day of the training session.

The core of the celebration consisted of setting a tall candle in the middle of the room and letting the trainees come up, take hold of it, and make their act of commitment.

Many of them came forward. There were so many who wanted to make their commitment that there came a moment when it seemed preferable to do it collectively. They all held out their right hands toward the candle, and held onto the gospels in their left, while we recited the creed together.

But what left the strongest impression on me was the personal commitment one of them made. Facing the candle confidently and firmly, he gazed at the flame and said in a strong voice, "I want to continue the work in the community toward the liberation of my people. And in this work I commit myself to death, with God's help."

In that man I could see a new Christian: someone who was ready for martyrdom. A church that can produce persons like that, men and women ready to give their life for their brothers and sisters as Jesus did, is a church that is really led by the gospel.

New Ministries for New Ministers

The training session is ending. Among these trainees I can see leaders who could be given a greater pastoral responsibility, one that could be officially recognized.

It's obvious that there's a priest shortage. Here the sisters are taking the place of a pastor, but there aren't many of them. Why not consider having some lay leaders be trained to be ministers of baptism, marriage, and some day, who knows, of the Lord's Supper?

Those at the top of the institutional church don't see it. They don't see it, because they don't experience the problem. And they don't experience the problem, because they don't live among the people, at the bottom.

What should we do? Begin down below with new, serious and responsible experimentation. That will eventually benefit the whole church.

The issue isn't just that of forming a "native clergy" with the established patterns. It's a matter of forming "native patterns" to produce different kinds of priests and other ministers.

How far behind we are in all this! Pastoral practice is so far behind the doctrinally sound possibilities that the theology of ministry has developed! The church's discipline is so out of step with both doctrine and the times!

For example, I look at Zeli and Luís, who are together leading this assembly of more than eighty persons. They're very competent and quite self-assured in front of the rest. They speak clearly, frankly, and confidently. They command attention, respect, and attention on the part of all.

Why shouldn't they receive a greater recognition from the church for their ministry, so their leadership will be more firm and more permanent?

Who Rules Brazil?

For the next training session the lay leaders suggested several topics:
1) Family life.
2) How to organize the people.
3) The four gospels.
4) Who rules Brazil?
This last topic arose because of the presidential election scheduled for 1984.

A vote was taken and the result was that the main topic would be, "who rules Brazil?" connected with "how to organize the people." A secondary theme would be "family life." They like to combine things—so everyone will be satisfied.

The True Interests of the People

This kind of survey ("What topic do you want to deal with in the next training session?") is risky or at least ambiguous. The *consciousness of a class* is one thing and *class consciousness* is another—a distinction made by Adam Schaff. The consciousness of a class is its *empirical* consciousness, the way it actually is. That's what you get in a survey and what the statistical average reveals what the group in question explicitly wants.

By contrast, class consciousness is the kind of consciousness that *corresponds* to the real situation and true interests of a class.

Take soccer, for example. It is obviously part of the interests of *favela* dwellers in Rio, in their psychology and social behavior. But is it part of their socio-economic and political interests? They *are interested in* soccer but is soccer *in their interests?*

It's true that the notion of the "real," "true," "objective" interests of the people often disguises a lot of manipulation and just serves as a mask for the interests of one group, a political party, the military, economic interests, etc.

And yet to accept the face-value interests of a people as its true interests means giving way to all kinds of ambiguities.

What should we do? It seems to me that from a *pedagogical* viewpoint we *always have to start* from the explicit and subjective interests of the people taken at face value. *But where should that lead?* Today we certainly need a theory to guide a political approach, a process, but it should always be discussed and worked out with those who will be affected. Now, isn't that what Marxism strives to be (I'm not saying that's what it is)?

It's clear that to some degree a people's interests are already inside its consciousness and to some degree they're outside, or out ahead of it. The truth of the true interests of the people comes out of the dialectic between what the people wants and what it "ought" to want or to do for its own good. All this goes on in the process of history, rather than in anyone's head.

The Bible is on the mark when it speaks of the "cry of the people." For a cry is not discourse. It's something that has to be discerned and interpreted, similar to what a cry of pain means to a doctor.

My brother Leonardo has defined liberation theology as "the cry of the people elaborated into discourse."

Bonds of Communion

I'm on my way back to Rio Branco by bus. We've made a half-hour stop at the halfway point, the station in Araxá. It's 3:30 P.M.

How did the training session end? The whole morning was devoted to practical matters. The lay leaders were picking up material they needed for the next few months: the bulletin *Nos Irmãos* ["we brothers"], the Christmas novena, calendars for next year (the one put out by the CPT and the one they fight over, the Sacred Heart of Jesus Calendar), song sheets, etc. A whole load of material, in other words.

By the end of the morning the training center looked more like a market place, with everyone coming and going, putting notes on the walls, assigning reading matter ("Christian Family," CPT bulletin, *Nos Irmãos,* etc.), making arrangements for the next meeting or trip, etc.

Later on, near lunchtime, we had a short prayer of thanksgiving. I took advantage of the moment to ask them to forgive me for times when I had been nervous, and to show my appreciation and admiration for the wonderful work and vigorous witness of faith and dedication they all had given: lay leaders, coordinators, catechists, ministers of the sick, and others.

As a finishing touch we sang the "training center song": "Our rights will be respected, and if they're not, Brazil will be the loser." Everyone started swaying back and forth, and moved into the center of the room dancing uninhibitedly. It was a festive sign, and the whole thing was quite moving.

When it was time to go, many had tears in their eyes. No wonder. Most of them spend almost the whole year in isolation, living in very narrow circles and faced with a kind of life that is very hard, in terms of both nature and society.

So when they spend a few days together studying, praying, discussing things, singing, and even kidding around, the relationship created is so rich and warm that it really hurts when they have to return to the same harsh life.

It's true that faith isn't just experiencing the Father and struggling for the kingdom. It's also human friendship and affection. The gospel that frees from everything harmful and saves the heart as well!

The closing of the training session was tying a beautiful ribbon to a crown of flowers!

XI

A Church under Construction

Here I'd like to give a picture of some of the kinds of work I found myself involved in during periods when I was staying in Rio Branco, the seat of the local church. These activities were quite varied and vital, and taken all together they suggested the idea of a work site with many persons involved. Hence the title for this chapter, "A Church under Construction."

Monday, September 19: Marizal, Candóia, and Panquecas

FIRST COMMUNION IN MARIZAL

The cathedral parish has responsibility for a large area of settlements or villages around Rio Branco. The day before yesterday, Saturday, we went out to visit some of them. We went as a team of four, two novices of the Sisters of St. Joseph, Leontina and Léia, and two priests, Father Bruno and myself.

Marizal was the first settlement we stopped in. It's about 25 kilometers from Rio Branco. We found a simple community center, open on all four sides, and with a packed earth floor, but very well kept up. It was all decorated for the first communion that was to take place at the end of the morning. Pennants and streamers fluttered in a breeze that provided a little relief from the intense heat of the day. Around the outside you could see carefully planted flowers.

Cosma, a lay leader and catechist, welcomed us very pleasantly. It is this dark, young woman, both humble and lively, who gives impetus to the whole life of the local community.

In her low-keyed but active way, she had prepared everything: the decorations in the center, water to drink, and a treat for the children.

The children began to arrive and took their places on the benches. There were thirty-three of them from three communities—Marizal, Candóia, and Panquecas. When they had all arrived they welcomed us with a song made up by members of the community. That's the sort of creativity you always find.

Next, Cosma put on a demonstration for us of what the first communicants had learned. She wanted to show how seriously they had been prepared. She was using a small catechism with questions and answers. It's one of those catechisms with formulas that are simple, clear, and sharp—unquestionable virtues—but, as good as they might be in doctrinal terms, they're not very existential, and not at all socially minded. I was surprised that this was the kind of catechism they were using. But I could see that the children weren't badly prepared—not at all. They had learned to think, with those well-polished formulas as their starting point.

When Cosma asked what the sacrament of orders meant, no one knew. Finally one child took a chance, "That's when you get an order from your daddy, your mommy, or your teacher to do something."

Cosma was satisfied, or seemed to be. So I felt obliged to step in, "Yes, it is an order but it's a very special order: the order of Jesus Christ when he sends someone to be the pastor of the people, and that someone is the priest." So things got fixed up.

The confessions went very well. The children made their preparation together. Then the two priests received each child individually. Sitting on a tree stump next to a big bush, I took them one by one, as did Father Bruno, sitting under a thatched roof.

At the end of the morning there was a festive Mass. The children were all decked out, some with a wreath on their heads and flowers in their hands, and the boys with a ribbon on their necks or arms. That's the way of the people.

It was a joyful celebration, full of singing and with enthusiastic participation. After the Mass there was the usual swirl of persons who wanted to take pictures of their children, especially together with the priest.

Events like these are milestones for the people. Everyone wants to remember them forever. Celebrating first communion is a way to affirm your own dignity, your own worth. Faith humanizes by divinizing.

What Does It Mean to Be Anointed? Look at the Lay Leader!

After having lunch in Cosma's house, we left to go to another community, located at kilometer 18. There we found some twenty young persons who were going to be confirmed the next day, Sunday.

The one in charge was Raimundo Nem. I was impressed by his attitude and the control he exercised. I could see in him what it means to have authority without dominating. His authority is made up of kindness and generosity, and yet it reflects how demanding the gospel is. I could see the people's respect for him as a leader and how well prepared he is.

Raimundo did a lot of singing. He had done a good job of preparing his charges for confession. The confessions, simple and quite specific, went very well. The young persons we were dealing with showed an amazing integrity and purity of spirit. I heard one young woman's confession, for example, and her life seemed so unsullied that I could scarcely believe she was being sincere. I asked her to prepare better and come back again but she didn't. In the meantime I was speaking to a catechist and to other young persons and I realized that I had been mistaken. The catechist summed it all up by saying, "All she does is work at home with her mother."

Raimundo asked me to speak to the group. I spoke about the anointing of confirmation. What does it mean to have been anointed? It means you're a person who has been strengthened by God, and you are filled with the Holy Spirit for the sake of a mission. All I had to do was to point to the living example of Raimundo Nem himself, a man full of the energy provided by the gospel, and of commitment to serving the people and its liberation.

Why go far away looking for something that's so close? Persons living an ethical life are more powerful than abstract formulas. There are persons of spirit, and of the Spirit, right in our midst!

Life Is Full of Meaning

Toward the end of the afternoon we stopped again in the community of Cruz Milagrosa, "miraculous cross." It's called that because a poor rubber-gatherer who died tragically due to human wickedness is buried there. A rubber dealer forced him to carry a load that was too much for him and it did him in. Everyone venerates him as a saint and comes to his tomb to make promises or fulfill them. That's how the poor canonize their saints. In fact, they are all poor saints, oppressed and put to death by the powerful of this world. This is a kind of theodicy: accounts are squared for the innocent.

In that community also there were some young persons who wanted to go to confession. They were going to be anointed the next day.

The team in the community was a group that worked together well: Eva, a young married woman: *Seu* Schons, a rancher who came here from Rio Grande do Sul; and one they called Barbudo, "bearded." It's always reassuring to see persons taking charge of the church, everywhere you go. Of course, they are weak, and don't have a lot of experience, like seeds that are just sprouting, or seedlings that have just been transplanted. But this church is vigorously taking root and calls for care, respect, and sensitivity, like the way a gardener treats his plants.

At the end of the day we came back home. It had been a very full day. And the night was going to be more of the same, as I'll describe in a moment. The four of us in the car were returning with an overflowing feeling of satisfaction. We were talking about what had happened during the day and we were singing. It's marvelous to live for something that's bigger than life itself! To live for liberation and a more abundant life for men and women! Is there any life that's more noble, pure, and great? In this kind of service you feel a joy and happiness beyond compare. The meaning of your life is devoting your life to meaning!

A Night Walk

I came back home, got washed up, and headed over to the Imaculada church in zone 2 of the city. That was to be the starting point for a walk at 7 P.M., organized by young adults to commemorate the 750th anniversary of the founding of the Servite Order, which has been in charge of the church in this area since 1920.

There they were, noisy and ready to go, about two hundred of them. They asked me to start things off. I spoke for about twenty minutes, emphasizing the ideal that the seven founders of the order had, what they proposed to do with their lives. They had been wealthy merchants in Florence, Italy, but they had gotten rid of their possessions and dedicated themselves to serving the outcast. Having become poor themselves, they went out to the edge of the city to live the gospel together. They broke with an evil system and went to live at Mount Senario, 18 kilometers from Florence. That was the starting point for the whole gospel-inspired movement that became the Servite Order. I stressed that such an ideal is not the exclusive property of any group, but that it belongs to all Christians. It is not just the Servite communities who continue the work of the seven founders, but also base communities and all persons who live inspired by the same aim of standing up to mammon, serving the poor, and following Jesus along the pathways of history. That was what the walk was all about.

The night walk came off quite well. They walked more than twenty kilometers, both inside the city and outside. The march stopped at various points where local communities welcomed the marchers with songs, skits, and something to eat and drink.

The walk wasn't just religious in nature but was fiestalike, had a family sense, and even a political thrust. They sang, recited poetry, shouted "Long live this!" and "Down with that!," denounced the injustices of the system, had friendly conversation, and spent moments in religious silence. The whole night went by that way.

About one hundred fifty young persons arrived at the cathedral for Mass at 6 A.M. Dom Moacyr welcomed them, and by now they were dead tired. But they were still able to join in with the other worshippers there, and enliven the Sunday Mass (which was being broadcast). Finally at 7 A.M. they went home. They had been on a moving vigil for practically twelve hours.

For the young it was an unforgettable experience. Besides showing the church's drawing power, it showed what the young are capable of if they are motivated by new ideas that demand something. There were very few who dropped out, especially when one considers that the organizers didn't expect more than fifty of them for the march.

For me, however, the work I had begun Saturday morning wasn't over yet. I still had to give a talk on the gifts of the Spirit to those who had been anointed. I took up Galatians 5:22–23: "The fruit of the spirit is love, joy, peace. . . ." Although I was extremely tired, I was going full steam, more inspired and creative than ever. It was the Spirit.

Wednesday, September 28: Rio Branco

A TALK WITH RAIMUNDO NEM, ORGANIZER

Raimundo is staying in our house. He came for a medical checkup. I've taken advantage of the occasion to have a chat with this leader I've run across so many times and in whom I've always seen someone hard at work battling for the people of the kingdom.

Here's what I've pulled out of our conversation:

"The leader who called me was Father João Rocha. I began as a catechist's aide. That was in 1975 in a settlement named Custódio Freire, about 17 kilometers from Rio Branco.

"I took part in two training sessions to prepare for being a catechist and a lay leader, and I began to take part in pastoral movements. In 1977 the assembly of the parish of Santa Inês chose me as number three coordinator from that area. Then they elected me to be general coordinator of the whole area where I was living, Cruz Milagrosa, because the communities were in very bad shape there. That area has now come under the responsibility of the cathedral.

"This year (1983) I'm working together with another coordinator, Zé Maria. I focus my attention on work in the area of Carão. I'm coordinating twelve communities: Cruz Milagrosa, Braslíndio (at kilometer 12), San José (at kilometer 18), Mário Lobão, San Jorge, Candóia, Marizal, Panquecas, Vertente, Quartéis, Alto San José, and Vaza-Barril.

"It's my obligation to visit these communities every two months. That's the way I spend my weekends—two or three communities each time.

"I'm not very likely to be home Saturdays and Sundays. Only if I'm sick or have a very serious problem in the family.

"Lay leaders come looking for me to solve a problem. It may be a fight, backbiting, problems with a child or with school, or a legal problem, a family being pushed off its land, or other things. So I give advice and guidance. Or I take them to the legal defense center in Rio Branco. When I reach my own limits, I take the matter to the church, to the pastor, or even to the bishop.

"I don't get involved in union work, because I don't have time. But I do tell others to go there and to struggle.

"Plantation workers also come looking for me. But that's only when they're in a fix. I advise them to get organized, to go to the union and battle for their rights. Even when they're not in one of the communities they come looking for me. I tell them not to trust the boss, especially when they've been ordered to pay him a fine after a court judgment. After all, you know what the bosses are like around here.

"The big landowners don't want anything to do with me. They don't let their workers come to my meetings. The farmworkers are the ones who least take part: the bosses won't let them.

"During the electoral period a well-known landowner used to come around to see me a lot, hoping to win me over. He was supporting the PMDB candidate, the one who won the governorship. But I didn't go along with him at all.

"The lay leaders like me to visit them. When one of them has been slipping, I pay a surprise visit. And then I point to the example of the prophets. I try to encourage everyone, and I point out how important our meetings in common are. They often miss those meetings in the parish, which take place once or twice a month. What makes it hard is transportation: they don't have the money. A round trip from Carão to Rio Branco costs 1,000 cruzeiros. And they have to spend the night here, with some relative or someone they know. I sometimes end up spending as much as 2,000 cruzeiros for transportation on one weekend.

"When I get to a community, that always makes them quite happy. And they always lay out a problem for me. But I make it a point never to be the first to speak. I wait for them to start things out. Then when I see a good opening, I move in. I don't like to be the first. They should first give their opinions.

"But when the priest comes, ideas seem to evaporate from villagers' heads. Try as hard as they can, they can't seem to remember things. It's because they're not used to it. They're scared. It's like what you saw when you went to kilometer 18. And like what happens to me when I go to speak on the radio—I almost forget how to speak. I'm just not used to it.

"I'm very fond of singing. That really encourages the community. When we get into the Bible, I sing only at the end. That's because Bible work shouldn't be interrupted. I translate God's work into prayer and explanation. Then at the end, we liven things up with song.

"The men don't participate as much. They always bring up reasons for not coming. They prefer to have the women come. They go out to play soccer or simply stay home. Or go fishing or hunting.

"Last Sunday I got all the men who were going out to play soccer together. I read to them the gospel story of St. Lazarus. I explained how there was a division into rich and poor. I used the lesson Dom Moacyr had given in his radio sermon that morning. He pointed out how the rich man had gone to hell not for being rich but for being selfishly rich. Lazarus had been rewarded for being a simple and humble poor man.

"They paid attention for the whole meeting. And the meeting lasted more than an hour. At the beginning I explained that before playing soccer they should prepare their spirit so they'll avoid violence and be sure everything ends in peace. They nodded their heads in agreement.

"The men come to Mass. But it's hard to get them to meetings. Sometimes the only men in the meetings are old Simeão and myself. That old guy always states his mind.

"There isn't much talking in the group. Only two or three speak up. It's hard to get them to open their mouths and say what they're thinking. They sit there listening. You always have to wait for them to speak. It's easier for those who come more often. They also accept a commitment to share in the work of the community. Everyone expects the lay leader to do most of the talking.

"There are those who complain when the lay leader asks the group to explain the gospel. Some of them say 'What do you mean?—we've come here to learn!'

"I always ask, 'What did Jesus Christ want to tell us with this saying?' Then they ask for an explanation. The trick is to explain it in a way that will get them to start talking.

"There are those who will say something that is different from the gospel, and almost the opposite. When that happens, you have to pick it up and use it somehow so as not to make the person feel bad.

"In the community of Pedro Eurico one woman made a statement that was rather confused. The lay leader corrected her and said, 'That's not what it means,' and so forth. He really chewed that woman out. Two days later she became an Evangelical. That was a horrible setback for the community.

"But she's been the only person who's gone over to the Evangelicals during my time as coordinator. I myself have a brother who was a deacon in the Assembly of God church. Later on, he was expelled because he was trying to find out something about their ministers. . . . And he stood up to say it in the meeting of the assembly. The pastors took him to a mental hospital. They put him in twice. Now he's working with the lay leaders. He's a schoolteacher and folks are very fond of him.

"When I got here, everyone was an Evangelical or becoming one. Now there are very few Evangelicals any more. The pastor even sold his place and left.

"In the whole area there's only one man who's an Evangelical. His son comes to our meetings, but he hasn't made up his mind yet. He's a leader among the young and is always coming around the community. But when they begin to say the creed, he gets up and leaves.

"The community holds meetings and also has catechesis. But the catechists are very slack about it. When they get their materials they're enthusiastic, but then they don't do anything more about it. The materials stay packed away somewhere. They don't prepare themselves and they don't show any concern. There seems to be some kind of sluggishness about them. As a result they give a little bit of catechism to the children but there's not much life in it.

"The way kids are in the countryside, if someone doesn't really put a lot into it, they don't think it's important.

"I also go out on trips outside my area, together with the priests. That means four or five, even ten days away, out on rivers or in the jungle. Sometimes it's even without a priest, just on our own as lay persons.

"Individuals come up and introduce themselves and we start talking. When the priest is along, they pay more attention. It's the old business of the people not trusting the people.

"We divide up responsibilities between ourselves and the community. You always work by dividing things up. And when you leave, they always ask, 'When are you coming back?'

"Sometimes on these trips you find persons you knew ten or twenty years ago. That always makes you happy!

"When the priest is along, the villagers always prepare a special meal, and provide transportation. They always show special treatment in everything. When it's just you as a lay leader, they show respect, but things are different.

"When I was young, until I was thirty-five, I used to drink and have a good time. Now I'm dedicated to the things of God. A woman who saw me on the last trip out was saying to another woman, 'How did it happen that this man who used to drink and carouse so much is now involved in work with the gospel?'

"At that time, my life was really far away from the law of Christ. I even left my own family and went off with another woman. My first wife, my true wife, managed to keep the family going. Later on God came closer and closer and set me on the right road. Since then I haven't fallen back into spiritual disaster.

"Work in a settlement gives workers and their families only enough to eat. There's nothing left for anything else. When you get sick that's when it really gets tight. That's when it gets hard. You get knocked off balance. You work only to keep going, and that means forever running from one place to another. There's never any money left over, to buy a little calf, for example.

"The community and the church help me out, with goods and even with money, thank God.

"Last year when I was sick, I thought God was going to take me out of this life and end my service to the mission of the gospel. Okay, I was content and willing to go. The only thing that bothered me was the fact that my family wasn't in harmony with God. I have six children. The youngest is six and the oldest is twenty-two. The two oldest aren't that willing to follow the gospel. They work in the field only when I'm with them. When I'm away, unless I leave a very clear order, they don't have any direction. Every day I ask God to set them on the road to serving the community. I'm confident that some day he'll hear me.

"The only one who goes along with me is my 17-year-old daughter, to help with catechism. She's a good student, is obedient, and is good-natured. Now she's working as a domestic with a family here in the city.

"But the older children aren't very interested in the community. So I say to them, 'How can I give example to the people, if you don't go along with me?' My son wanted to be confirmed, but he didn't take part regularly in the meetings. So he wasn't confirmed.

"I want to stay calm about them, and not do anything rash or unwise. But they don't hold me back from the work of the gospel. Sometimes they come to a meeting, but they never stay to the end. They leave early.

"This all bothers me. The thing that makes me happiest is to see many community members listening to the word of God, and speaking of their life in the faith.

"My wife gets nervous. When things aren't going well, she gets to feeling anguished. So I tell her, 'We have to be patient with suffering, dear, so God can see that we're not just folks who want things to go well, but we also accept it when we don't have something we need.' "

That's what I could pick up from talking with this man who is so valiantly struggling for the kingdom of God in this world. His clear words have been tested and purified in the crucible of struggle and suffering, and are full of the breath of the Spirit. This is the new kind of Christian now coming forth: deeply rooted in the people, in the world, and in history, and deeply immersed in mystery, in the gospel, in God.

Saturday, October 1

PASTORAL WORK FOR THE WHOLE POPULATION

I generally ride a bike from our community house to the cathedral. That gives me ten minutes of good exercise, spiritual as well as physical, because I can think about the homily I'm going to give during the Mass, or about pastoral matters, or things having to do with the people.

Tonight, when I was going over to celebrate the 7 P.M. Sunday Mass, I was noting that I didn't come across anyone I knew, and no one seemed to know me.

Actually our groups and communities are like droplets of oil on a huge body of water. We have to recognize the fact that we don't have any organized kind of mass pastoral work.

I wonder to myself: how is this multitude to be reached by the gospel? Perhaps through the customary parish pastoral work: Masses celebrated seven days or thirty days after death, baptisms, weddings, processions, novenas, and so forth. On these occasions, especially when they bring a child to be baptized or a man and woman to get married, they are told that they have to take part in the communities. Sometimes that demand takes the form of a law, a necessary precondition. They put up with this test, taking part in the groups, just so they can have their children baptized and not because life in communion with the church is inherently worthwhile to them. Afterward, most of them in effect say "Good-bye," or "See you next time."

Actually, the church doesn't have a hold on the people the way it is sometimes supposed. Its grassroots work reaches scarcely 5 percent of the population. No doubt it does have a great deal of drawing power. But developing and making it real so that the whole mass can be fermented is something else again.

We do need pastoral work on a large scale. But it has to be a new kind, one that is different from the traditional form, a kind of mass pastoral work that will enable the masses to become a people, a people that is an active agent in history and in the life of the church.

Sunday, October 2

CHURCH GIVING BIRTH

Vocational work in the local church of this diocese is growing remarkably. There are already a half dozen theology students, novices, and young members of religious orders, both male and female, as well as two groups of young persons considering vocations, some fifty of them altogether.

All vocational promotion is done in common, so the young gradually head toward the particular type of life to which they feel most attracted.

A church that provides its own priests, sisters, and lay ministers is a church that is alive and adult. It's a church that has reached motherhood.

It's only natural: if BCCs produce good Christians, they will also produce priests, sisters, and ministers. That's a sign of the fruitfulness of the BCCs, a fruitfulness rooted in the gospel and in the life of the church.

Today I was in a settlement called Souza Araújo, about 20 kilometers from Rio Branco, for a meeting with a group of young persons considering a vocation. There were about twenty of them. I gave them a talk on sin. I gave a general introduction on the biblical idea of sin (breaking the covenant, the "heart" as its source, etc.). Then I spent some time on two points that are being emphasized in the awareness of the church today: sin as a breaking of one's "basic option," and the question of "social sin." Both these aspects are very rich, but they haven't yet reached the theological and pastoral clarity they need.

With regard to "social sin" it seems to me that in addition to being caught up in the "sin of the world" that is objective and part of history, there is such a thing as becoming responsible for it oneself (subjective responsibility). I think it can happen on three levels—1st level: taking part directly and personally in "social sin" (unjust laws, evil mechanisms, tyrannical governments, etc.); 2nd level: complicity or indirect collaboration; and finally, 3rd level: omission, letting things go their own way, or remaining neutral.

Thursday, October 6

COMMUNITY CONFESSION BASED ON A PENTALOGUE

Today at 7 P.M. in the cathedral I presided over the community confession that takes place every first Thursday of the month. The church was two-thirds full.

I put confession in the context of one's "basic option" in life. That option can be expressed in terms of living the faith, following Christ, doing the Father's will, seeking the kingdom and its justice, etc. Conversion means turning toward this central core of the gospel, of being a Christian. I tried to explain this by means of St. Augustine's famous statement, *Amores duo fecerunt civitates duas*, "Two loves have founded two cities"—self-love to the point of contempt for God, and love for God to the point of surrendering oneself.

Then I broke this basic life-project down into a kind of decalogue. For local pastoral reasons, it was a "pentalogue." We did the "examination of conscience" on the basis of these five points:

1) *Love for God*: participation in the life of the community (meetings, activities, etc.), hearing or reading the word of God, personal prayer, etc.

2) *Respect for life*: violence, slander, petty intrigues.

3) *Personal self-control*: vices of drinking, gambling, drugs, smoking, carousing, etc.

4) *Honoring the body*: chastity, male-female relationships.

5) *Struggling for justice*: respect for the rights of others, especially workers; omission, not being involved in struggling for a new kind of world, whether out of conformity or fear.

These are, in fact, the most common failings among our people. But if we are to avoid pharisaic casuistry, we have to set all this under the great rainbow of love for God and for neighbor, as did Christ, St. Paul, St. John, and the whole New Testament. That is, we have to situate all our *acts* within this basic *attitude*, this basic option, which is that of "walking before the Lord," "living with God," in a word "following Jesus Christ," or "walking according to the Spirit."

Friday, October 7

TFP AND LBV

This past Monday the bishop and the presbytery had asked me to prepare a statement that could explain to the people the nature of the programs that the Legion of Good Will (LBV) is putting out on the local television station, and on the campaign that the Tradition, Family, and Property (TFP) is conducting in our streets and plazas, strongly attacking the base communities.

I got the information I could gather together and drew up a flyer. The bishop and priests read and corrected it and it's going to be passed out tomorrow and the next day (Saturday and Sunday) during Mass. Community members have been asking for information on these two movements, and some Catholics are being swayed by them.

The statement points out that both movements have taken a line that is incompatible with Christian faith and with the guidelines of the church, especially because they oppose any effort toward transforming society—that is, toward social justice. No wonder that the dominant classes in our society support them, despite the fuss these organizations make about being politically neutral.

Sunday, October 9: Baixa da Colina

MARRIED COUPLES MEET

This afternoon I took part in a meeting of married couples organized by the parish of Santa Inês and held in the community of Baixa da Colina.

It began at 2 P.M. and the heat was infernal. You had to be deeply motivated to come to a meeting at that time of day.

The lay leader in the community, *Dona* Joana, welcomed us with the joy and sensitivity that are so much a part of her. She lives for the people. She's separated from her husband, who lives with another woman, and she lives with her daughter, who is also separated from her husband. It is the thrust of the gospel that holds life together for both of them.

There were a lot of men present. The issue of family and marriage is something they're really concerned about. All together, there were about forty couples there.

One by one, they introduced themselves. It was the first time some of them were stepping out into public life, onto a stage in society. Their lives are confined to their own family circle and the persons who live directly around them. For them even to introduce themselves is a kind of public action. When they do so, they take on something of a social personality, and thus they emerge into history, a history they are beginning to shape themselves. They say who they are, stammering and embarrassed. But gradually they catch on and they learn how to stand up before others, now as agents in society. From that point on, they exist and speak socially, and they no longer just live alongside others.

When they begin their experience of community in groups, they aren't used to it and they still speak in a conversational tone. They keep their voices low, and there's little expression; they get lost in details, and have no qualms about interrupting each other, they speak at the same time, etc. Later on, they become more disciplined and learn to dialogue: to listen and to speak. Dialogue is the golden mean between informal conversation and the discourse of politicians or the media. It's an authentic expression of true social relationships.

It's good for married couples to get together. These meetings are a space, a rare space, in which to exchange ideas, speak about specific problems, and liberate that repressed and oppressed area that is married life in all its complexity. Where can they find any place to give vent to their feelings constructively? These meetings are schools where one faces one's partner as both student and teacher. This is what I said to them so they would become aware of it.

I noticed that a particular middle-class couple, thoroughly devoted to pastoral work with ordinary people, was here and helping move things along. He used to be a high state official. Now he was recounting his own life story in order to encourage other couples to tell their experiences so all could learn from them. He said that before being converted to Christ, he drank a lot, was living with another woman, and took the easy road of graft, etc., until God came to meet him head on, and stopped him from continuing on his mistaken way.

Other personal testimonies followed. There emerged the major problems of marriage, which can be summarized under the following headings: 1) men having two households; 2) violence, machismo; 3) the vices of alcohol and carousing.

The social conditioning of these problems also came out: living and working conditions, the lack of schooling for children, families broken up for sheer economic survival, etc.

At a certain point the question of the validity of being married "only in front of a judge" was raised. Someone formulated it in a way that I found quite perceptive: "Marriage before a judge is sacred. Marriage in the church is consecrated." Someone else added, "A household is something that always demands respect. It's a blessing. But with the sacrament, we're consecrated to the church and to the kingdom of heaven."

At the end they asked me to speak. All I did was encourage them. I urged them to keep going. Then I took the famous "hymn of love" in 1 Corinthians 13 and made comments on it, urging them toward a love of self-giving and forgiveness, as the love of God and Christ has always been.

Together we talked about some familiar scenes in family life, had some laughs, and then we stood up to pray. Finally, we said good-bye.

I'm convinced that family pastoral work is something that the church must take on, but it has to happen in a new perspective, that of liberation. That is the appropriate perspective for our age, and for the "new way of being church" that BCCs represent. This realm of family and marriage is one that must be liberated and itself become liberating. Liberation is either integral or it's not really liberation.

Sunday, October 16: Rio Branco

EVALUATING THE LOCAL THEOLOGY PROGRAM

Today six of us professors and twenty of the students in our theology program held an all-day meeting. Nilson, the course coordinator, kept a good grip on things as he led the meeting. He has already been the general pastoral coordinator of the church, and the Worker's Party candidate for governor, and he soon intends to do postgraduate work in sociology at the University of São Paulo.

The program has been going on for two years. What's been done so far isn't bad at all—actually quite good, in fact. It has three component parts: *intensive courses* in theology during the months of January, February, and July (where the subjects are explicitly theological: Bible, christology, and subjects related to pastoral work, such as popular religion, popular education, basic elements of law, history, theory of social analysis, etc.); *study teams* made up of three or four students during the interval between courses, to review the material studied in the intensive course, write papers, or do projects (where the idea is to compare what they have learned with what their pastoral experience has shown) and discuss assigned readings; finally, *a night course in theology for the people* during the month of January, a course run by students who have finished the basic three-year cycle (which is followed by a two-year cycle of further study and which is obligatory for those students who aim to become priests).

The students are more or less equally divided into seminarians, sisters, and lay persons. Some of the students in the course are from neighboring diocesan churches.

Nilson directed the discussion toward finding a way to put some internal order into the program. There is now a feeling that the basic minimum structures have to be formulated in order to put some continuity and objectivity into the program. Otherwise, there will be a danger that things will always keep changing and matters will simply depend on the arbitrary decisions of one or another individual. Still, we were aware that this order has to always remain flexible and open, and never dogmatically predetermine the experience and life of the program itself.

By the end of the day we had the basic lines of the order worked out. It was an initial hardening or institutionalizing of the theology program.

A new coordinating body, made up of students and professors, was also chosen. Ana Rosa is going to replace Nilson. If Nilson led the way to a first effort to declericalize theology, with Ana Rosa there is going to be a first attempt at "demachoizing" it. That's all for the good.

Other more practical questions were also discussed: budget, new students, setting up study teams for the periods between courses, the possibility of getting accreditation by connecting up with a recognized theology department, the problem of participation by lay persons who can't come because of their work (the question of holding the courses at night was raised), the problem of exams, or how to check what students have gotten out of it, etc.

I think this program is a basic element in our church, and it is contributing toward helping our church assume its own legitimate autonomy. It represents the womb wherein the different kinds of ministers our local needs will be formed.

I've been surprised to see how quickly the program has taken root. Our whole church has accepted responsibility for it: bishops, priests, and people, and it has really gotten moving. It has come to stay. Next year will be its third year in operation and the last year of the basic cycle. After that it will turn to the two-year cycle. Even next year I think I can remain in the south and it won't hurt the program at all.

It's now walking on its own two feet. Thanks be to God!

Sunday, October 23: Back from Santa Catarina

MANY BRAZILS WITHIN THE ONE BRAZIL

I've just gotten back today from a trip to Santa Catarina, where I went as a consultant for a regional meeting of the Conference of Religious Orders of Brazil and to give talks in the Instituto Filosófico in Santa Catarina, and also in the Instituto Teológico. I also took advantage of the occasion to visit the hills of Florianópolis, where there are more and more *favelas* on the outskirts. Santa Catarina is where I was born.

The difference between Santa Catarina and Acre is striking, in nature as well as in the economy and culture. You wouldn't think it's the same Brazil. As I was going by car through those beautiful fields, all planted, with the houses so nicely fixed up, I had to ask myself, "But can this be the Brazil the liberation theologians talk about?" It looked more like a transplant of Europe than a piece of the Third World.

Still, there are contradictions bubbling away behind the apparent order and integration—the contradictions of the capitalist system that prevails all over our country. True, they're not as sharp and clear as they are elsewhere, but they're there. And they're there in a specific way, one that has to be figured out. I didn't sense a great deal of effort in that direction on the part of the church personnel I came in contact with. Their vision of things is general and abstract. So I stressed the need to produce a theology, and a kind of religious life and pastoral activity, specifically for Santa Catarina, so that the church can really be *barriga-verde* (literally, "green belly," a nickname given to persons from Santa Catarina).

To do that, however, you have to carry out a careful examination of the way things are there, how the contradictions of the system are manifested there, and the specific areas where the situation in Santa Catarina raises religious and pastoral challenges for lay Christians, religious, and pastors.

In fact, I found out that the much touted orderliness of *barriga-verde* society is actually falling apart under the impact of advancing capitalist relationships of production, which are leaving lots of people with no land and are turning urban areas into shantytowns.

What it means is that when the development of the contradictions of a social system reaches a certain point, contradictions that have previously been "visible" only through theory or analysis become empirically visible. That's the moment when the injustices of a society can no longer be hidden: they're just too obvious. What is already a fact in the most urbanized centers of Brazil, like Rio and São Paulo, and in the whole northeast, is beginning to happen also in the south, and particularly in Santa Catarina.

These are "signs of the times," and they demand that the church in the region wake up and "heed the Spirit's word to the churches" (Rev. 2:11, 29, etc.).

Tuesday, November 15

THE POOR IN EUROPE

Three of us were talking for a while today, two Italian priests, Primo, who is now working in Abaetetuba, and Guido, who is from the diocese of Lucca (Italy), and myself. We were comparing the experience of the church in Latin America (and especially Brazil) with the European church.

The main thing we talked about was the question of "the people" in Europe. Space within society is organized into elites in such a way that the people, considered as the base of society, is left out. That's true of church and government, political parties and labor unions. "The people" is a real entity, and the people often takes initiatives, but it cannot find adequate political channels for expressing itself. That's the case with volunteer movements, with solidarity with the Third World, and with the peace and ecology movements.

Guido was saying that he found ordinary persons very much interested in speaking about issues of social change and issues relating to peripheral countries, and getting involved in those issues. He was also saying that the great lesson he was drawing from our church was the way everything was being done *with* the people, so that the people would become an agent of its own destiny and history. He said the process is slow, but it is the surest way toward creating an egalitarian world.

In Europe it is especially young drug addicts and older pensioners who make up the poor, but the poor also continue to be workers, especially foreign workers, and everyone who doesn't count with those who run society. Europe's misfortune is that it has set up a society that has now been crystalized in its institutions, its apparatus, and its elites for centuries, and it has now reached a point of stagnation in the midst of all its contradictions, primarily at the cost of the Third World, which it exploits and dominates.

The European church, which is too much a part of the existing system, could nevertheless be the "weakest link," and thus allow the people to emerge onto the stage of history. That's what Guido thinks. But that can happen only when the European church opens up more space for lay persons, who are really the people of God inasmuch as they are the overwhelming majority. But they mustn't be coopted by ecclesiastical elites serving clerical aims; they must be autonomous agents in the church. There should be a special emphasis on those coming from the more marginal sectors of the population.

Sunday, November 20

ST. PAUL, APOSTLE PAR EXCELLENCE

I spent the whole morning with thirty-five or forty lay leaders in Imaculada parish in the city. They were making a retreat on problem areas in their apostolic service to the people.

When you go into a situation like that, you see a body of women and men seasoned in group work. You get a sense of power and authority coming out of their eyes, their faces, and their whole personality. I thought to myself how much time and care it must have taken to form such a group.

They are poor and simple persons, with teeth missing and scars on their bodies, dressed very modestly, and in sandals. These suffering and struggling persons have not seen justice win out very often, accustomed as they are to being knocked down to the ground, but always getting up and moving ahead, against the way things are at present. When you run your eye over the group you don't see anyone from the privileged classes in society. This is a church of the poor, and it is a poor church, where the poor are church and they evangelize. Viewed as a social phenomenon, it is a "popular church."

They've asked me to help out with this retreat. Besides meetings dealing with organization (planning and evaluation) and meetings for reflecting on the word of God and on life, it is certainly important to have meetings during a retreat. They feed the heart, strengthen the will, reactivate the impulses of freedom, nourish the underlying motives for one's mission, and fertilize and water the hidden roots of the life of faith and love.

Only that way can persons be formed not just to be activists but to be convinced Christians rooted in the mystery of Christ. Unless they are so rooted, persons active in pastoral work can easily go over to the Evangelicals or to some ideological movement or political party.

I chose the figure of St. Paul, the model for every Christian apostle. Together with the retreatants, I read through some of the most expressive passages of Paul's most autobiographical epistle, the Second Letter to the Corinthians.

I drew out seven of Paul's traits, traits that could also be found in any leader or anyone working for the church. I took advantage of Paul's penchant for metaphor:

1) Paul is "an aroma of Christ" (chap. 2).

2) Paul is aware that he is an "earthen vessel," carrying the treasure of the faith and of the gospel (chap. 4).

3) Paul is "impelled" by "the love of Christ": love for Christ and love like Christ (toward the lowly, etc.) (chap. 6).

4) Paul remains firm in trials and persecutions (chap. 6 and 11).

5) Paul has a sense of communion, of working together with others (chap. 7, 8, 9).

6) Paul is so zealous for the community that he can no longer be married except to Christ (as we can't be married to our own person, to the system, etc.) (chap. 11).

7) Paul trusts in the power of grace, despite the "thorn in the flesh," and the "angel of Satan" who "beats" him—that is, despite his weaknesses, even humiliating weaknesses (chap. 12).

I could see that Christian ethics is more *typological* than nomological. Duméry, Ricoeur and biblical scholars have already recognized that. And I could see that you do a lot better pastorally, especially with ordinary persons, when you present types rather than insisting on norms, laws, or rules.

We spent the whole morning at this. They all took part, mentioning their own experiences, motivated by the presentations others made. From time to time we broke out into a hymn or song connected with our joint meditation.

Friday, December 9

AUTOGRAPH NIGHT FOR THE PEOPLE

Last night in the Meta School, Maria Lúcia Régis celebrated the publication of her book, *A coragem de viver* ["the courage to live"]. There were some one hundred persons present, most of them from the communities. The government wanted to take over the ceremony, with TV and everything, but Maria Lúcia spotted the trap and refused.

I was watching this humble housewife, who is a lay leader and a leper, as she signed autographs. She grasped the pen firmly with her hand, which was "pruned," as Bacurau, another leper, put it. A few years ago he had put out his own autobiography, *À margem da vida* ["on the edge of life"].

"That hand is more beautiful than the hands of many artists," I whispered to Bacurau standing next to me. And he added, "And it's tougher than lots of boxers' hands." It's true: with their own hands lepers are tearing down tons of oppression weighing over them, a heavy oppression thousands of years old.

With all the penmanship she could muster, Maria Lúcia was writing long, fancy dedications. You didn't see in her anything of the arrogance and pretension of so many professional writers, who haughtily pick up a pen, jot down two or three words that are formal or clever, but almost always empty, and then sign their name illegibly, as though they were mysterious gods, whose name had to remain hidden.

They asked me to introduce Maria Lúcia's book because I had pushed for it to be published. I spoke along the following lines.

The People as Publisher

"My friends, there is a joyful atmosphere here on this autograph night, and that atmosphere is very much centered on the people. It seems it is the people itself, in the person of Maria Lúcia, that is publishing and signing its own book. And that's not just an impression.

"In fact, Maria Lúcia's book mirrors the life of the people. This book breaks the mirror that the powerful, with their mercenary scribes, offer the people to look at itself. That mirror is distorted and distorting. The mirror of so many famous writers who presume and pretend to speak *of* the people and *for* the people (but not *with* the people); the mirror of the media, and especially the TV screen. There the poor come across as dirty and scab-covered undesirables who are good only for working, being servants, and dying.

"There's no book that deserves an autograph night with ordinary persons more than this book by Maria Lúcia. Autograph sessions with many famous writers are formal and stilted. Their books are often like snakewood trees— they're big and fat, but they're empty and offer little shade and no fruit. Maria Lúcia's book, like books coming from the people, is like the *coumarou* tree, strong, full of sap and solid wood. Outwardly, her book may seem humble, in its grammatical expression and even the way it's printed, but its substance is rich. It is a love letter in a modest envelope, a humble package with a precious gift inside.

"Besides that, the kind of book Maria Lúcia is publishing comes close to the kind of writing we find in the books of the gospel, unpretentious literature, popular literature. The word of God has taken on a literary flesh that is frail and mortal. It did not become incarnate in the glorious body of sophisticated epic poetry such as the *Iliad* or the *Odyssey*. Absolute Meaning comes to us wrapped in the poor swaddling clothes of simple, popular writing.

"Maria Lúcia's book also comes close to the gospel in that it is a book that tells of the life and passion, death and resurrection, of the people in the person of a humble woman who besides everything else is a leper. That's not what the media show: they only show the tip of the iceberg of the suffering and hope of the oppressed, and nothing more.

"Maria Lúcia's experience of always being on the move is the same thing that goes on throughout the masses: moving from one place to another, changing work, changing partners, etc. She is but the sign of a whole people expelled, exiled in its own land, living under a foreign social system that alienates.

"But the similarities between Maria Lúcia's book and the gospels don't stop there. It is also similar insofar as it tells of the struggle and resurrection of the people. In that sense, it is good news. Its message is bright and affirmative, one of life and triumph.

"Not that we should now make an idol out of the people and turn Maria Lúcia into a saint. Not at all. The masses have their sins as does the people of God (Israel and the church). And Maria Lúcia doesn't hide her faults and failures. She courageously acknowledges and assumes them all, without making excuses. 'The rich man does wrong and boasts of it, the poor man is wronged and begs forgiveness' (Sir. 13:3).

"This book records the memoirs of an oppressed woman—a symbol of millions and billions of oppressed persons. It tells of her pain and her death, but even more of her struggle to stand up and resist being crushed and made an outcast. For the oppressed, what is life all about? It's not the endless show we see in the memoirs of public dignitaries, politicians, intellectuals, artists, and performers. It's not the senseless game we see in the comings and going of those frivolous elites high above us. For the poor, life means courage and battle, hope and the resurrection of the dead.

"Hence the sense of what is real that you get when you read Maria Lúcia's book. The poor don't speak words, but things. Their words touch reality like your teeth touch your tongue. They are rocks, not clouds. There's no distance between speaking and living—unlike the way it is with so many intellectuals.

"What you can see in Maria Lúcia's book is her profound humanism. The way she relates to others breathes forth tenderness, mercy, and solidarity. The way she relates to ongoing history is full of power and of the spirit of resistance.

"The poor are finally beginning to speak and write on their own, with their own tongue and their own hands, without any go-betweens, representatives or defenders—the whole crew of do-gooders, who pretend to live *for* the poor, when in fact all they're doing is living *off* the poor. The lowly are breaking forth onto the stage of public cultural life with what they have produced themselves. They are emerging as creators of a word whose own inherent power gives it authority. Of course there will be those who are going to make the kind of remark already anticipated in Sirach:

> A rich man speaks and all are silent,
> his wisdom they extol to the clouds.
> A poor man speaks and they say: "Who is that?"
> If he slips they cast him down [13:22].

"But when the tongue of the poor is loosed, who will be able to tie it down again?

"The fact that the poor can write is itself a challenge to the bourgeois way of being a writer, and bespeaks a revolution in the way writing is done, as well as in the way it is published. With regard to the way it is done, Maria Lúcia has thanked a whole host of friends who helped her write her book, including those who encouraged her and suggested topics, as well as those who provided paper, did the typing, corrected her Portuguese, divided the book up into chapters and paragraphs, and so forth. This has obviously been a collective effort.

"Then there's the way such a work is published: if the poor are putting it out, the usual criteria will not apply. That has to do with the kind of cover, the paper, the type (bigger letters), layout, distribution, price, and so forth. That obviously means that books produced by the people and for the people will mean a revolution in the way books are published and sold—and that will be possible only in a different kind of society.

"A further characteristic of this book is that the author is a leper. She didn't write it so others would feel sorry for her, but to draw attention to both the strengths and the rights of lepers. She shows how being a leper is primarily a cultural and political problem rather than a problem of health care. That's the philosophy of the leper movement that is sponsoring our meeting here.

"Finally, this book is especially a witness of faith. It is an expression of this 'new agent' in the church, the people. Here it is that faith begins to have the aroma of the people and thus the aroma of prophecy and liberation. This is one of the high points of the book, encountering faith, a faith that affirms humankind and means dignity for the lowly. In her book Maria Lúcia tells how it was faith and the church community that started her on her way to lifting up her head, loosening her tongue, and speaking on her own. The reason is that faith not only makes persons Christians, but in so doing, it refashions them as human beings. It humanizes as it sanctifies. It revolutionizes as it evangelizes. That is what the medieval scholars called *gratia sanans*—healing grace—when they reflected on the restorative and humanizing function of grace. Hence in the church the leper is not only saved, but also freed, restored not only to grace but to life in common with others.

"Finally, I'd like to express my desire that Maria Lúcia keep going, not so much as a successful writer, but as someone struggling. May she not be affected by vanity over having a book published, but keep on believing that life is worth more than all books put together, and that the kingdom and its justice is worth more than life itself."

Seu *Raimundinho, Mystic of the People*

Riding back home on a bike as usual, I stopped at the house of *Seu* Raimundinho, the sacristan and porter at the cathedral. I speak of him in *"Deus e o homem no inferno verde"* ["God and humanity in the green hell"] as a "mystic of the people." I wanted to know how he was, because he was soon to have an operation for a stomach ulcer.

I found him in bed, the operation already completed. "How are you?," I asked. "Marvelous," he responded, and then went on, "God is too good to me." He kept gazing at the picture of the Sacred Heart hanging on the wall in front, with the steady serious gaze of a rubber worker, but also full of the most holy tenderness. Over and over he kept telling me that God was too good to him, that he didn't deserve so much, that he only wanted to get well so he could go back to the church, pray his endless rosaries, and read the sacred scriptures in peace and quiet.

He told me that for the operation he had to spend five days on a strict fast. "The nurses, sisters, and doctors all had their eyes peeled on me," he said. But he would fool them by picking up a bottle of serum in his hands, going into the bathroom, and having a little drink of water. "And nothing disastrous happened to me," he added with a crafty look. And then he compared himself to Jacob: "There was no one as tricky as he, and yet he was God's favorite. That's how I am and that's how God treats me," looking once more at the Sacred Heart high up on the wall.

I don't know what he sees in that picture. Only God knows. Some critics would raise a lot of questions about that picture, that it's too sweet and syrupy, that it doesn't convey prophetic vigor, and who knows what else. But none of that concerns *Seu* Raimundinho. In that picture he sees what his critics can't see. For him the picture says more than all the criticism. That's so because the picture goes beyond itself to speak of the person of Christ and of his infinite passion for human beings and their world.

Saturday, December 10: Brasiléia

THE PEOPLE'S GENEROSITY AND OURS

This morning I started out for Brasiléia, to speak on radio about our work there. I would deal with the two hottest and most prophetic topics at the moment: the subhuman conditions the colonizers have to live in, and the murder of Jesus Mathias. I would describe what residents of Brasiléia had been saying, seeing, and doing. Perhaps the radio broadcast would give these problems a wider hearing, so our silent candlelight march for peace and justice would have a greater impact and for a longer time.

When I got to Brasiléia, after five and a half hours on the road, I was asked to do the program not that day but the next, and at first I refused, not happy at all with the unexpected delay. "This is just too much." But then I changed my mind, although it cost a lot. The fact is that the people of God is worth any sacrifice. "One should give everything to the people and ask for nothing, not even sympathy"—that's what Siqueira Campos, a Brazilian president in the early twentieth century, said about our country. If the people, despite its sins, indeed because of them, has been "deserving" of the death of the Lord, what should it not deserve from us?

Besides that, I felt the lay leaders in Brasiléia were ready to keep going forward in their work, even though it was definitely affected by the murder of

Jesus Mathias. Texts like "Do not fear those who can kill body and soul, but nothing more," and "He who wishes to save his life will lose it, but he who loses it for my sake will save it" kept coming up when they spoke with me, and those texts obviously expressed deep convictions that were decisive in their lives. Those words fill them with an enormous strength, and shine like stars in the dark night of the oppression those lay leaders endure.

It's really true that the poor convert us and force us to improve.

Sunday, December 11: Rio Branco

LAY MINISTERS OF BAPTISM

There are twenty ministers of baptism in the prelature. Today they met in the training center to go over the ritual that was prepared especially for lay ministers, but which priests also use now.

Only ten came because the rain was coming down in buckets. It had created a huge swamp out of the street leading to the center. These are simple, serious, hardworking persons. Only one couple could be said to be well off. I had the impression that they had all matured in their work with the church. Four of those present were women.

One has to see them as they baptize. They take on their role with conviction, even with middle- or upper-class persons present, whether politicians, public officials, or landowners. Thus the great are forced to listen to the small, at least in church.

That is usually the way it is with popular religion. It is the humble who say what has to be done, and the "important" ones go seeking their "services." Access to Mystery is not given to those who have more, know more, or can do more, but to those who are humble, open, and committed—and thus the poor are more eligible.

Practical Suggestions

At the end of the day some practical suggestions were drawn up and I think they're worth recording:

1) Ministries, especially the ministry of baptism, should be extended to more remote areas and communities.

2) There should be more room for women in ministries; they are proving to be so dynamic and responsible in local work.

3) It would be good if ministers of baptism could use a special garment, or something of that order, when baptizing, to show that they are acting in the name of Christ and of the church. It would be valuable for ministers from a psychological and social viewpoint, besides making their sacramental function clearer.

I can see how lay persons are refashioning ecclesial ministries, starting out from their true theological meaning and seeking to meet the social and cultural demands of the situation.

A People's Principal in a People's School

Seu Nicó, a minister of baptism, is a BCC veteran. He is, as it were, the father of the BCC he leads in the area of Palheiral. Not long ago he told me how he had been elected principal of the school in his barrio.

In the voting of the Parents and Teachers Association, his name was third and last on the list but he got 92 votes out of the 128 cast. He got a telegram of congratulations from the former secretary of education, Iris Célia, who is now an alternate senator for the Social Democratic Party.

Seu Nicó told me that it was members of the local base community who had started the Áurea Pires school, to which he had been elected principal. They had presented their demands to the state Department of Education, taking with them a list of 300 children who weren't going to school. The government shipped in the material and the people supplied the labor. The school was built in 90 days.

Seu Nicó is now waiting for his election to be approved by the authorities. He's afraid they may refuse him, because he's only in the second grade in the adult education program.

It's always the same story: they require a piece of paper (whether it's a legal document or a school diploma) so they can disregard the human being.

Government and the People

While the group of lay ministers was meeting, the officers of twenty neighborhood associations were taking part in a training session.

We were together at lunch and I got to know about their work. The Center for the Defense of Human Rights is encouraging the formation of these associations. Center personnel organized this training session. They brought in government officials to explain to the association leaders how a government works and is administered: finances, who is in charge of what, etc. That's very good, because it leads to mutual enrichment, such as what took place last night at the Meta School.

For the discussion on colonizers from the south, there were two agronomists from INCRA who are responsible for projects dealing with organized settlements in the area. The officials got an earful from the colonizers, and the colonizers got a chance to hear the government's position. The government representatives provided good information and got to know what the real situation was. They have a good attitude, and are well intentioned. They can struggle as those who are "willing to stand by the workers," as Leo XIII put it in *Rerum Novarum*.

It is essential to combine work with the people, in connection with projects they carry out on their own, and work with the government, where citizens claim their rights. For this kind of work, you have to have trustworthy allies within the power structure.

The church is in a position to work out relationships with officials in various sectors of the government, criticizing from within. That relationship should not just be one of prophetic confrontation, but also one of promoting the common good.

Monday, December 12: On the Way Back to Rio

A COUPLE MARRIED TO THE PEOPLE

Last night at Mass in Volta Seca, I ran across Luísa and Antônio, at whose marriage I had officiated two years earlier. I recalled that at the celebration, as the couple were receiving their wedding rings, they committed themselves to remain closer than ever to the community movement—to be married to that community, in a sense.

Luísa and Antônio continued to be active within the church, even going on visitations over rivers and through jungles.

At one point, though, they had left for Rondônia, in search of employment. However, in their hearts they were still linked with the work with the people that the church in Acre was doing. In Rondônia they didn't find any way of working with the people, in either the church or society at large. So in the end they came back. That was the only reason.

"Although we're earning less," Antônio confides, "it's better here, because we can do grassroots work. That's what's important in life, rather than filling your pockets with money and making others unhappy, and yourself as well."

That's an example of how marriage can open and liberate persons for the work of the gospel, even in its political dimension.

Gospel, Politics, and Feeling

The Mass I celebrated last night with the community of Volta Seca was my last one this year in Acre. Usually the liturgy prompts the degree of vitality in the community. But sometimes the community has more life and participation than its liturgy. That's what I observed at Mass last night.

Some of the older women came up to pay their respects with that pure tenderness that only they, the suffering mothers of the people, can show. They kissed my hands and face, and asked where I had been, and whether I would stay longer in the community, and so forth.

You get the same kind of friendliness and affection from children and young adults. Working with them may be hard, but it produces fragrant, colorful flowers. It's true: struggling with the people on the bottom has a powerful impact on integrating your feelings. It certainly demands sacrifice, abnegation, and forgetting yourself, but it also centers and integrates your feelings. This kind of work generates so much friendship, and there is so much affection that comes out of meeting and relating to others, and engaging in dialogue.

I've always believed that one of the remarkable things about liberation pastoral work is how it stimulates the formation of teams of colleagues (for action) and also communities of brothers and sisters (for communion). Church communities bring persons together not only in their work, but also—and especially—in their hearts, through what they are deep down inside. This is true and deep fellowship. Only faith and love can produce it—no political ideology or undertaking.

So I'm now feeling sorry that I have to leave these Christians in whose hearts this marvelous affection has taken root. You don't love *in order to be* happy; you love and *then* you're happy. Happiness doesn't come from justice; it comes from grace.